Heikki Rinne and Lasse Mitronen
Empowering Employee Engagement

Heikki Rinne and Lasse Mitronen

Empowering Employee Engagement

—

Reignite Commitment through Shared Responsibility

DE GRUYTER

ISBN 978-3-11-220981-3
e-ISBN (PDF) 978-3-11-220983-7
e-ISBN (EPUB) 978-3-11-220985-1

Library of Congress Control Number: 2026933760

Bibliographic information published by the Deutsche Nationalbibliothek
The Deutsche Nationalbibliothek lists this publication in the Deutsche Nationalbibliografie;
detailed bibliographic data are available on the internet at http://dnb.dnb.de.

© 2026 Walter de Gruyter GmbH, Berlin/Boston, Genthiner Straße 13, 10785 Berlin
Cover image: Alisa Zahoruiko/iStock/Getty Images Plus
Typesetting: Integra Software Services Pvt. Ltd.

www.degruyterbrill.com
Questions about General Product Safety Regulation:
productsafety@degruyterbrill.com

Preface

Employee engagement has shifted from a "nice-to-have" concept to a strategic imperative in today's workplace. As organizations navigate hybrid models, tightening labor markets, and rising employee expectations for meaning and autonomy, engagement is emerging as a key differentiator for performance and resilience.

There are three compelling reasons for us to write this book on employee engagement.

First, employee engagement is a critical driver of organizational success. A substantial body of research and practical evidence demonstrates that high levels of engagement lead to improved performance outcomes—including increased productivity, lower turnover, enhanced customer satisfaction, and stronger financial performance. According to Gallup, highly engaged teams are 23% more profitable than their less engaged counterparts (Gallup, 2020). As Doug Conant, former President and CEO of Campbell Soup Company, insightfully stated: "You can't expect a company to perform at high levels unless people are personally engaged" (*Fast Company*, 2014). In today's competitive environment, engagement is not a luxury—it is a strategic imperative.

Second, there remains a significant opportunity to improve engagement in many organizations. Recent data shows that only about 21% of global employees are engaged at work—the lowest level in a decade. Unlike fixed assets or market constraints, human engagement is dynamic. It is neither predetermined nor static. The level of employee engagement can be meaningfully influenced by the daily choices and actions of individuals, leaders, and teams. This is the central thesis of this book: engagement is both a conceptual framework and a practical discipline. We present actionable guidance and evidence-based strategies that individuals at all levels of the organization can use to improve engagement and build a more energized, high-performing workplace culture.

Third, the perspectives offered in this book are grounded in decades of academic research, executive leadership, and global consulting experience.

Dr. Heikki Rinne earned his business degree from Brigham Young University, followed by an MBA from the University of Oregon and a PhD from Purdue University. He spent more than two decades in academia before transitioning to C-level executive and board roles across multiple industries. He later founded and led a global consulting practice focused on employee engagement, working with teams and leaders on five continents. This unique combination of scholarly insight, executive leadership, and consulting experience provides Heikki with a multidimensional understanding of engagement—what it is, why it matters, and how it can be transformed into a sustainable organizational advantage.

Professor Lasse Mitronen brings complementary experience from academia, corporate leadership, and consulting. He holds an M.Sc. (Econ.) and is a Docent and Professor of Working Life at the University of Tampere. Prior to his academic roles, he worked at Kesko for 24 years in positions spanning responsibility, market research, business concept development, and corporate strategy, ultimately serving as Vice President of Corporate Planning and Strategic Development. Over the course of his career, Lasse has led and contributed to numerous domestic and international projects in retail development, service innovation, training, and research. His interdisciplinary perspective enriches the insights in this book, particularly in translating theory into practice.

Together, we offer this book not just as a scholarly exploration, but as a practical guide for leaders and teams committed to unlocking the full potential of their people. We hope it equips you with the insights and tools to build a culture where improving engagement becomes not only possible, but a part of your everyday business.

Contents

Preface —— V

Introduction —— 1

Part 1: The Concept of Engagement

Chapter 1
Employee Engagement Matters: Engaged Employees Produce Better Results —— 11

Chapter 2
Levels of Engagement —— 18

Chapter 3
Multidimensional Engagement —— 23

Chapter 4
Engagement Profiles —— 30

Part 2: Improving Engagement

Chapter 5
Engagement by Choice —— 43

Chapter 6
Engaging Leaders with Impact —— 62

Chapter 7
Engaging Teams —— 87

Chapter 8
Strong Engagement to Company —— 98

Chapter 9
Employee Engagement and the Customer —— 106

Part 3: **Emerging Themes in Engagement**

Chapter 10
Dealing with the Disengaged —— 117

Chapter 11
Remote Work and Employee Engagement —— 125

Chapter 12
AI and Employee Engagement —— 132

Chapter 13
International Multiculturalism and Employee Engagement —— 140

Chapter 14
Making it Happen —— 150

References —— 157

List of Figures —— 169

List of Tables —— 171

Index —— 173

Introduction

Why Engagement?

> "Engaged employees are your greatest competitive advantage."
> — Cheryl Bachelder, former CEO of Popeyes Louisiana Kitchen

A few years ago, while serving as the CEO of a multinational industrial company, one of our Asian partners asked how we managed operations in more than 30 countries with such a small central organization. After reflecting on the question, we concluded that in locations where we had engaged leaders and employees, operations flourished. Conversely, we faced challenges where engagement was lacking. This realization led us to focus on empowering engagement across the organization.

We soon recognized that our responsibility, as top leaders, was to prioritize and empower engagement. We needed to create a work environment where people wanted —and chose—to be engaged. We found that when employees chose to be engaged, their self-initiated engagement empowered them, and their teams. Empowering engagement became a dual strategy: a leader's responsibility to foster an engaging workplace, and an individual's opportunity to be empowered through their commitment.

Employee engagement—the emotional commitment and enthusiasm employees have for their work—is the invisible force that can make or break organizations. In a hypercompetitive and rapidly evolving business environment, engagement is no longer a "nice to have "—it's a strategic imperative.

Employee engagement refers to the emotional commitment an employee has to their organization and its goals. Employee engagement has been described both in practice and in academic literature. Kevin Kruse (2012), *Employee Engagement 2.0*, defines employee engagement as the emotional commitment an employee has to the organization and its goals. In contrast, Kahn (1990), who first introduced the concept in academic literature, defined engagement as the harnessing of the self to work roles, in which individuals "employ and express themselves physically, cognitively, and emotionally during role performance." Taken together, these perspectives highlight both the internal psychological conditions that enable engagement (Kahn) and the outward commitment to organizational success that engagement produces (Gallup)

Business leaders often equate engagement with satisfaction or happiness, but this is a mistake. Engagement is not about making employees happy—it is about making them feel committed, energized, and purposeful. Engaged employees go the extra mile not because they have to, but because they choose to.

Right now, full employee engagement is in short supply. Recent data shows that only about 31% of U.S. employees are engaged at work—the lowest level in a decade (Gallup, 2025). In Europe the number is even lower at a mere 13% engaged. Globally, according to the Gallup Global Workplace Report, only 21% of employees feel engaged. Manager engagement is at 27%, while individual contributor engagement is at 18%.

According to Gallup 62% are "not engaged" and 17% are actively disengaged. This isn't just an HR concern—it's a strategic crisis, draining productivity and potential. Gallup estimates that low engagement costs the global economy nearly $9 trillion annually.

Employee engagement is a challenge!

In the current era of rapid change in the workplace, remote work, and the "Great Resignation" (coined by Professor Anthony Klotz of Texas A&M University in May 2021; the term describes a structural shift in workforce dynamics, where resignations were not simply a short-term response to the pandemic, but part of a deeper reassessment of how, where, and why people work) (Klotz, 2021), leaders can no longer treat engagement as optional. It is the cornerstone of performance and resilience. Engagement is not only good for business—it is the engine of business excellence. Employee empowerment creates a clear competitive advantage for organizations where employees choose to be engaged. Engagement in the current workplace challenges old views on management and leadership. True engagement replaces old views of control, rules, and just showing up.

Workplaces are also rapidly developing with technology and the use of AI, and as noted by John Clifton, the CEO of Gallup:

> We are witnessing a pivotal moment in the global workplace—one where engagement is faltering at the exact time artificial intelligence is transforming every industry in its path. While few employees have harnessed AI's full potential, its rapid advance will force every organization to adapt, whether they are ready or not. This presents a defining challenge for leaders and managers: Will they seize AI's opportunities to energize their workforce, or will they risk falling behind? (Gallup 2025, p. 4).

Given these developments, and many engagement challenges facing organizations, our aim is to provide insights that leaders, teams, and employees can practice to create better, more engaging workplaces.

What This Book Will Do for the Reader

This book is designed to:
1. Help readers understand the importance of engagement.
2. Provide specific tools for conceptualizing and measuring multidimensional employee engagement.
3. Show specific actions individuals, leaders, and teams can take to improve employee engagement.
4. Discuss the role of employee engagement in the current, rapidly developing workplaces.

Although many examples in the book are drawn from the business world, the principles apply equally across academic institutions, nonprofits, government, and even religious organizations.

This book is not intended to be a comprehensive literature review of all recent scholarship on employee engagement. So, even though this is not a comprehensive book review, we have researched references to describe the current academic and management consensus view on engagement, and have provided the citations, so the reader can find the sources and information for themselves, if interested. The number of references also illustrates the significant academic and leadership interest in employee engagement and related topics. While this book is grounded in academic research and supported by empirical work, our goal is to translate those insights into practical strategies that work in real workplaces.

Our recommendations are based on work and past research of real examples from numerous organizations around the world where we have consulted over the past several years.

If we succeed in helping even a few readers learn something new, and experience even one "aha moment," this book will have fulfilled its purpose.

Conceptual Contributions of this Book

This book makes several important contributions to the field of employee engagement:
1. **Multidimensionality of Engagement**: Recognizes that engagement is impacted by five key forces—(1) company, (2) leadership, (3) teams, (4) individual work assignments, and (5) customers—and must be measured and addressed accordingly.
2. **Measurement and Visualization**: Introduces a measurement approach and graphical model for assessing and understanding engagement across different organizational levels.
3. **Individual Responsibility**: Emphasizes the role employees themselves play in shaping their own engagement and provides practical tools for self-directed improvement.
4. **Engaging Leadership**: Highlights that leaders must not only be engaged themselves but also become engaging to others. Specific steps are provided to help leaders build environments where employees choose to engage.
5. **Team Dynamics**: Shows how high-functioning teams contribute to individual engagement and offers actionable tools to enhance team operations and culture.
6. **Engagement in Current Workplaces**: Focuses on improving engagement in today's rapidly changing workplaces, shaped by cultural divides, remote work, and the increasing impact of technology and AI.

The book also offers new perspectives on the link between employee engagement and customer loyalty and provides a blueprint for creating lasting cultural transformation. As such, it is a valuable resource for business leaders, HR professionals, and academics alike.

Key Findings

In our work at Sitoumus LLC over the past several years—across 15 countries on five continents, with hundreds of teams and numerous companies and industries—we have learned ten important aspects about employee engagement:

1. **Engagement is multidimensional**

Engagement is not merely about work satisfaction, turnover, Employee Net Promotion Scores (ENPS), or any other one-dimensional measure. Given the multidimensional nature of engagement, it must be measured multidimensionally to be fully understood and to be actionable.

We have found that there are five key forces of engagement that impact employees' level of engagement.
1. The organization (or company) they work for
2. Leadership (both senior leaders and immediate supervisors)
3. Their team
4. Their own work
5. The customers

People may be highly engaged in some areas and disengaged in others, and the concept of multidimensionality in this book is represented in Figure I.1. and described in detail in Chapters 2–4.

2. **Employee engagement matters**

Employees and teams with higher engagement across all five forces consistently deliver superior results than teams with lower engagement scores. Research consistently shows that highly engaged employees, teams, and organizations perform better, with fewer quality mistakes, lower absenteeism, and lower turnover. In a meta-analysis of 7,939 business units across 36 companies, Harter, Schmidt, and Hayes (2002) found that units with higher employee engagement achieved significantly better outcomes—including higher productivity and profitability, as well as lower turnover and absenteeism—compared to less engaged units. Subsequent Gallup analyses have quantified these effects in terms of percentage gains in profit margins and productivity. Higher engagement leads to higher productivity, more sales, and greater profitability.

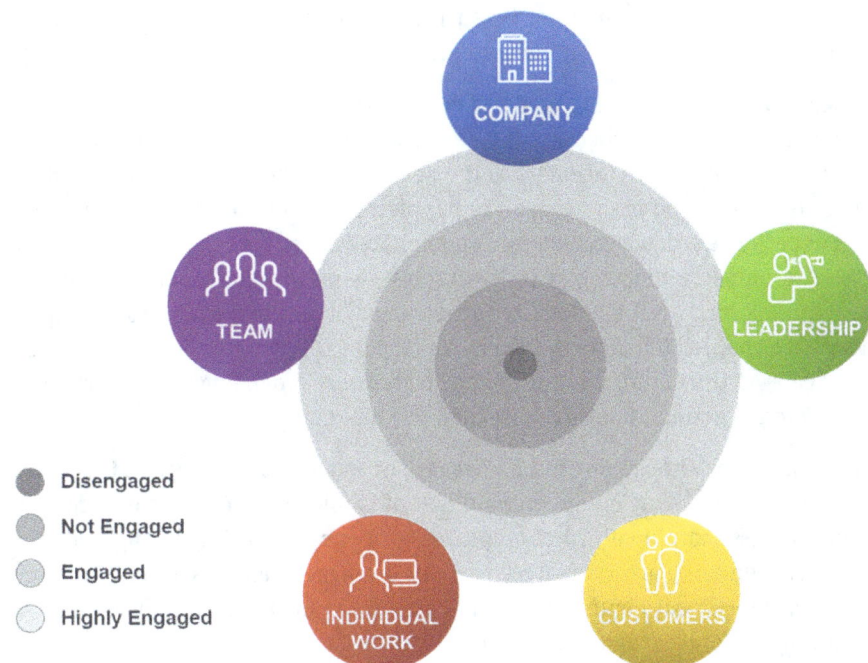

Figure I.1: Multidimensional representation of employee engagement.

3. **Engagement is a choice**

Everyone is responsible for their own engagement. Engagement defines people's enthusiasm, attitude, and behavior—all of which are choices individuals make every day. Many leadership coaches observe that while leaders can set the stage for engagement, the choice to engage ultimately lies with each individual employee. This managerial perspective affirms that while culture and leadership matter, individual agency decides engagement. In our work this has been one of the most important principles for organizations to understand, and often almost a revolutionary thought.

4. **Choosing to be engaged is a WIN-WIN-WIN proposition, with real benefits**

We often treat employee engagement as if the greatest beneficiary is the company, and potentially the leaders. However, almost everyone benefits when employees choose to be engaged: the customers, the company, the work team, and the person choosing to be engaged. Only the competition is likely to suffer, since employee engagement is a sustainable competitive advantage that is difficult to copy.

Gallup's meta-analysis shows that business units with the highest employee engagement achieve significantly stronger outcomes: 18% higher sales productivity and 23% greater profitability, along with increases in customer loyalty and organizational citizenship. Mvuyana et al. (2025) also found an inverse relationship between employee engagement and counterproductive work behaviors.

Even though the results may not be surprising, they clearly show that engagement is not only a soft HR issue—it makes a measurable bottom-line difference.

5. **People who choose to be engaged are real beneficiaries**
Even with all the benefits to the company, the customers, and the work environment, the greatest beneficiary of engagement is the person who chooses to become and remain engaged. People who are engaged are happier, healthier, more satisfied in their work, and experience greater well-being at home. Actively engaged employees—those who choose to immerse themselves in their roles—experience a broad spectrum of benefits including improved job satisfaction, stronger intent to stay, and higher productivity. Also, Schaufeli, Bakker, and Salanova (2006) validated the Utrecht Work Engagement Scale across countries and demonstrated that work engagement is negatively related to burnout and positively related to well-being.

6. **Many employees choose not to be engaged, or even to be disengaged**
Based on Gallup research, as many as two-thirds of employees are either nonengaged or disengaged. Less than one-third of employees are engaged or highly engaged. The distinction between these groups is stark and this disengagement has a significant impact on performance, and incurs significant costs to organizations and even society. We have unfortunately learned that the actively disengaged can cause disproportionate damage to the morale and culture of engagement.

7. **The impact of the disengaged can be significant!**
Almost every workshop we have held over the years, the impact of the disengaged has seen the greatest interest around the topic of disengagement. Participants almost universally identify the wider negative impact of only one or two disengaged, negative team members. Unfortunately, most participants can also recount experiences where disengaged individuals have negatively affected them personally, as well as their workplace. Webb and Greer (2021) review the literature on disengagement and show that it is consistently linked to negative organizational outcomes, including reduced performance and higher costs across industries and functions. Also, Gallup has estimated a cost of $8.8 trillion loss to the economy in lost productivity (Gallup, 2022). Also, organizations with higher rates of disengagement have 37% higher absenteeism, and just one disengaged employee costs an organization $2,246 per year (ActivTrak 2024), as shown in Figure I.2:

8. **Teams play an important role in people's level of engagement**
We have found, globally and consistently, that positive teams significantly contribute to creating work environments where people choose to be engaged.

Research by Gallup (2015) highlights a striking gap in engagement across teams: managers alone account for 70% of the variance in employee engagement, meaning that high-functioning teams led by effective managers are far more engaged than poorly managed teams. Thus, building positive, well-functioning teams becomes a critical strategy for developing higher engagement levels across any organization.

Annual Cost Of Disengagement

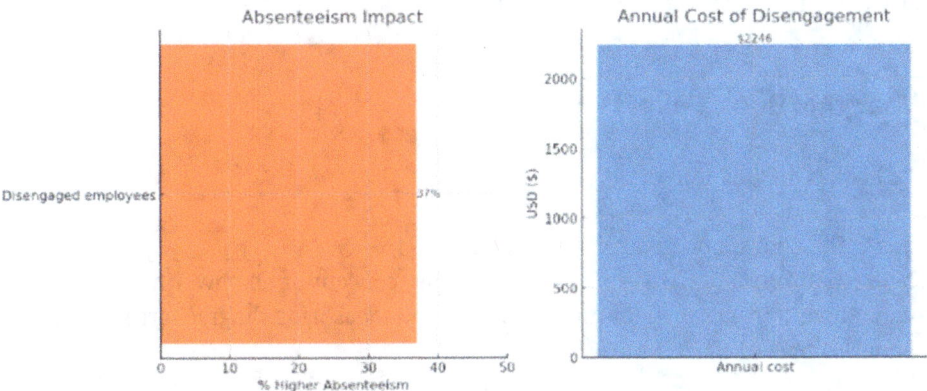

Figure I.2: Annual cost of disengagement.
Source: ActivTrak (2024). *Exploring the True Cost of Disengaged Employees*, 4 July.

9. **Leaders have a significance impact on employee engagement**
Leaders create an engaging environment where people choose to be engaged. It is not enough for leaders to be engaged—they must be engaging. For many leaders, this represents a paradigm shift: not just being engaged themselves, but actively creating an environment where others want to and choose to engage. As noted, Gallup shows that managers account for 70% of the variance in team engagement—highlighting that the behavior and support of leaders have the most profound influence on team morale and performance (Gallup 2015).

Often, leaders and supervisors are chosen based on their individual engagement and results, yet they receive little training on how to create an engaging environment for others. Without this understanding, leaders may overwork themselves, trying to use their own engagement, and end up doing everything, and burn out without recognizing what went wrong.

10. **There are concrete actions employees, leaders, and teams can take to improve engagement**
The key focus of our work is to help:
- Individual employees become more engaged
- Leaders create environments where people choose to be engaged
- Teams become more positive and engaging

Our experience shows that people want to work with engaged colleagues and teams. Generally, people want to be a positive force in their workplace and among teammates. However, many do not know how to improve their own engagement, be more engaging leaders, or foster positive teams that lift engagement for everyone.

Helping employees, leaders, and teams understand and take action to improve engagement has been, and continues to be, our core mission and the key motivation for writing this book.

What this Book Covers

The book is divided into three parts:

Part 1: The Concept of Engagement (Chapters 1–4)
This section introduces the importance and the concept of empowering engagement and outlines a framework for understanding and measuring the five forces and levels of engagement.

Part 2: Improving Engagement (Chapters 5–9)
This section focuses on the role individuals, leaders, and teams play in improving the level of engagement and provides strategies for individuals, leaders, and teams to permanently improve engagement, as well as to deal with actively disengaged employees. This section also explores strategies for embedding engagement across the organization and creating a culture where future employees can thrive, even in the face of evolving workplace dynamics. Also, in this section we discuss how we can make the company a stronger force for engagement. In addition, this section describes how to improve an organization's focus on the customer, and how engagement with customers benefits the customers and the organization.

Part 3: Emerging Themes in Engagement (Chapters 10–14)
Engagement is an important issue in the current, rapidly developing workplace, where remote work, AI, global developments, and increased demands on employees impact employees and their engagement. This section will specifically address the key issues facing organizations, leaders, and employees as they continue to improve employee engagement in their organizations, including dealing with the disengaged, the challenges and opportunities of remote work, and the evolving AI, multinational engagement issues, and leading a permanent change to a more engaged workforce and culture.

Part 1: **The Concept of Engagement**

Chapter 1
Employee Engagement Matters: Engaged Employees Produce Better Results

> "To win in the marketplace, you must first win in the workplace."
> — Doug Conant, former CEO of Campbell Soup Company

Engaged employees produce better outcomes and are happier in their work than non-engaged or actively disengaged workers. Research shows a clear relationship between employee engagement and positive outcomes. In this chapter we will make the following key points:
- Engagement improves outcomes.
- Engagement fuels innovation.
- Engagement impacts customers.
- Engagement enhances employee well-being.
- Employee engagement is low.
- It is possible to improve employee engagement.
- Engagement across all five forces matters.

The key focus of this book is to discuss ways to improve engagement and culture at all organizational levels (employees, teams, and leaders), as well as across the five forces of engagement (the company, leadership, teams, own work, and customers), as illustrated in Figure 1.1, and discussed in detail in Chapters 3 and 4.

Engagement Improves Outcomes

Gallup's 10th meta-analysis (2020), drawing on 465 research studies across 276 organizations in 54 industries and 96 countries, confirmed the robust work-unit-level connection between employee engagement and 11 performance outcomes. These include customer loyalty, productivity, profitability, turnover, absenteeism, quality, safety, and employee well-being.

Gallup's 10th meta-analysis (2020) compared top- and bottom-quartile business units and found striking differences in outcomes: 81% lower absenteeism, 58% fewer patient safety incidents, 18% and 43% lower turnover in high- and low-turnover organizations, respectively, 28% less shrinkage, 64% fewer safety incidents, 41% fewer quality defects, 10% higher customer loyalty, 18% higher sales productivity, and 23% greater profitability. Gallup also reported that companies with more engaged workforces achieved higher earnings per share (EPS), demonstrating a tangible link between engagement, stock performance, and investor value.

Figure 1.1: Improving organizational engagement across the five forces of engagement.

Yes, engagement matters. Big time! "Each percentage point gain or drop in engagement represents approximately 1.6 million full- or part-time employees in the U.S. Trends in employee engagement are significant because they are linked to many performance outcomes in organizations" (Gallup, 2024).

Engagement Fuels Innovation

Innovation is the lifeblood of sustainable success. Whether it's developing a new product, improving a process, or finding a creative way to serve customers, companies in the long run rise or fall on their ability to innovate. Here's where engagement plays a pivotal role. Engaged teams are far more innovative because people who are enthusiastic about their work seek out ways to make things better. They're not just punching the clock—they're thinking about how to solve problems and invent new solutions, often even when they're off the clock. In contrast, disengaged employees, at best, tend to stick strictly to their job descriptions and avoid extra effort or risk, stifling innovation. Companies with engaged employees see more creative ideas, which in turn lead to innovation and competitive advantage.

> Satya Nadella, CEO of Microsoft, who famously shifted Microsoft's culture from a knowing-it-all mentality to a learning-and-engaging mentality. When he took the helm in 2014, Microsoft was seen as a stagnating giant. Nadella championed a growth mindset and encouraged employees at all levels to share ideas and learn from failures. He often says, "Listen more, talk less, and be decisive when the time comes." By listening to and engaging employees, Nadella unlocked a wave of innovation—from the cloud business Azure to AI initiatives—that revitalized Microsoft. The company's market cap and product portfolio soared in the years that followed, a testament to how engagement and an innovation culture go hand in hand.
>
> Indra Nooyi, as CEO of PepsiCo, focused on engaging employees' hearts and minds, even writing personal letters to employees' parents to thank them for the "gift" of their child's work. This unusual gesture made employees feel deeply valued and proud—a level of personal engagement that translated into greater loyalty and willingness to contribute ideas. Under Nooyi's tenure, PepsiCo introduced innovative healthier product lines and saw sustained growth.

These, as well as many other examples, underline a key lesson: when leaders create a workplace where people choose to, and want to, be engaged, employees respond with commitment and creativity. New ideas and innovation flourish because people feel safe and motivated to push boundaries.

Engagement Impacts Customers

One specific area where employees and employee engagement make a big difference is in their impact on customers. Engaged employees directly influence customer satisfaction, loyalty, and engagement. Engaged employees enjoy connecting with and serving customers (both external and internal), and customers are more loyal and engaged with organizations where they are served by engaged employees. Most of us have encountered service from both engaged and disengaged employees, and these experiences are memorable—leaving strong emotional reactions. These are the experiences we tell others about, whether they are good or bad.

> Some years ago, while serving on the Halton Group Board, the Board traveled to Singapore for a meeting. Upon arrival at the airport, we were asked to fill out immigration papers. While waiting in line, a local immigration officer came to check that the papers were filled out correctly. When they reached the Finnish group and saw their passports, they enthusiastically declared, "FINLAND!" and proceeded to sing the Finnish national anthem. Later, when they saw my wife's American passport, they exclaimed, "AMERICANS!" and sang Frank Sinatra's *Strangers in the Night*. I asked why such enthusiasm for a job that simply involved checking papers. The officer replied, "I am the first Singaporean you meet, and I want to welcome you to Singapore. Anyone can check the papers, but I want to be the person you remember welcoming you to my country." No one minded the long line—we were all entertained and impressed. That employee's strong engagement left a lasting positive impression on all of us.
>
> However, another airport experience wasn't as positive. Years ago, I missed a flight in Helsinki and was quite frustrated. I found an alternative route and approached an airline employee, saying, "I'm sure you could help me." Their response: "I could help you, but I do not want to." At the time, one of

> the airline's leaders had just published a book on the importance of customer service. I asked about it, and the employee said, "Yes, they write these books, but that's not how we act." Needless to say, the experience—and the disengagement—made a lasting impression, and I haven't used that airline since.

Engagement matters to customers—engagement and disengagement can leave a lasting impression. Unfortunately, negative experiences tend to stick longer and spread wider than positive ones. That's why it's imperative for leaders to focus on fostering employee engagement and building an engaging culture to serve the customers.

Engagement Enhances Employee Well-Being

Robertson and Cooper (2010) argue that employee engagement is closely linked with psychological well-being. Engaged employees are more likely to report positive mental health, lower stress levels, and a stronger sense of purpose in their work. They are less likely to suffer from burnout and more likely to experience positive emotions at work.

Engaged employees often find deeper meaning in their work. According to Kahn (1990), employees are more engaged when they perceive their roles as meaningful and connected to organizational goals, fostering a stronger sense of purpose and psychological fulfillment. Steger, Dik, and Duffy (2012) found that meaningful work is strongly associated with intrinsic motivation and higher psychological well-being, underscoring the role of meaning in preventing disengagement and fostering positive mental health.

Employee Engagement is Low

It is well known that the COVID-19 pandemic caused lasting disruptions to work worldwide, affecting the engagement and well-being of millions of employees. Gallup's latest data show that U.S. employee engagement stagnated at the end of 2023, following a slight uptick in the first half of the year. However, in 2024 the global percentage of engaged employees fell from 23% to a low 21% as shown in Figure 1.2. (Gallup, 2025a). Employees still feel lonely after the COVID pandemic—whether they work remotely or not—resulting in a historically high level of disengagement, absenteeism, turnover, and increased employee health care costs (Hadley and Wright 2024).

During the pandemic and after, the most dramatic decline in engagement occurred among the younger generations, and especially the older group of millennials (born between 1980 and 1988). The percentage of these engaged millennials declined by seven points, from 39% to 32%, while the percentage of actively disengaged older millennials increased by five points, from 12% to 17%. This means the engagement

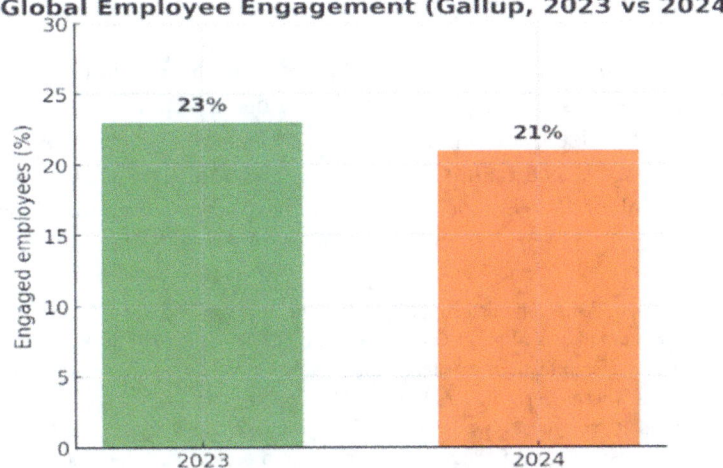

Figure 1.2: Global employee engagement (Gallup, 2023 vs. 2024).

ratio (engaged/disengaged) plummeted from 3.3 to 1.9—i.e., for every actively disengaged employee, there are now only slightly more than two engaged ones. This trend could have a negative long-term impact on U.S. workplaces and competitiveness unless it is reversed.

However, one powerful positive example of engagement breeding resilience also came during the COVID-19 pandemic. Many companies had to pivot overnight to remote work and new business models. The ones that navigated this successfully often reported that their employees showed extraordinary adaptability—volunteering for new roles, learning new skills, and helping colleagues juggle responsibilities. Why? Because those employees were engaged—they cared about helping the organization survive. They had built up a reservoir of goodwill and connection that they could draw on under stress. Gallup's research during this period found that teams with high engagement had significantly lower reports of burnout and maintained higher well-being, even amid uncertainty. Engaged employees were more likely to feel their company had their back—and in turn, they had their company's back. This reciprocal trust is the essence of resilience.

Deborah Perry Piscione and Josh Drean emphasize that many employees are less disconnected from work—they feel a gap between their tasks and the greater purpose. If leaders ignore this preference for meaningful work, they risk losing top talent (Perry Picone and Drean 2025).

It is Possible to Improve Engagement

Even though Gallup's data show that the world's workplace is not headed in the right direction, there is hope. The data also show a productivity boom opportunity if employees, teams, and leaders seize the moment. Gallup estimates that if the world's workplace were fully engaged, $9.6 trillion in productivity could be added to the global economy, the equivalent of 9% in global GDP. The best practice organizations have 70% employees engaged, compared to the global average of 21% (Gallup 2025).

> A great case study on engagement is the Campbell Soup Company. The company had lost half its market value in 2000 when Doug Conant was hired as CEO. From 2001 to 2011, he led a dramatic turnaround. He transformed the leadership team, restructured the portfolio, cut costs, reshaped the culture, and made key investments. These efforts delivered top-tier shareholder returns.
>
> Doug Conant understood that "you must have talented people who are highly engaged in their work to have any chance of winning in the marketplace." His mission to achieve superior employee engagement became a cornerstone of Campbell's success and the foundation of the Conant Leadership Flywheel. Under his leadership, employee engagement went from one of the lowest in the Fortune 500 to among the best. His philosophy: "Be tough-minded on standards and tender-hearted with people."
>
> Campbell Soup Company took three major steps to reach world-class engagement:
> 1. Created "The Campbell Promise"—valuing people and trusting they would, in turn, value the company
> 2. Staffed leadership positions with the best qualified leaders
> 3. Measured engagement, based on the principle that "you can't manage what you can't measure"
>
> Over time, they increased their ratio of highly engaged to nonengaged employees from 2:1 to 17:1—a truly world-class outcome. The Campbell story shows that engagement can be improved, and that it pays off.
>
> (For Doug Conant's full story in his own voice, see: https://conantleadership.com/the-campbell-soup-story/)

Engagement Matters

Every leader knows that talent is precious. In today's knowledge economy, people are an organization's greatest asset—and losing great people physically or emotionally is costly. High turnover or low engagement drains momentum, drives up recruiting and training costs, and erodes institutional knowledge. Why do employees stay or leave? Increasingly, it's about whether they feel engaged and appreciated.

A striking Gallup statistic reveals the truth: when asked why they left their last job, the #1 reason wasn't money—it was "engagement and culture." In total, 37% cited cultural fit or engagement issues, compared to only 16% who left for better pay (Gallup, 2025b). In other words, people are over twice as likely to quit because they feel uninspired or unsupported, rather than underpaid. While fair compensation is essential, keeping top performers requires engagement: engaged employees are 87% less likely to leave than their disengaged peers (PeopleThriver, 2025), highlighting how engagement often matters more than pay in retention

Employee engagement isn't a luxury. It's essential. Research consistently shows that engagement drives performance, innovation, service quality, well-being, profitability, retention, and shareholder value. Improving the current declining employee engagement isn't just a "nice to have"—it's possible, and a business imperative. Engagement matters!

Key Questions
1. Why does employee engagement matter to your organization?
2. What are the key benefits of a high level of employee engagement to your organization?
3. In your experience, how has employee engagement impacted you as a customer?
4. What is the potential impact of high employee engagement on your employees?
5. How could your organization benefit from increased employee engagement?

Chapter 2
Levels of Engagement
Level of Engagement for Individuals Varies and Impacts Results

> "Engagement is not a binary state. It is a spectrum that reflects how employees relate to their work, their team, and the organization."
> — Kevin Kruse, entrepreneur and leadership expert

The level of engagement of individuals, teams, and departments varies, and understanding how engaged employees are is critical in order to know how to improve employee engagement.

Gallup, the premier company measuring engagement globally, makes a strong case for the importance of measuring engagement, and recommends strongly measuring employee engagement so leaders understand employee sentiment and needs

In the following three chapters, we present a unique, conceptual framework for engagement, which we believe is critical for managers seeking to improve employee engagement in their organizations:

- In this chapter (Chapter 2), we discuss the different levels of engagement and describe how these levels impact individual performance. We specifically divide the engagement levels into four groups: the actively disengaged, the nonengaged, the engaged, and the highly engaged, also describing the typical characteristics of each group.
- In Chapter 3, we present and discuss in detail the five forces of engagement (company, leaders, teams, individual work, and customers).
- In Chapter 4, we combine the levels (from Chapter 2) and forces of engagement (from Chapter 3) into a measurement tool and visual model to help management understand engagement across different parts of the organization. This is shown in our multidimensional graph represented by the five forces of engagement shown in Figure 2.1, and explained in more detail in Chapter 4.

Understanding the Continuum of Engagement

Employee engagement is often spoken about, and even measured, in simple terms: either employees are engaged or they are not. In reality, engagement exists along a continuum, ranging from active disengagement to high engagement. Understanding these different levels is essential for leaders who aim to build high-performing, resilient, and innovative workplaces.

Gallup has conducted decades of research into employee attitudes and behaviors. Their framework divides employees into three broad categories: engaged, not engaged, and actively disengaged. However, we, as well as many experts and organiza-

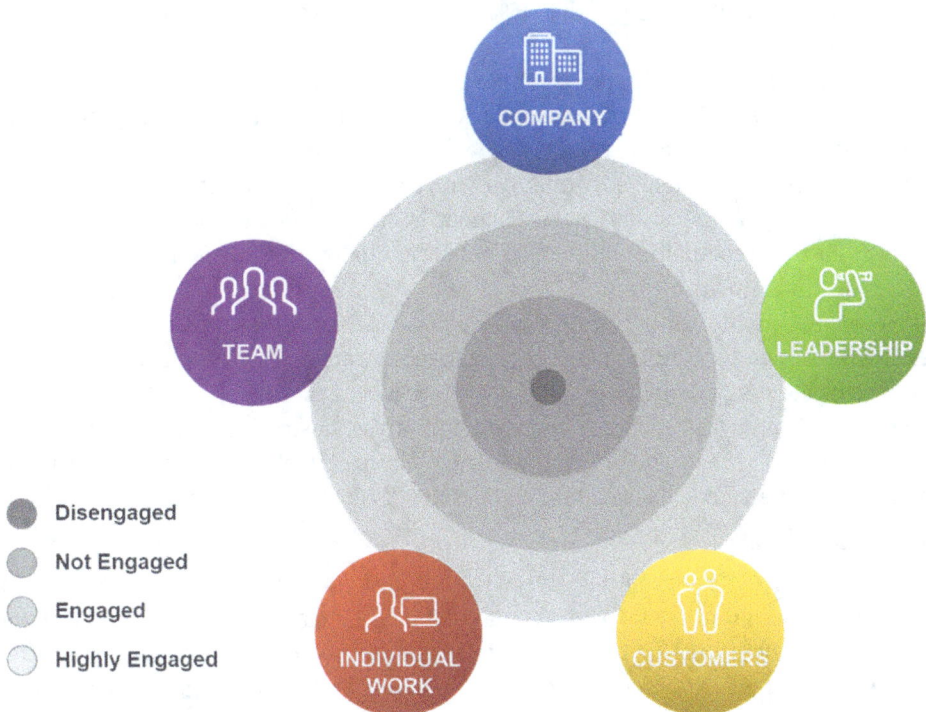

Figure 2.1: Multidimensional representation of employee engagement with the four levels of engagement.

tions, further segment this into four levels, adding a fourth tier: the highly engaged employees.

Employee engagement is commonly understood as existing along a continuum, with the four distinct levels that reflect the degree to which employees are emotionally and behaviorally invested in their work. These levels include actively disengaged, not engaged, engaged, and highly engaged.

This chapter explores each of these four levels, using academic insights and real-world examples to highlight their significance and implications.

The Four Levels of Engagement

1. The Actively Disengaged
Disengaged employees are not only unhappy at work—they act out their dissatisfaction. These individuals may undermine their colleagues, resist leadership initiatives, or spread negativity throughout the workplace. Gallup estimates that in the U.S., 17% of employees are actively disengaged—the highest level recorded in a decade (Gallup,

2025). Globally, Gallup reports that 15% of employees are actively disengaged (Gallup, 2024).

"Actively disengaged employees aren't just unhappy at work; they're busy acting out their unhappiness. Every day, these workers undermine what their engaged coworkers accomplish."— Gallup (2020)

Actively disengaged employees can have a corrosive impact on morale, productivity, and customer relationships. The Engagement Institute estimates that disengaged employees cost U.S. companies up to $550 billion annually in lost productivity (InStride 2022; The Engagement Institute 2017).

For example, a customer service agent who dislikes their job may respond to customers with sarcasm or indifference. One negative interaction can ruin a customer's experience, potentially costing the company future business.

Disengaged employees sabotage company initiatives, destroy team effort, and often cause more harm than good over time. They talk negatively about company values, disrespect leaders and colleagues, and generally do less than expected.

2. The Nonengaged

This "nonengaged" group of employees is often described as "checked out." They do the bare minimum to get through the day. While they may not actively sabotage the workplace, they are not emotionally invested in their work or the organization. The following statement has been attributed to Gallup 2013 Employee Engagement Checklist, and has been qupoted by numerous third party sources. "Not engaged employees are essentially sleepwalking through their workday. They put time—but not energy or passion—into their work." — Gallup Workplace Research (2013)

The nonengaged often form the largest segment in most organizations. They are at the greatest risk of turnover if a better opportunity arises—not because they are actively dissatisfied, but because they lack any strong ties to their current role. In the 2025 *State of the Global Workplace*, Gallup estimates that 62% of employees are not engaged.

For example, a mid-level analyst may consistently meet deadlines and produce acceptable work but never contribute ideas or volunteer for stretch projects. They coast along, and their potential contributions are lost.

Nonengaged employees are indifferent. They do not put in extra effort to move the company forward, are apathetic toward the mission and values, and merely tolerate their team members. They approach work as just a job.

3. The Engaged

Engaged employees are enthusiastic, committed, and connected to their work. They show up not just for a paycheck, but because they care about their performance and the performance of their company. They are more productive, have lower absenteeism, and are more likely to stay with the organization.

"Engaged employees are highly involved in and enthusiastic about their work and workplace." (Gallup 2022)

Saks (2006) found that employee engagement is positively influenced by perceived organizational support and job characteristics. Drawing on the Job Characteristics Model, this suggests that organizations providing meaningful work, autonomy, and recognition are more likely to foster higher levels of engagement.

For example, an engaged marketing associate who brainstorms new campaign ideas, volunteers to lead initiatives, and celebrates team wins embodies engagement. Their engagement and enthusiasm often lift those around them.

Engaged employees move the company forward. They support the mission, respect leaders, work well with teammates, and consistently meet organizational expectations.

4. The Highly Engaged

"Highly engaged" employees differ from merely engaged employees. They have an outsized impact on their teams and the company. They are passionate, accountable, trustworthy, collaborative, and relentlessly focused on development—their own, their team's, and the organization's. They consistently promote the company's mission, co-operate with teammates, and drive leader strategies forward.

The highly engaged are the ambassadors, innovators, and informal leaders within an organization. They not only perform at a high level themselves but also inspire others to do the same.

Highly engaged employees are strongly emotionally connected to the company's mission and often go above and beyond expectations. They act as multipliers, enhancing their teams' performance and helping drive cultural transformation.

For example, consider an engineer who not only excels in technical work but also mentors new hires, proposes process improvements, and influences company strategy through cross-functional collaboration.

"When people are financially invested, they want a return. When people are emotionally invested, they want to contribute." — Simon Sinek

Gallup finds that when companies can increase the rate of highly engaged employees, they achieve, on average, 147% higher earnings per share than their competition (Gallup 2014).

Leaders must identify these individuals early and create opportunities for them to grow, mentor others, and influence culture. Neglecting their development can lead to attrition and a broader decline in engagement levels.

Engagement Levels Matter

Understanding and managing the different levels of employee engagement is critical for strategic success. Actively disengaged employees can harm morale and performance, while nonengaged employees represent untapped potential. Engaged employees deliver strong, consistent results, and highly engaged employees can transform organizations.

Leaders must tailor their strategies to meet employees where they are along the engagement spectrum. Recognition, career development, meaningful work, and emotional connection all play vital roles in moving people from disengagement toward high engagement.

As Doug Conant, former CEO of Campbell Company, famously has stated in many of his speeches and interviews (Conant Leadership, 2015):

"To win in the marketplace, you must first win in the workplace."

By fostering engagement at all levels, organizations not only create better workplaces—they create a culture of sustainable competitive advantage.

 Key Questions
1. Why is it important in your organization to understand the different levels of engagement?
2. What has been the potential impact of the actively disengaged in your organization, or in any other organization you know?
3. From your experience, can you identify anyone you would think is highly engaged? What has been his/her impact on the organization?
4. What are the key differences between the nonengaged and the engaged employees?
5. Why would you look for the highly engaged in your organization to support the organization's innovation effort?

Chapter 3
Multidimensional Engagement
The Five Forces for Engagement

> "When people are financially invested, they want a return. When people are emotionally invested, they want to contribute."
> — *Simon Sinek*

Employee engagement refers to the level of enthusiasm, commitment, and involvement an individual has in their work and organization. Kahn (1990) first conceptualized it as the emotional, cognitive, and physical investment of the self in work role performance. Later research has expanded this view, showing how engagement connects not only to an individual's tasks but also to their leaders, teammates, the organization, and even the customers they serve.

Saks (2006) found that employee engagement is shaped by multiple antecedents, including job characteristics, organizational support, and procedural justice, suggesting that engagement emerges from a combination of influences across the workplace environment. In other words, an employee's engagement is shaped by multiple "forces" acting together. Markos and Sridevi (2010) argue that employee engagement is shaped by multiple organizational factors acting together. When these conditions are positive and aligned, employees are more likely to go beyond their formal roles, resulting in stronger performance outcomes.

This chapter explores and discusses the five key factors or "forces" for engagement that we have found together create the overall engagement experience for employees. These forces are the Company (or organization), Leadership (and management), Teams, Own Work assignment, and Customers. Each represents a distinct domain of influence:

1. **Company:** The overall organization, including its culture, values, and policies.
2. **Leadership:** The influence of managers, supervisors, and leaders through their actions and decisions.
3. **Teams:** The relationships and dynamics among coworkers and teams.
4. **Own Work:** The nature of the job role and tasks, and how meaningful and motivating they are.
5. **Customers:** The interaction with and impact of serving customers (internal or external) or end-users.

Each of these forces plays a critical role in shaping employee engagement. In this chapter we will examine how each force contributes to engagement and why a holistic approach—addressing in turn each of the five forces—is essential to sustain high levels of workforce engagement. These five forces are represented in Figure 3.1.

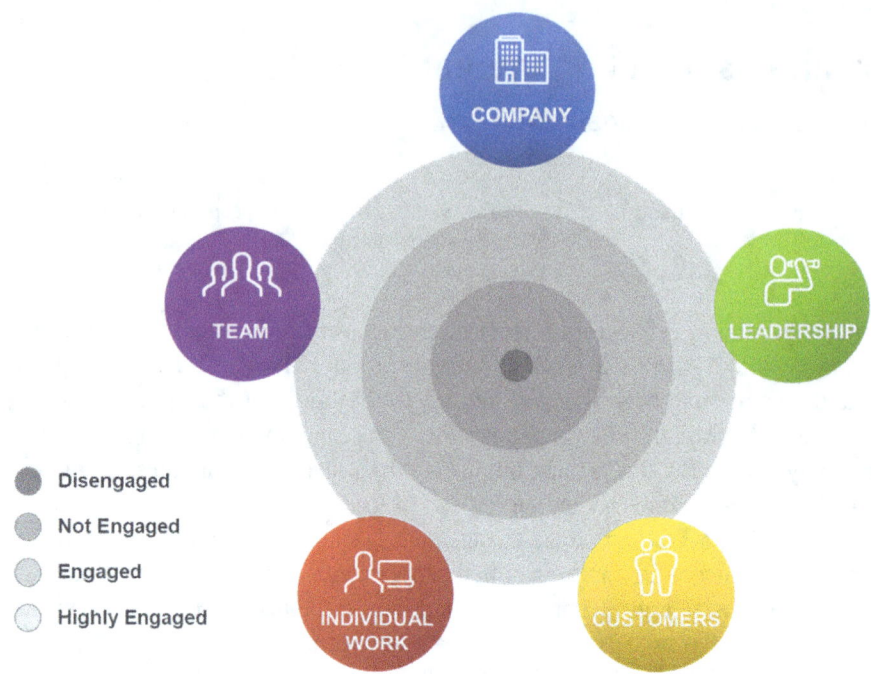

Figure 3.1: Five forces of employee engagement.

Company

The first force is the company itself—the wider organizational environment in which employees operate. This includes the company's ownership, brand, culture, values, mission, and the support structures that the organization provides. Employees tend to be more engaged when they feel proud of their organization and believe in its values, direction, and purpose. A positive organizational culture—one that aligns with their own values, and promotes trust, fairness, and a sense of belonging—lays the foundation for engagement. When the company clearly communicates its vision and values and aligns them with daily practices, employees are more likely to feel connected to a common purpose.

Organization's support is a key aspect of this force. Employees who perceive that their company is fair, and genuinely cares about their well-being and development, will typically exhibit higher level of engagement. For example, providing opportunities for growth, recognizing employee contributions, and maintaining fair policies can all strengthen an employee's commitment to the organization. Saks (2006) demonstrated that perceived organizational support is a significant antecedent of employee engagement, underscoring the role of reciprocity in the employee–organization relationship. In practical terms, this means that if the company invests in its people—

through training, supportive HR practices, and a positive work climate—employees reciprocate with greater loyalty, engagement, and effort. Conversely, a dysfunctional or negative company culture can undermine engagement, even if other factors like interesting work or good teams are present. Thus, the company's overall environment acts as a force that can either enable or hinder the other drivers of engagement. Chapter 8 discusses the company impact on engagement in more detail.

Leadership

Leadership is the clearly major force for engagement and refers to the influence of both senior executives and direct managers on employees' engagement. Leaders set the tone for what it feels like to work at the organization. Effective leadership builds trust, instills confidence, and provides clear direction—all of which are essential for strong engagement. Employees are more engaged when they trust their leaders and feel that management is competent and cares about their welfare. Open communication, transparency in decision-making, and demonstrating integrity are leadership behaviors that strengthen this trust.

Immediate supervisors also play a particularly crucial role. It is often said that "employees leave managers, not companies," highlighting how a poor relationship with one's direct boss can damage engagement. In fact, studies indicate that leadership quality, particularly the behavior of direct managers, is one of the strongest influences on employee engagement (Xu and Thomas, 2011). Leaders who empower their team members—by providing a strong vision, values, feedback, coaching, and autonomy—tend to foster higher engagement levels among employees. By contrast, a leadership style that is short sighted, authoritarian, unsupportive, or inconsistent can disengage employees, even if those employees are passionate about their work.

A supportive leadership approach involves recognizing employees' accomplishments and addressing their concerns. When leaders show appreciation for hard work and give credit where it is due, employees feel valued and motivated to maintain high performance. Additionally, clear and inspiring communication from leadership about how each person's work contributes to the organization's goals can reinforce a sense of meaning and engagement. In summary, leadership serves as a major force that can amplify engagement by creating an environment of trust and empowerment, or diminish it if mismanaged. Chapter 6 will discuss in more detail ways leaders can improve employee engagement.

Teams

The third force, teams, encompasses the relationships and social dynamics among coworkers. In our work with companies around the globe, we learned that humans everywhere are social creatures, and the quality of interpersonal interactions at work significantly affects how engaged team members are. A collaborative, supportive team can motivate individuals to be more involved and committed, whereas a tense or isolating team environment can erode enthusiasm. When employees have strong, positive working relationships—characterized by trust, empathy, mutual respect, and camaraderie—they often report higher levels of engagement. Feeling part of a cohesive team gives employees a sense of belonging and accountability to one another, and to their work.

Peer support is a crucial element here. Colleagues who help each other, share knowledge, and provide encouragement contribute to a culture where engagement thrives. Research on workplace engagement has found that social support from coworkers is associated with increased engagement and better performance outcomes (Salanova et al., 2005). In settings where teamwork is integral, engaged teams can even experience a sort of collective engagement, where enthusiasm and effort become contagious. This is why many organizations invest in team-building and fostering an inclusive culture—the benefits are not just better morale, but tangible improvements in how engaged employees are in their tasks.

Multiple studies indicate that teams functioning better—through strong leadership, psychological safety, trust, feedback, shared decision-making, and collaboration—are environments where individual employee engagement thrives more than in poorly functioning teams. For example, Mazzetti et al. (2022) demonstrated how team resources catalyze both team effectiveness and individual engagement, revealing that well-supported teams foster higher motivation and involvement at work.

On the other hand, negative team dynamics—such as lack of trust, conflict, lack of cooperation, or feeling excluded—can be highly detrimental. If employees dread interacting with their team or feel that their contributions are not valued by peers, their engagement will likely suffer. Thus, the team environment acts as a force for engagement either by reinforcing positive work experiences or by exacerbating disengagement when team relations are poor. Effective teams celebrate successes together and navigate challenges with a shared mindset, which boosts each member's commitment to the work. Chapter 7 discusses ways teams can promote behaviors to improve team members' engagement.

Own Work

The fourth force is an employee's own work assignment—the nature of the job itself and the intrinsic satisfaction it provides. Even within the same company, with the same leadership and team, an individual's engagement can vary greatly depending on whether people experience their work as fulfilling. Key aspects of the work itself include how meaningful the tasks are, the level of challenge and variety, opportunities for skill use and growth, and the degree of autonomy or control one has over their work. When a role is designed well and aligns with an employee's strengths and interests, it can ignite personal passion and dedication.

Employees are most engaged when they find personal meaning in what they do. Psychological research shows that meaningful work is a powerful driver of engagement. Kahn (1990) argued that people are more engaged when their work feels worthwhile, while May et al. (2004) found that psychological meaningfulness was the strongest predictor of engagement in their empirical study. For instance, jobs that allow creativity, problem-solving, or helping others tend to generate higher engagement because they tap into core human motivators like mastery and purpose.

Autonomy is another important factor: having the freedom to make decisions about one's own work can enhance ownership and intrinsic motivation, which in turn fuels engagement. The Job Demands–Resources model of work engagement highlights job resources—such as autonomy, feedback, social support, and opportunities for development—as key drivers of engagement (Bakker and Demerouti, 2008).

Feedback and recognition related to the work also play a role. When employees can see the results of their efforts and receive acknowledgment for good work, it reinforces the value of their contribution. If, however, a job is monotonous, overly micromanaged, or doesn't utilize an employee's capabilities, disengagement can set in. People disengage when work feels pointless or when they have no say in how it's done. Therefore, ensuring that each employee's work is enriching and well-structured, aligning with their skills and values, is vital. The force of "Own Work" highlights that even in a great company with supportive leadership and teams, the day-to-day job experience must itself be engaging for the employee to truly thrive.

Customers

The fifth key force, customers, might seem outward-facing, but it has a profound feedback effect on employee engagement. This force represents the impact of serving customers (or clients, or end-users) and how that interaction influences employees' attitudes toward their work. For many employees, seeing how their work makes a difference for customers can be a powerful source of motivation. When employees interact directly with customers, positive customer feedback and satisfaction can boost an employee's pride and commitment to their job. Even employees who do not interact with customers personally can feel more engaged if they understand how their work ultimately serves or benefits the end-user.

Organizations that successfully link employees' roles to customer outcomes often create a stronger sense of purpose. For example, knowing that one's efforts lead to a happy customer experience or solve a client's problem gives meaning to day-to-day tasks. Engaged employees are often described as those who "go the extra mile" for customers, and this customer-focused mindset can reinforce their own engagement in a virtuous cycle. Research confirms that companies with higher employee engagement tend to achieve better customer satisfaction and loyalty, demonstrating that employee engagement and customer outcomes are closely linked (Harter, Schmidt and Hayes, 2002). This pattern is often described as the "service-profit chain" (Heskett et al., 1994), which explains how engaged employees deliver better customer experiences, ultimately driving customer loyalty, revenue growth, and profitability. In a well-documented case, Sears found that improvements in employee attitudes translated into measurable gains in customer satisfaction, which subsequently drove revenue growth (Rucci, Kirn and Quinn, 1998). This illustrates the mutually reinforcing nature of the employee–customer link.

From the employee's perspective, being able to witness satisfied customers can validate the importance of their work. It's motivating to know that one's effort has real-world impact. Some organizations involve employees in hearing customer testimonials or seeing how products benefit users in order to strengthen this connection. However, if employees are shielded from customer impact or if they frequently face unhappy customers without support, this force can turn negative, leading to frustration and burnout. Thus, fostering a strong connection between employees and the customers they serve—through feedback loops, a customer-centric culture, and empowerment to resolve customer issues—can significantly enhance engagement.

The Five Forces of Engagement

Employee engagement is a multifaceted phenomenon shaped by the interplay of the five forces: Company, Leadership, Teams, Own Work, and Customers. Each force contributes a vital piece to the engagement puzzle. A company with a positive culture and supportive policies creates the groundwork for engagement. Strong and inspiring leadership then builds on that foundation, guiding and motivating employees. Positive team relationships add a layer of social support and belonging that can boost morale and commitment. Meaningful, well-designed work provides the personal motivation and fulfillment that sustain individual engagement. Finally, a clear line of sight to customers and the impact of one's work adds purpose, reinforcing why the work matters.

For maximum engagement, organizations must pay attention to all five forces. They are interdependent; weakness in one area can undermine strengths in another. For instance, even a passionate employee (high Own Work engagement) can become disengaged if the leadership is poor or the company's culture is toxic. Conversely, an employee-friendly company and great manager might not fully engage someone whose role is dull or disconnected from any clear purpose. By ensuring alignment across company values, leadership behaviors, team culture, job design, and customer connection, employers can create a work environment where engagement flourishes on multiple levels.

When the five forces for engagement are all positively aligned, the result is a workforce that is not only satisfied, but engaged—employees who are loyal, enthusiastic, and willing to give their best effort. This multidimensional engagement drives better performance, innovation, and customer satisfaction, creating a competitive advantage for the organization (Markos and Sridevi, 2010). Leaders and HR professionals should thus evaluate and strengthen each of these areas as part of a comprehensive engagement strategy. By understanding and leveraging the five forces for engagement, organizations can sustain high engagement even in challenging times, leading to improved outcomes for both employees and the business as a whole.

Key Questions
1. What elements in your company or organization could likely strengthen employee engagement?
2. In your own assessment, how engaged are employees by the leadership in your organization?
3. Is the team you are currently part of motivating and engaging you? Why?
4. What could your organization do to strengthen employees' engagement with their own work assignments?
5. How could employees' engagement with customers and customer service improve customer loyalty and satisfaction for your organization?

Chapter 4
Engagement Profiles
Combining Levels and Forces of Engagement

> "Highly engaged employees make the customer experience. Disengaged employees break it."
> — Timothy R. Clark, Founder and CEO of LeaderFactor

Employees' level of engagement is shaped by multiple interconnected forces that influence how employees think, feel, and act at work. These five key forces were discussed in Chapter 3. *The company* culture sets the foundation—when values, communication, and policies align with purpose and fairness, employees are more likely to invest themselves. *Leadership* plays a pivotal role by fostering trust, recognition, and development opportunities, directly influencing motivation and emotional connection. Within *teams*, collaboration, support, and shared goals create a sense of belonging that fuels engagement. Equally important is the *individual's commitment to their work* and customers—when employees find meaning in their tasks and see the impact of their contributions, they are more energized, loyal, and willing to go the extra mile. Focus on *customers* is a critical part of determining engagement. Together, these five forces form a dynamic system that either amplifies or erodes engagement levels across the organization.

In this chapter, we combine the two concepts: the levels of engagement from Chapter 2 and the five forces of engagement from Chapter 3 into a conceptual model and graphic representation to clarify how these concepts interact. This is particularly useful for leaders to understand what engages different parts of the organization, so they can focus on what individuals, leaders, and teams can do better to improve the culture and level of engagement.

The success and versatility of our profile model stems from combining the two dimensions described in Chapters 2 and 3—the levels of engagement and the five multidimensional forces of engagement. These dimensions address two fundamental questions of engagement: "How engaged are people?" and "What engages (or disengages) them?"

How can the model be interpreted?

In the model, the different rings represent the levels of engagement, and the closer the graph is to the outer ring, the higher the level of engagement is relating to the specific force identified by the five balls around the model; that is, if the graph is close to the outer ring on the company, it shows high engagement to the company force, and on the other hand, if the graph is close to the center (disengaged) on any of the dimensions, it reflects low engagement, or even disengagement in relation to that engagement force.

How were the graphs developed and measured?

The graphs were developed by a questionnaire with a total of 30 five-point Likert scale questions relating to the five forces (six questions for each force), plus some demographic questions defined by the specific company and unit. The questions were aligned closely to the Gallup questionnaire, as well as other engagement questionnaires, to improve the validity of our surveys. Individual responses were then averaged across the different units to get unit-specific results. No units with fewer than five valid responses were aggregated or reported.

Creating this engagement profile with the five elements of engagement and the four levels of engagement adds a better understanding of the engagement drivers, and presenting this in an engagement profile has been an eye-opener for many, as shown in Figure 4.1.

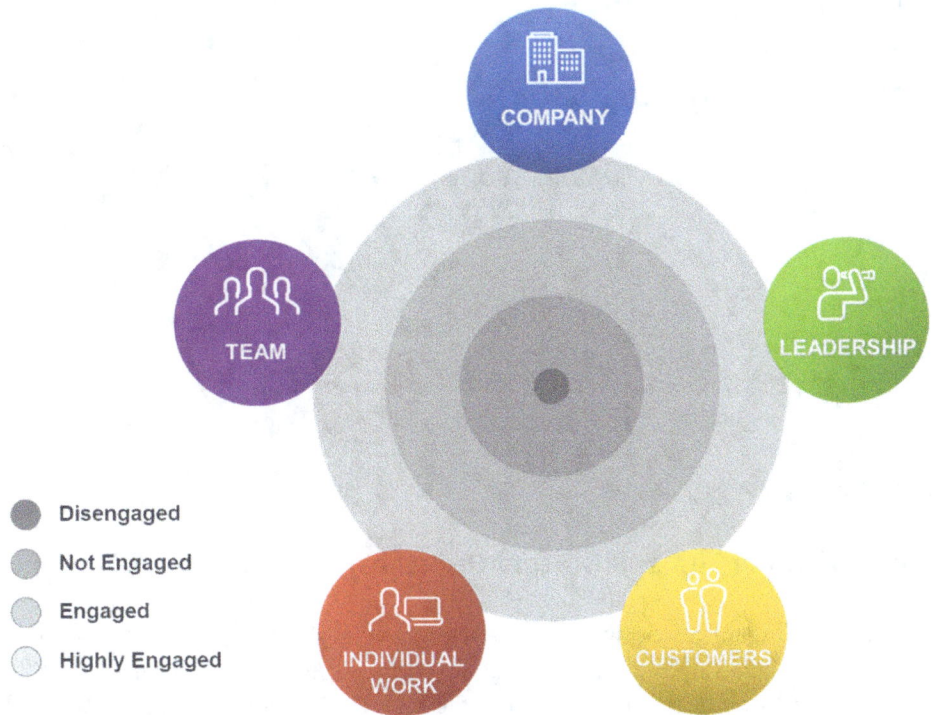

Figure 4.1: The Model: Levels of and Five Forces of Engagement.

This profile, which combines both the different levels of engagement and the five elements of engagement, is a significant contribution to the concept of engagement and gives us both interesting and useful insights into employees and organizations. Using this model, we can compare, and better understand, the engagement profiles of different organizations, departments, and teams. These profiles provide insights to management on how to better manage and engage the employees in their organization.

Comparison of Total Organizations

Figure 4.2 presents profile comparisons for two large customer service organizations. Even though both organizations have a rather strong engagement, clearly, organization 1 employees are more committed and engaged across all the engagement elements than organization 2, and the customer service organization 1 is likely to perform at a higher level than organization 2. Even though unit 2 has consistently lower levels of engagement across all the elements, it is particularly low in the company, where organization 1 is highly engaged, and organization 2's engagement is at a nonengaging level.

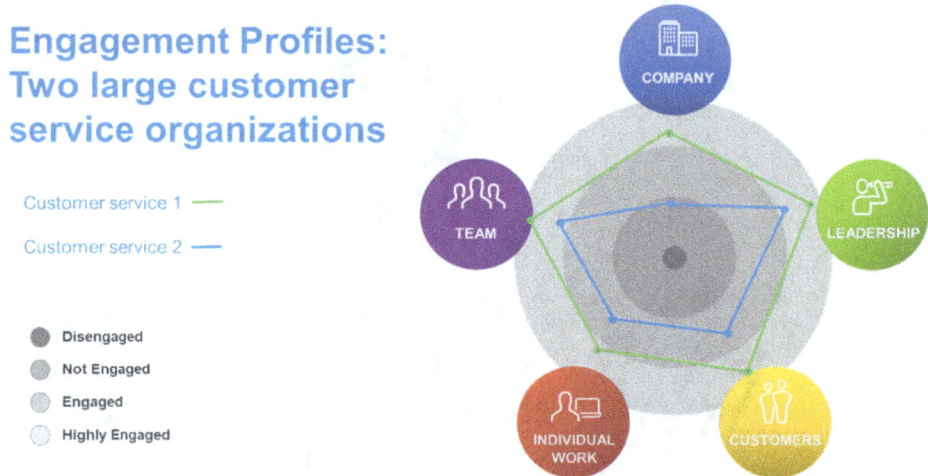

Figure 4.2: Comparison of Organizations.

Comparison of Top and Bottom Quartiles

In comparing organizations, we often see significant levels of engagement differences between the highest and lowest levels of engagement. As shown in Figures 4.3, and Figure 4.4. in two different organizations, the highest 25% and the lowest 25% of engagement scores in the same organization are significantly different. In these profiles, we can see how the top 25% is highly engaged across all elements, whereas the lowest quartile is at a nonengaged level across all the elements, except the company, where they are even at the disengaged level. This is likely to have a significant negative impact on the performance and motivation of the lowest 25% of employees.

This figure is very typical for most organizations we have worked with, signifying that even in the highly engaged organization, there is generally a significant portion of people who are not engaged, or even disengaged, across several of the five forces of engagement.

Organization lowest 25% and highest 25% engagement profiles

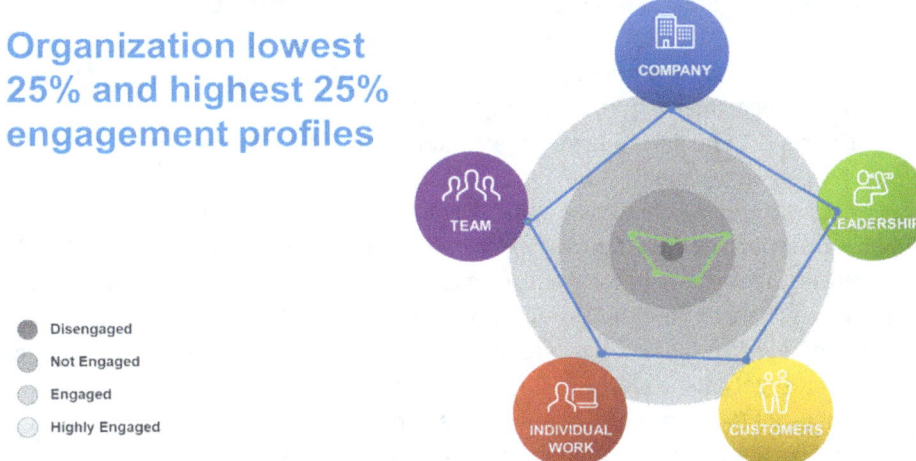

- Disengaged
- Not Engaged
- Engaged
- Highly Engaged

Figure 4.3: Top and Bottom Quartile Engagement in the Same Organization.

To illustrate this in a rather positive organization, the comparison of the top 25% and lower 25% looks somewhat different, where even the lowest 25% is highly engaged with the customers, and at least somewhat engaged with their own work. However, the bottom 25% is not engaged with the company, leaders, or their teams, and this likely has an impact on the organization's performance.

Highest and lowest 25% for a customer service company

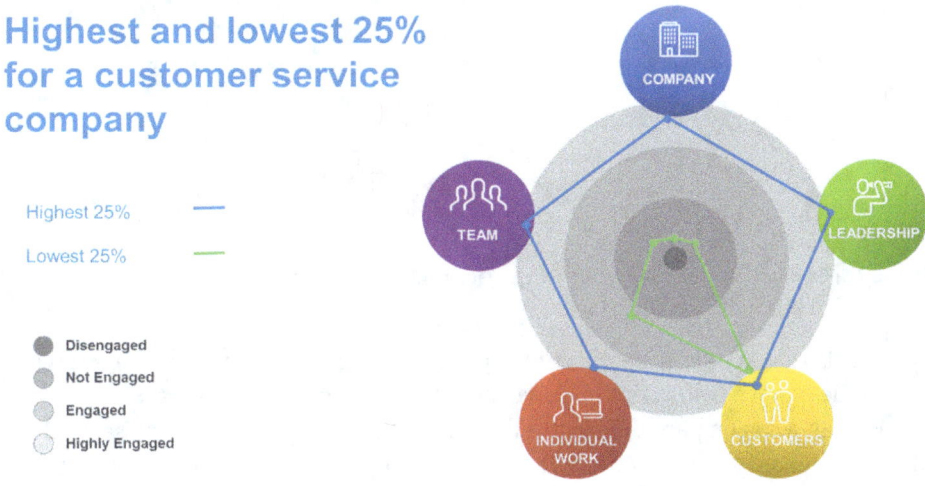

Highest 25% —
Lowest 25% —

- Disengaged
- Not Engaged
- Engaged
- Highly Engaged

Figure 4.4: Top and Bottom Quartile Engagement in the Same Organization.

Comparison of Departments, Organizations, and Roles

Furthermore, the model can also give us significant insight into how engagement differs between departments in the same organization.

In Figures 4.5 and 4.6 we have added another measure: the proportion of people in each level of engagement.

Figures 4.5 and 4.6 show two approximately the same-sized departments in the same organization. In these figures, we compare the profiles of the groups in the different engagement levels, and have also given the size of these different groups, from the highly engaged to the disengaged. Comparing these profiles, we see clearly different levels of engagement and likely different performances as well. Department 1 has much lower engagement levels and a much higher level of disengaged (17% vs. 0%) and nonengaged (60% vs. 28%), and we can say that there is likely a significant measurable difference in the performance between departments.

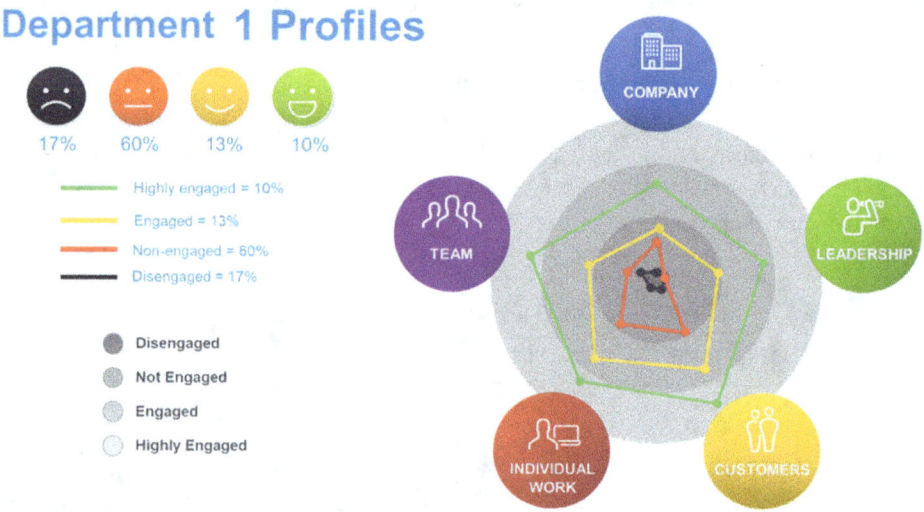

Figure 4.5: Comparison of Groups in Different Engagement Level Groups—Department 1.

We can also see similar differences in departments in a retail setting, as we can see in the profiles shown below for two departments in the same store (Figure 4.7).

We can also compare different retail store profiles (Figure 4.8) in the same chain of stores and see the differences. These levels of engagement also correspond to different performance levels in these stores, which is not surprising.

Or, we can see different levels of engagement based on the functions in the organization, such as office and factory workers, shown in Figure 4.9.

Furthermore, in our experience in most organizations, managers tend to be more engaged than the rest of the employees, and staff tend to be more engaged than fac-

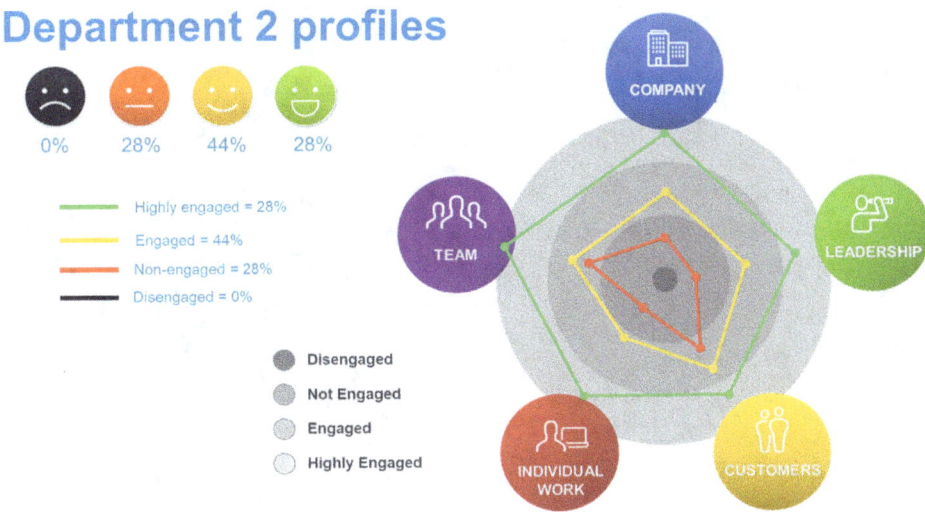

Figure 4.6: Comparison of Groups in Different Engagement Level Groups—Department 2.

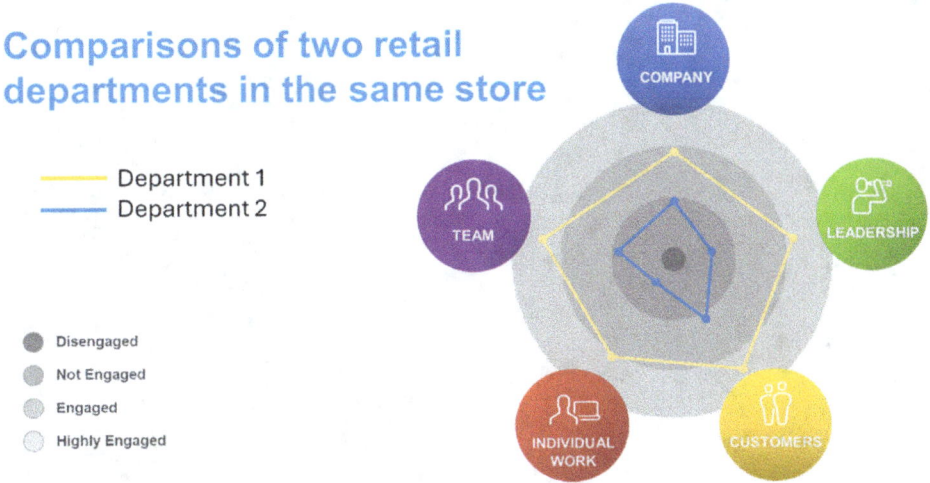

Figure 4.7: Comparison of Engagement Profiles in Two Departments in the Same Retail Store.

tory workers, as shown for a U.S. manufacturing organization below in Figure 4.10. Unfortunately, in many organizations, managers assume that everyone is as engaged as they are and manage accordingly without recognizing the different engagement profiles for the different levels of the organization.

As these examples well demonstrate, the profiles provide information that single, unidimensional engagement measures do not capture. It has often been said that we cannot improve things we cannot measure, but it is also true that we cannot manage

Comparison of two retail stores' engagement profiles

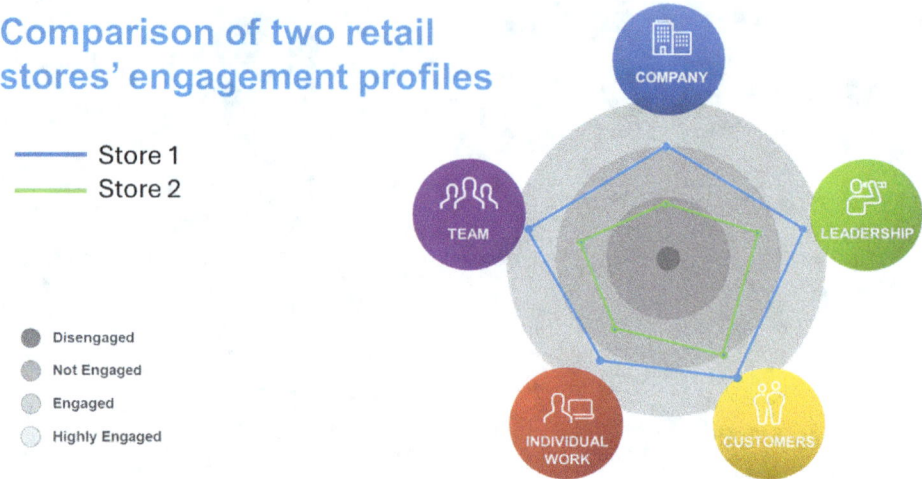

Figure 4.8: Comparison of Employee Engagement in Two Similar Retail Stores in the Same Chain.

Engagement profiles

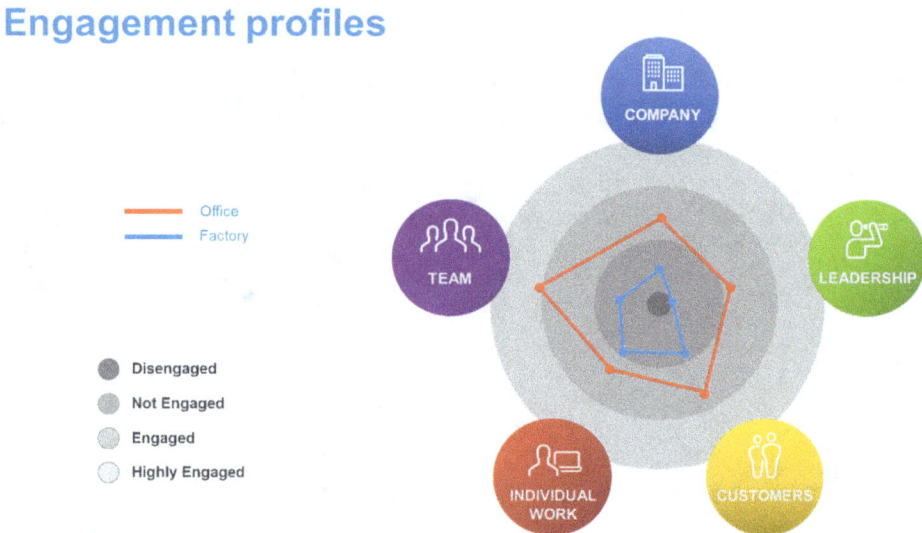

Figure 4.9: Comparison of Office and Factory Worker Engagements.

things we do not understand. It has been our experience that managers are often unable to act on simple measures and that multidimensional engagement measures are more likely to give actionable information to management and even to the employees themselves.

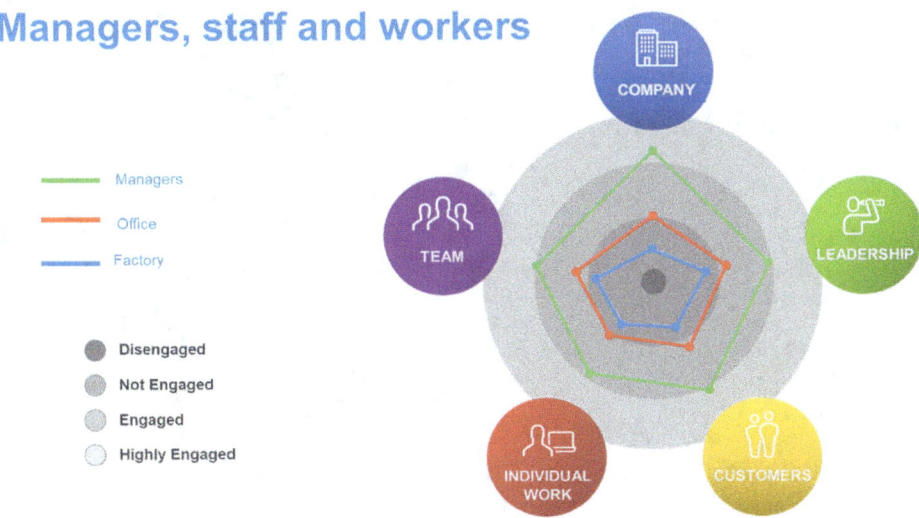

Figure 4.10: Comparison of Managers, Staff, and Factory Worker Engagement.

Comparison of Individual Engagement

Even though we do not report any individual engagement scores, it may be enlightening to show a few individuals with different levels of engagement for the different elements. Below are profiles for two individuals with rather negative attitudes, but for different reasons. Individual 1 (Figure 4.11) sees themselves as customer-oriented with some respect for their managers but with truly negative attitudes toward their team, the company, and even their own work. On the other hand, Individual 2 (Figure 4.12) is very negative toward the customers, their leaders, and the company, but very positive toward their team and somewhat positive toward their work. However, both individuals are seen rather negatively by their leaders and teams, and yet have very different reasons for their negativity.

Interestingly, based on unidimensional measurement classification, Individual 1 would likely be classified as "nonengaged" rather than "disengaged," even with the negative and quite destructive attitudes toward leaders, the company, and their teammates.

Also, if one wanted to help these individuals become more positive and engaged, understanding their "gripes" may be beneficial, and it is unlikely that the same treatment would work on both of them in the same way.

All this shows how important it is to understand the multidimensional character of engagement in order to develop ways to understand, lead, and improve engagement for different organizations, departments, teams, or even individuals.

In this chapter, we have introduced our multidimensional model of engagement, combining both the five forces of engagement as well as the four different levels of

Individual 1

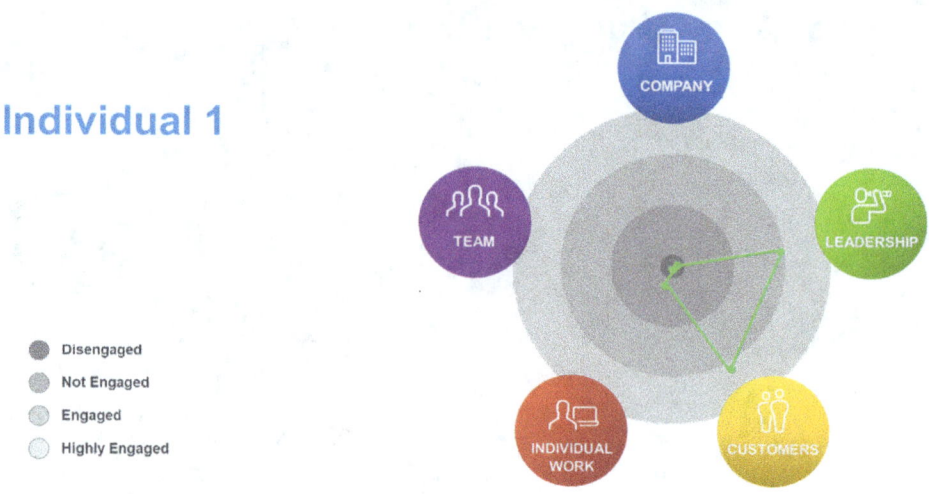

Figure 4.11: Example of an Individual Engagement Profile—Individual 1.

Individual 2

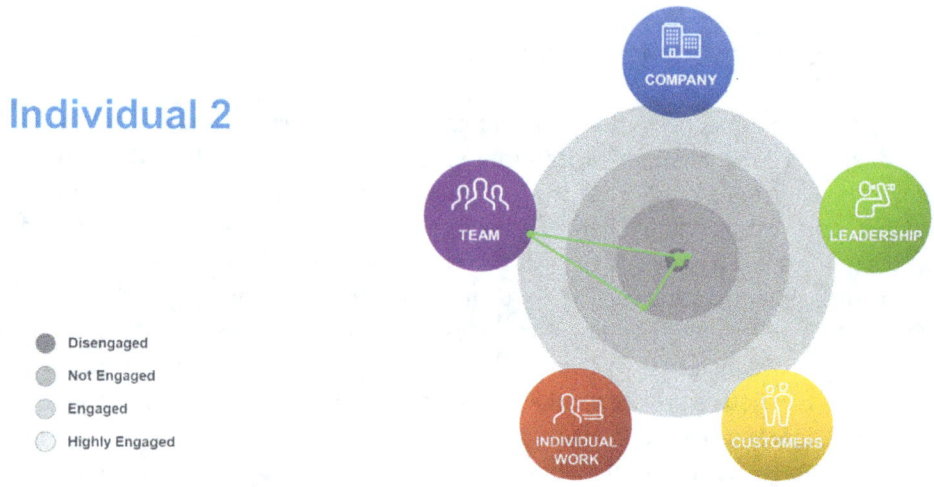

Figure 4.12: Example of an Individual Engagement Profile—Individual 2.

engagement. Understanding the multidimensional nature of employee engagement helps us to gain a deeper understanding of the engagement of individuals, teams, business units, and the entire organization. This understanding is crucial for management to develop ways to improve engagement at all of these levels and to improve the performance of individuals, teams, business units, and the entire organization. We are convinced that unidimensional engagement measures, even if helpful, do not provide enough depth to plan actions to improve employee engagement.

This chapter combines two key engagement concepts (the level of engagement from Chapter 2, and multidimensional engagement from Chapter 3) into an easily understandable model, which serves as an important tool for any organization or leader wishing to improve employee engagement.

Key Questions
1. What do you honestly think your own personal engagement profile looks like?
2. What do you think the engagement profile of your team looks like? Why?
3. Where in your organization profile do you see the most room for improvement?
4. How do you think your organization could improve the employee engagement profile?
5. If you were able to improve the engagement profile for your team/organization, what would be the greatest benefits?

Part 2: **Improving Engagement**

Chapter 5
Engagement by Choice
Cultivating Passion, Accountability, Collaboration, and Transformation

> "The greatest day in your life and mine is when we take total responsibility for our attitudes. That is the day we truly grow up."
> — John Maxwell

The first part of this book (Chapters 1–4) discussed the importance, construct, and measurement of employee engagement. This, the second part, focuses specifically on how individuals, leaders, and teams can improve their own engagement, as well as the culture of engagement in their organizations. The following four chapters specifically address the following issues:

- Chapter 5: Individual responsibility and behaviors to choose to be engaged
- Chapter 6: How leaders become not only engaged, but engaging leaders who create an environment where employees choose to be engaged
- Chapter 7: How teams become a source and power for positive engagement
- Chapter 8: Ways to deal with the actively disengaged

This chapter, Chapter 5, specifically focuses on the responsibility each individual has to be engaged, and how choosing to be *passionate, accountable,* and *collaborative and choosing to continually transform ourselves* help us to be more fully engaged, and how the person who chooses to be engaged is the greatest beneficiary of that choice.

Responsibility for Our Own Engagement

> A while ago, I asked the CEO of one of the early adopters of our engagement improvement process what he thought was the most important principle he learned. His response, without any hesitation: "Individual responsibility for engagement." This has consistently, over the years, been the most important and first principle of "empowering engagement." Each person has to understand and accept that they are responsible for their own engagement, and that when they choose to be engaged, they are the greatest beneficiary from that choice.

Individual employees—not just the leaders —can actively foster their own engagement by cultivating four key personal drivers: passion, accountability, collaboration, and transformation or development (PACT). These drivers represent personal attitudes and behaviors that make work more meaningful and energizing. An employee who actively ignites their passion in their work, takes accountability for outcomes, builds collaborative relationships in the workplace, and continually transforms themselves by developing new skills is far more likely to be engaged. When employees make this choice to be fully engaged with their own PACT across the five forces of engagement, the benefits accrue not only to themselves in terms of greater job satisfaction, growth, and purpose, but also to their teams and organizations in higher performance, innovation, and retention. As individuals focus on these behaviors, they are able to improve their engagement across all five forces of engagement, as noted in Figure 5.1.

Figure 5.1: Multidimensional representation of employee engagement with individual PACT responsibility.

Employees play a critical role in shaping their own engagement at work across all five forces. While organizations and leaders can create conducive environments, engagement ultimately stems from individual choice, mindset, and behavior. According to Saks (2006), employee engagement functions as a form of social exchange: when employees perceive organizational support, fair procedures, and enriching job conditions, they tend to reciprocate by becoming more engaged in their job or organization. This means that while external factors influence engagement, employees retain the final agency in how they respond. Engaged employees proactively seek meaning, take initiative, and build positive relationships that enhance their experience. Kahn (1990) emphasizes that psychological presence—being fully attentive and connected to one's role—emerges when individuals feel conditions of meaningfulness, safety, and availability. Under these conditions, employees are more willing to be authentic, involved, and emotionally invested in their work roles. Moreover, Bakker and Demerouti (2008) argue that personal resources such as self-efficacy, optimism, resilience, and self-esteem help employees remain engaged, even under challenging or less-than-ideal work conditions. In addition, job resources such as social support, opportunities for development, and collaboration with colleagues further reinforce engagement. Thus, taking ownership of one's engagement is not only a sign of taking responsibility but also a strategic act that contributes to personal fulfillment and organizational success.

> Before becoming CEO of Microsoft, Satya Nadella joined the company in 1992 as a young engineer. Despite starting in a mid-level role, Nadella quickly stood out—not merely for his technical skills, but for the deep level of personal engagement he brought to his work. Rather than waiting for direction or limiting his contributions to assigned tasks, Nadella took the initiative to understand broader business goals, collaborated across teams, and consistently sought opportunities to learn and improve.
>
> One key instance of this engagement was his role in driving the success of Microsoft's Cloud and Enterprise group. Instead of passively executing directives, Nadella immersed himself in understanding customer needs, championed innovation, and actively shaped the group's strategy. His decision to take ownership of outcomes, seek feedback, and advocate for change—even when it required challenging the status quo—demonstrated a high level of self-directed engagement.
>
> When asked about leadership and performance, Nadella has emphasized curiosity, energy, and posture of learning as hallmarks of someone who chose to be engaged, not because he had to, but because he found meaning and purpose in the work itself.

This example of Mr. Nadella illustrates that engagement is not solely a product of a supportive environment—it's also a personal choice. Nadella's journey reflects how choosing to be engaged can lead to both personal growth and organizational transformation.

> One of the great examples of someone choosing to be fully engaged was Chris (example and name used with his permission). Chris was a financial controller in one of the company's global units, and had done a great job in his work. But he wanted to advance and take more responsibility, and came to me one day asking if he could move to manage production so that he could learn more about the company, and learn more leadership skills. Initially, it seemed like an odd request and an unusual move, but given his desire to be more fully engaged, he moved to become a production manager in one of the manufacturing units. His engagement helped him succeed in his job, and he soon became the plant manager, and eventually the director of one of the new global businesses. Chris's full engagement has always been a great example to me of what people can accomplish when they want to be engaged. His story, like many others, demonstrates that engagement is not solely bestowed top-down; it can be actively cultivated from within, and is a choice.

In our work with organizations, our first priority is to help everyone in the organization understand and accept that they are responsible for their own level of engagement. And also, to help them realize that they are the greatest beneficiaries when they *choose* to become engaged!

In this chapter, we delve into each of the four drivers of engagement—*passion, accountability, collaboration, and transformation*—illustrating how employees can nurture these elements in themselves.

Passion

One of the most powerful drivers of engagement is passion—that intrinsic spark which makes work feel personally meaningful. From business leaders to athletes to everyday front-line staff, passion is often cited as a key ingredient in high engagement and achievement.

Passion and enthusiasm for our work stem from understanding and internalizing the meaning and mission of work and finding sources of joy in what we do. We find that as people strive to succeed and even exceed specifically their own expectations, they find more passion in what they do. Meeting and exceeding our own goals builds passion and enthusiasm for our work.

To increase passion, we have identified three behaviors everyone can choose to improve their passion and engagement. We have identified these three behaviors to help people with concrete actions everyone can choose to take, and they are not meant to be all-inclusive, but are meant to be examples of what employees can do. The three behaviors to increase passion, each discussed below, are:
1. Identify meaning
2. Find joy
3. Exceed expectations

Identifying Meaning

In today's fast-paced corporate world, many employees find themselves asking a deeper question: Does my work really matter? For many, the answer isn't always clear. Yet research shows that employees who find meaning in their jobs are more engaged, more resilient, and more fulfilled—both personally and professionally (Rosso et al., 2010). They are not just more productive; they experience higher levels of satisfaction and well-being. In fact, research highlighted by *Harvard Business Review* in Lysova et al.(2023) indicates that meaningful work is more important to individuals than compensation, promotions, or working conditions. Also, Cascio (2019) emphasizes that meaningful work and quality of work life are critical components of employee motivation and retention.

If you've ever felt disconnected or unmotivated at work, it may not be the tasks themselves that need to change—it might be time to reconnect with a deeper sense of purpose. The good news? One does not have to wait for your manager or company to change. There are specific, research-backed steps one can take to find more meaning in work—starting today.

Every employee has the potential to infuse their job with passion by uncovering a deeper sense of meaning in their daily tasks. Increasingly, research confirms that employees are motivated not only by compensation or career progression, but by a desire for personal significance and purpose in their professional roles as well. Research shows that employees thrive when they are able to align their personal values with their work, transforming routine responsibilities into sources of fulfillment and resilience (Rosso, Dekas and Wrzesniewski, 2010; Bailey and Madden, 2016; Lysova, Fletcher and El Baroudi, 2023). This pursuit of meaningful work is echoed in timeless advice from visionaries such as Steve Jobs—"The only way to do great work is to love what you do"—and mythologist Joseph Campbell, who urged people to "follow your bliss." Meaningful work does not necessarily require a dramatic career shift; rather, it often comes from reframing how one sees their contribution. Employees who recognize how their work supports a greater mission, improves others' lives, or reflects their personal values report higher levels of engagement, well-being, and sustained motivation (Wrzesniewski et al., 2003). Passion, then, is not something passively discovered but actively cultivated through a thoughtful connection to purpose.

> Companies have started recognizing the power of purpose in driving passion. Global consumer goods giant Unilever, for instance, launched a program to help employees identify their personal purpose and link it to their role in the company's sustainability mission. Many Unilever employees reported higher engagement after discovering how their daily tasks helped to improve health or environmental outcomes in communities—aligning their daily work with what they personally cared about.
>
> Similarly, outdoor apparel maker Patagonia explicitly hires people who love nature and activism; the company even encourages employees to take paid time off to volunteer for environmental causes. This alignment of job and personal passion creates a workforce that is highly energized and loyal—employees feel, "I'm not just selling jackets, I'm saving the planet," which spurs them to advocate for the brand and innovate eco-friendly solutions.

So, how can one do that? Start by reflecting on the aspects of the job that connect to your personal values. Do you enjoy helping others? Do you take pride in solving problems or building something? Think about the "why" behind the daily tasks. Who benefits from your work? What would be missing if you didn't do it well? Reframing your role in this way can shift your perspective and renew your sense of purpose. Even in a corporate setting, where goals and structures are clearly defined, one can draw personal significance from how the work contributes to a larger mission, team, or especially the customer experience.

Ultimately, finding meaning in work is not a passive experience—it's an ongoing process of reflection, intention, and small, strategic action. While organizations and leaders do play a role in shaping culture and purpose, each employee holds the power to redefine how the job connects to what matters most. When one takes ownership of the meaning at work, they find greater energy, creativity, and satisfaction—not just in daily tasks, but in the entire career journey. As Viktor Frankl has been quoted, saying, "Life is never made unbearable by circumstances, but only by lack of meaning and purpose." (attributed to Viktor Frankl; precise origin unverified). The same is true for work. Choose to seek out meaning—and you may find more than just engagement. You may rediscover joy.

Finding Joy

In our seminars around the world, when employees are asked to choose one thing they would like to do to increase passion in their work, the most common response, especially for experienced workers, is to find more joy in their daily work.

Many people experience peaks and valleys in their passion for work. It's easy to get caught up in daily stresses and lose sight of what once excited us. Yet joy—that feeling of genuine pleasure and meaning in what we do—is not a trivial extra; it's a key driver of engagement and performance. In fact, happiness at work is strongly linked to positive outcomes: companies with happier employees tend to see better productivity, customer satisfaction, and even financial results. If we can rediscover the joy in our work, we can rekindle our passion and become more engaged, motivated, and creative in our roles. Both employees and managers have a part to play in making this happen, through small daily actions and broader cultural shifts. We'll explore why joy in the workplace matters and how it can be nurtured from the ground up and the top down.

Joy might sound like a soft, subjective idea, but its impact on work is very real. Psychologists define employee engagement as being deeply involved in and enthusiastic about one's work—essentially, finding joy and meaning in what you do. Engaged employees feel energized and passionate; disengaged ones feel bored or resentful. Positive emotions like joy fuel engagement by broadening our thinking and helping us build resources to succeed.

While organizations and leaders shape the culture and working environment, each employee can take proactive steps to rediscover more joy in their own work. One does not have to wait for someone else to "fix" their job—small mindset shifts and actions in the daily routines can reignite your enthusiasm. Employees can focus on the more enjoyable part of their work, and focus on those aspect of their work, celebrate their achievements, and encourage fun and humor in the workplace.

One powerful way to increase joy at work is through job crafting, which means redesigning your own job (formally or informally) to make it more engaging and meaningful. Professors Amy Wrzesniewski and Jane Dutton define job crafting as *"the physical and cognitive changes individuals make in the task and relational boundaries of their work"* (Wrzesniewski and Dutton 2001, p. 179).

In simple terms, it's a proactive mindset where you alter what you do, who you interact with, or how you perceive your tasks, so that your job better fits your interests, strengths, and values. By taking ownership of aspects of your role, you can transform even mundane duties into sources of motivation. Notably, research indicates that job crafting behaviors are linked to higher joy, job satisfaction, performance, and engagement (Moreira et al. 2022). Shaping your job to find more joy not only makes work more enjoyable but can also enhance your own engagement and success at work.-

One can apply job crafting in several practical ways:

- **Task Crafting:** Adjust *what you do* day-to-day. This could mean taking on new projects that excite you, dropping or minimizing tasks that feel draining (with permission, if needed), or finding more efficient ways to handle necessary chores. For example, if you enjoy creative work, you might volunteer to design a team newsletter or improve a process, infusing creativity into your role.
- **Relational Crafting:** Change *who you work with* and how you interact. You might seek out colleagues who inspire or teach you, build a mentoring relationship, or collaborate with others on cross-functional tasks. By increasing positive interactions (and reducing toxic ones), you shape a more supportive social environment around your job.
- **Cognitive Crafting:** Shift *how you think about your work*. Even if your tasks don't change, you can reframe them in terms of the bigger purpose they serve. For instance, a hospital janitor might view their role not just as "cleaning floors" but as *helping patients heal in a safe, clean environment*. This mental reappraisal can greatly increase the sense of joy and meaning in any job. Research finds that such changes in perception—seeing how your work contributes value—foster greater joy, engagement, and satisfaction.

Rather than waiting for a manager to redesign your job or assign the "right" duties, *you* take the reins in shaping a role you can truly be passionate about. Job crafting demonstrates that even within organizational constraints, employees often have more power than they think to improve the enjoyment and joy in their work.

Exceeding Expectations

Exceeding expectations fuels engagement through a profound sense of achievement and progress. Consider how motivated you feel when you not only meet a challenging goal at work but actually surpass it. Exceeding a target delivers a powerful rush of accomplishment that energizes you—it shows that your efforts are meaningful and that you're making real progress. In fact, achieving meaningful goals fulfills our innate need for mastery and competence, reinforcing the inner motivation to keep performing at a high level (Locke and Latham, 2002). Psychologists observe that when work feels purposeful and employees see clear forward movement, they become more enthusiastic and absorbed in their tasks. In this way, consistently meeting and exceeding goals gives people a tangible sense of purpose and momentum—the lifeblood of deep employee engagement.

High performance also invites recognition, strengthening employees' commitment. Exceeding expectations brings positive reinforcement that further heightens engagement. From a managerial perspective, recognizing and rewarding such high performance is essential—the simple act of acknowledging performance boosts employee engagement and encourages repeat excellence. Recognition effectively signals that their contributions truly matter, and it consistently ranks as a top driver of engagement; indeed, research shows that employees who exceed expectations, and anticipate praise are nearly three times more likely to be highly engaged at work. In turn, this sense of appreciation feeds a virtuous cycle: goal achievement leads to recognition, which fuels even greater engagement, motivation, and subsequent high performance.

Passion is a critical driver of engagement, and it is a choice. It's about bringing your whole self to work—your values, interests, and enthusiasm. Whether you're in Kuala Lumpur or London, a junior analyst or a senior nurse, you can choose to approach each day with a sense of purpose, joy, and high performance. Passionate employees don't just produce good results—they inspire those around them to be engaged, and find greater personal satisfaction. Employees can increase their own engagement by *identifying meaning*, *finding joy*, and *exceeding expectations* in their work.

Accountability

If passion is the heart of engagement, accountability is the backbone.

Winston Churchill has been quoted as saying: "The price of greatness is responsibility." Recognizing our own responsibility and accountability for our own results, as well as the results of our team, even though at times painful, builds our determination to accomplish our work well. As we show accountability by taking ownership of our work and lives, becoming even more trustworthy, and committing to continuously improving our own lives, we find that our own engagement increases.

To increase accountability, we have identified three behaviors everyone can choose to improve their accountability and engagement. We have identified these three behaviors to help people with concrete actions everyone can choose to take, and they are not meant to be all-inclusive, but are meant to be examples of what employees can do. The three behaviors to increase accountability, each discussed below, are:
1. Take ownership
2. Be trustworthy
3. Improve continuously

Taking Ownership

Taking ownership of one's work—in terms of responsibilities, decisions, and outcomes—is a critical driver that transforms an employee from a passive participant to an active, engaged steward of the business. Accountability means thinking and acting like an owner. It's exemplified by the employee who says, "This project's outcome, success or failure, rests in part on me, and I accept that responsibility," rather than, "I just do what I'm told." When individuals embrace accountability, they tend to invest more effort, anticipate problems, focus on the outcome, and find proactive solutions—behaviors tightly linked to higher engagement. Psychological ownership is a state where employees feel a sense of possession and responsibility toward their work and the organization. When employees feel a sense of ownership, they are intrinsically motivated, exhibit higher levels of commitment, and take initiative (Kerr 2024). They move from feeling like hired hands to feeling like vital members of a team on a mission.

> A striking real-world case of employee accountability driving engagement comes from the Netherlands, at the innovative home-care organization Buurtzorg. Buurtzorg is famous for its self-managed teams of nurses—an approach that radically decentralized decision-making in an industry typically known for rigid hierarchies. Each nursing team (usually 10–12 people) essentially runs its own small operation: they set schedules, divide tasks, coordinate patient care, and even handle hiring and minor discipline, with almost no middle managers to direct them (Bernstein and Sandino 2022). What has this meant for engagement? According to a *Harvard Business School* case study, Buurtzorg's nurses are *highly* engaged and "take full ownership of their work," often coming up with creative ways to serve patients because they feel trusted to act on their ideas. One nurse described the experience: "Working in an organization that trusts you and cares for you makes things possible you had not thought about before . . . You can get so much out of a person—they bring so much to the table—and it is so innovative to work this way" (Bernstein and Sandino 2022). In other words, by giving employees true accountability, Buurtzorg unleashed their initiative and motivation. The company's outcomes—patient satisfaction is 30% higher than competitors, with lower turnover and absenteeism—show that engaged employees owning their results can dramatically outperform more controlled environments. The Buurtzorg example, while in healthcare, has inspired businesses globally to consider how empowering employees can combat disengagement and even "quiet quitting." When people are treated as accountable adults rather than cogs, they rise to the occasion.

As a CEO of a multinational company, people often came to me and asked me to make decisions for some areas they were responsible for. My typical response always was that I was more than willing to make the decision, but they would still be responsible for the end results, even if I made the decision. Most of the time people may have wanted some advice, but did not want me to make the decision for them. They wanted to make the decision themselves, because they knew that they would ultimately be accountable for the outcomes. And evidence generally showed that when people made their own decisions and were accountable, they became engaged, and made better outcomes of their "bad" decisions than they did out of my "good" ones. Sense of accountability is a great motivator for stronger engagement.

From a psychological perspective, when you become accountable and own your work, you also own your engagement. James Kerr, a leadership coach, notes that "This sense of ownership transcends mere job duties, leading employees to care deeply about the outcomes and success of the organization." In a *Psychology Today* article, he explains that empowering employees with autonomy and growth opportunities helps instill this ownership mentality, which in turn drives higher commitment and initiative (Kerr 2024). In other words, being accountable is not just about shouldering burdens—it's about feeling *invested*. When you take personal responsibility for both outcomes, achievements, and setbacks, you start to identify with the organization's outcomes and take pride in them. This intrinsic investment is a hallmark of engaged employees. They talk about "my project, my client, my product" with genuine care. They are the opposite of the disengaged worker who might cynically mutter, "Not my problem." The engaged accountable employee instead asks, "What *else* can I do to make this better?"—an accountable attitude that inevitably leads to continual learning and improvement.

Accountability is a driver of engagement that any individual can activate by shifting their mindset from employee to owner. No matter your level, start viewing your work area as *your business*. Set personal standards of excellence, follow through on commitments, and step up to challenges instead of sidestepping them. This will not only make you more engaged (because you'll see your fingerprints on the results), but it will also likely get you noticed as a reliable, proactive contributor. When employees at all levels do this, organizations become more resilient and performance-driven. As the Buurtzorg case shows, even life-and-death decisions can be entrusted to employees when they are trained and prepared—and the employees respond with outstanding engagement and accountability. Choosing to be accountable is ultimately empowering: it means you acknowledge your agency to shape outcomes, which is both a heavy and a liberating feeling. In owning your work, you own your success and growth, which is deeply engaging.

Being Trustworthy

Being trustworthy is a foundational element of accountability, as it signals reliability, integrity, and a commitment to follow through on responsibilities. Trustworthiness builds confidence among peers and leaders, allowing for greater autonomy, collaboration, and efficiency in the workplace. Whitener et al. (1998) comment that when employees consistently deliver on commitments, admit mistakes, and act with integrity, they foster trust by demonstrating behavioral consistency and integrity. This trust serves as a foundation for accountability and an ethical organizational culture. Trustworthy behavior also reduces the need for micromanagement, enabling teams to function with mutual respect and shared responsibility. Costa et al. (2001) show that in high-trust teams, members coordinate more effectively and engage in cooperative self-regulation. This suggests that accountability can become self-regulated—employees hold themselves and one another to high standards because of the trust established within the team. Ultimately, being trustworthy is not just a personal virtue; it is a strategic contributor to a high-performance, high-engagement culture where accountability thrives.

Improving Continuously

The current, rapidly developing and changing work environment requires us to grow and adapt. A desire to continuously improve fosters a mindset of accountability and significantly enhances employee engagement by *aligning personal growth with organizational contribution*. When employees are committed to learning and development, they take ownership of their performance, actively seek feedback, and hold themselves accountable for progress and outcomes (London and Smither, 1999). This growth-oriented attitude to improve continuously reinforces accountability because it reflects a proactive commitment to meet and exceed expectations—not out of obligation, but out of intrinsic motivation. Moreover, Dweck (2006) demonstrates that individuals with a growth mindset—those who believe abilities can be developed through effort and learning—are more adaptable and resilient, finding satisfaction in mastery. Applied to the workplace, this perspective suggests that employees who continuously improve are also more engaged, as they derive purpose from their evolving roles. Thus, personal development and accountability are mutually reinforcing drivers of passion and enduring engagement.

Collaboration

A study, published in *Harvard Business Review*, found that "the time spent by managers and employees in collaborative activities has ballooned by 50 percent or more" over the last two decades and that, at many companies, more than three-quarters of an employee's day is spent communicating with colleagues (Cross et al. 2016, p. 74).

We as humans are inherently social creatures, and the workplace is a social environment. It's no surprise, then, that collaboration—the drive to connect, cooperate, and work together with others—is a fundamental pillar of engagement. While passion and accountability often start within an individual, collaboration is about the passion and energy sparked *between* individuals. When employees build positive relationships with colleagues and feel part of a cohesive team, their commitment and engagement to work improves. They no longer work in isolation; they are plugged into a network of mutual support and shared goals. As a result, they feel a greater sense of belonging and responsibility toward the group's objectives, which can make work far more enjoyable and meaningful.

There are a few jobs where collaboration is not important, and where better collaboration does not improve individual and team engagement. As we build relationships, the old African Proverb: "If you want to go fast, go alone. If you want to go far, go together." Such collaboration and teamwork are increasingly important for most workplaces. Furthermore, workplaces are becoming more and more diverse, and learning to value diversity, in all its forms, is critical for any team's success. As Maya Angelou has stated: "In diversity, there is beauty and there is strength." Individuals can enhance collaboration actively by *valuing diversity* in the workplace, by *building relationships,* and by actively *communicating* with colleagues. One of my favorite beliefs is that "Any connection is better than no connection."

To improve collaboration and connections, we have identified three specific behaviors that everyone can choose to improve collaboration and engagement. We have identified these three behaviors to help people with concrete actions everyone can choose to take, and they are not meant to be all-inclusive, but are meant to be examples of what employees can do. The three behaviors to increase collaboration, each discussed below, are:

1. Value diversity
2. Build relationships
3. Communicate

Valuing Diversity

In most workplaces we work with people who are not like us. Valuing diversity can enhance collaboration and our own engagement at work by broadening our perspectives, and deepening our sense of connection. When we actively appreciate the unique backgrounds, viewpoints, and strengths of our colleagues, we create more inclusive interactions that foster connections, trust, and mutual respect—conditions that boost our own emotional investment and satisfaction (Shore et al., 2011). Engaging with diverse teams encourages learning and personal growth, which increases curiosity, collaboration, and a sense of purpose. It also stimulates creativity, making work more stimulating and meaningful. Moreover, when we contribute to an inclusive culture, we reinforce our own values of fairness and integrity, which strengthens our psychological alignment with the organization (Roberson, 2006). In this way, valuing diversity is not only good for team dynamics and company performance—it also deepens our personal engagement by connecting us more authentically to the people around us.

Building Relationships

Building strong relationships in the workplace significantly enhances collaboration and an individual's own engagement by fostering a sense of belonging, trust, and emotional connection. Kahn (1990) argues that supportive interpersonal relationships with colleagues and leaders foster psychological safety, enabling employees to feel valued and secure. This, in turn, motivates them to contribute more fully and engage in their work roles. Social connections at work not only make daily tasks more enjoyable but also provide emotional resilience during stressful times, which helps sustain engagement over the long term. According to Gallup (2020), employees who report having a best friend at work are significantly more engaged, productive, and loyal to their organizations. Furthermore, relationships encourage collaboration, open communication, and shared learning—elements that make work more meaningful and fulfilling. In essence, relationships transform the workplace from a transactional environment into a community, where individuals thrive through connection, mutual respect, and shared purpose.

Communicating

Effective communication in the workplace is a vital driver of collaboration and individual engagement, as it fosters clarity, connection, and a shared sense of purpose. When employees communicate openly—with colleagues, supervisors, and teams—they better understand expectations, receive meaningful feedback, and feel more involved in organizational decisions. According to Bakker and Demerouti's (2008) Job Demands–Resources model, job resources such as clear communication, feedback, and social support reduce ambiguity and build confidence, enabling employees to engage more fully and intentionally with their work. Additionally, communication cultivates psychological safety—when people feel heard and respected, they are more likely to contribute ideas, ask questions, and take initiative. According to Gallup (2020), engaged employees frequently cite regular, honest communication with their managers as a core factor in their motivation and satisfaction. In short, communication transforms work from a series of tasks into a collaborative, purpose-driven experience that strengthens personal engagement and performance.

Collaboration isn't just about friendships, of course. It also encompasses effective teamwork, knowledge-sharing, and collective creativity. When people collaborate well, they achieve synergies that make work more rewarding. For example, consider a cross-functional product development team in a tech company with members from the US, India, and Germany. If each person worked siloed on their piece (coding, design, marketing) and only communicated minimally, they might complete the project, but likely without much personal attachment or innovation. Now imagine them actively collaborating—holding brainstorming sessions to solve problems together, learning about each other's cultures and expertise, and iterating based on group feedback. Not only is the end product likely to be better, but the team members will feel a greater collective pride and engagement. They'll each say, "We built this together," which is a hallmark of an engaged team. Employees in such high-trust, communicative, and collaborative environments report much higher engagement and innovation.

In summary, choosing to collaborate is choosing to be part of something larger at work—to draw energy from teamwork and to give energy back to it. The most engaged employees tend to have strong connections with their colleagues; they feel seen, heard, and valued by their team. Employees can improve their own engagement by valuing diversity in their teams, actively building relationships in the workplace, and communicating openly.

Transformation

The final key driver of engagement is continuous transformation and development—the pursuit of personal and professional growth. If passion gives work meaning, and accountability and collaboration give it energy and connection, transformation and development give work a trajectory. It's the forward-looking component of engagement: the feeling that "I am improving, advancing, and moving toward my potential through my work." Stagnation is the enemy of engagement. Conversely, when employees see a path to grow—new skills to learn, challenges to conquer, opportunities to progress—they are far more likely to invest effort and stay committed. Development feeds an intrinsic human motivator: the desire for mastery and competence, as well as the ambition for career advancement. It reassures people that their work today will continue to transform, and benefit their tomorrow.

For many, especially for the young workers, the ability to develop, grow, and advance in their work is more important than money. Contemporary workplace studies suggest that many younger employees today look for a reciprocal investment—support for development from their employers before fully committing their own contributions. A recent survey by Amazon and Workplace Intelligence found that 74% of Gen Z-ers and Millennials are contemplating a career change in the next 12 months due to a lack of career mobility and skill development options (Perna 2023). Younger workers prioritize working for employers who will provide them with development opportunities.

Based on *Training* magazine: "Various studies have found that Learning and Development opportunities are in-demand and increase employee engagement and job satisfaction (*Training* 2022):

- 57 percent of U.S. workers want to update their skills, and 48 percent would consider switching jobs to do it.
- 80 percent of employees said that learning and development opportunities would increase their engagement at work.
- Workers who feel they have access to the Learning and Development opportunities they need are 21 percent more engaged than workers who don't.
- Employees who see good opportunities to learn and grow at their organization are 3.6 times more likely to report being happy than those who don't.
- 71 percent of workers say job training and development increase their job satisfaction.
- 91 percent of employees want more training opportunities from their employers.
- 76 percent of Gen Z workers see learning as the key to advancement.
- 83 percent of Gen Z workers want to learn skills to perform better in their current roles.
- 59 percent of millennials say opportunities to learn and grow are significant to them when applying for a job.
- 66 percent of workers between 18 and 24 years of age ranked upskilling and reskilling as the third-most important benefit when assessing new job opportunities, behind health insurance and disability benefits."

"If employee disengagement and lack of job satisfaction are both causes and products of quiet quitting, then employers should take note of the above statistics to engage employees optimally" (*Training* 2022).

Specific behaviors to help employees improve their engagement through development are for them to take responsibility and own their own future, develop new, specific skills, and make bold, motivating goals for themselves. As the quote often attributed to Nelson Mandela states: "Education is the most powerful weapon which you can use to change the world," reflecting Mandela's enduring belief in the transformative power of education. And in almost all areas of business, rapid changes require employees to develop new skills in order to stay current and relevant. This allows employees to invest in their own transformation, and in turn to keep themselves engaged and motivated.

To make transformation a reality, we have identified three behaviors everyone can choose to improve their engagement and focus on development. We have identified these three behaviors to help people with concrete actions everyone can choose to take, and they are not meant to be all-inclusive, but are meant to be examples of what employees can do. The three behaviors to make transformation a reality, each discussed below, are:
1. Own your own future
2. Develop new skills
3. Make bold goals

Owning Your Own Future

Taking responsibility and owning one's own future is a powerful catalyst for personal transformation and deeper engagement at work. When you shift from a reactive mindset to one of owning your own future, you begin to see yourself as an active agent in shaping your career paths, development, and impact. This sense of autonomy fuels motivation, resilience, and purpose—key elements of sustained development and engagement, key elements described in the seminal work (Deci and Ryan, 2000; Bakker and Demerouti 2008). Employees who take responsibility for their own lives are more likely to seek feedback, pursue learning opportunities, and align their actions with long-term goals, which accelerates both growth and fulfillment. London and Smither (1999) argue that self-directed development enhances employees' sense of competence and control, thereby increasing their psychological investment in work. Building on their perspective, personal transformation occurs when individuals take charge of their own growth, turning engagement into a self-sustaining journey of development, contribution, and meaning.

For an individual employee, actively choosing development means taking responsibility and charge of their own future. In today's world, there are abundant resources to learn almost anything, from formal employer training programs to online courses, certification workshops, industry conferences, or even simply reading and self-study. Engaged employees tend to be continuous learners. They seek feedback to improve, volunteer for stretch assignments, and often pursue training even when it's not mandated. Not only will this make them more valuable professionally, but it also makes their daily work more engaging as they apply new knowledge. That self-driven development can be deeply satisfying. Learning is inherently motivating and engaging—think of the gratification in mastering something new—so "owning your future" by building learning into your work life is a powerful antidote to boredom and a strong source of engagement.

Developing New Skills

Most current work environments develop and change, and require new knowledge and skills. Engaged employees are continuous learners, and continuous learning improves engagement. Engaged employees seek feedback to improve, volunteer for stretch assignments, and often pursue training even when it's not mandated. If your company offers an internal training portal or subsidizes courses, make use of it! If not, consider investing some of your own time (and yes, possibly money) into learning skills that excite you or will advance your career. Not only will this make you more valuable professionally, but it also makes your daily work more engaging as you apply new knowledge. A good example is a marketing coordinator in Finland who took an online course on data analytics out of personal interest. As she started using those skills to analyze campaign results at work, she gained a fresh sense of competence and recognition from peers—essentially carving a growth path in a role that might otherwise have plateaued. This kind of self-driven development can be deeply satisfying. Learning is inherently motivating and engaging—think of the gratification in mastering something new—so building learning into your work life is a powerful antidote to boredom and a source of engagement.

Developing new, specific skills can significantly enhance employee engagement by fostering a sense of progress, mastery, and relevance in one's role. Bandura (1997) argues that acquiring skills that improve personal effectiveness strengthens self-efficacy—leading to greater confidence and a heightened sense of control. These psychological resources are foundational drivers of motivation and, by extension, employee engagement. Skill development also aligns work with personal growth, turning routine tasks into opportunities for learning and innovation. Macey and Schneider (2008) note that opportunities for growth and development are key antecedents of engagement, as they help employees feel more energized, committed, and connected to their work. Furthermore, gaining new competencies often leads to broader responsibilities and recognition, reinforcing the employee's value within the organization and encouraging ongoing investment in their role. In this way, skill development is not only a tool for career advancement—it is a vital lever for sustaining motivation and deepening engagement.

Making Bold Goals

Making bold, ambitious goals can help employees become more engaged by inspiring a deeper sense of purpose, challenge, and forward momentum in their work. Locke and Latham (2002) demonstrate that setting specific, challenging goals increases motivation, persistence, and personal investment, as the pursuit of meaningful achievement becomes energizing and rewarding. Bold goals encourage focus, resilience, and innovation—qualities that not only enhance performance but also reinforce a sense of progress and capability. According to Latham (2004), individuals who set specific and challenging goals are more motivated, perform better, and experience greater satisfaction from their accomplishments. These outcomes are foundational to employee engagement. Moreover, when employees own their goals, they are more likely to feel autonomy and alignment with their broader values, further strengthening their emotional connection to their work and organization.

Engagement at work is often portrayed as something leaders must *drive* into employees—through visionary speeches, incentive programs, or better perks. Certainly, leadership and organizational culture set the stage for engagement and play a major role in developing an engaged work culture. But as we've explored in this chapter, there is immense power in the choices of individual employees to cultivate their own engagement by focusing on passion, accountability, collaboration, and their own transformation. Employees at any level can become more engaged, and transform how they experience work. They can turn a mundane role into a mission by identifying what they love about it; they can become linchpins in their organizations by taking ownership; they can create supportive collaboration through teamwork; and they can keep their work life stimulating by constantly transforming themselves. In doing so, they not only enrich their own careers but also become role models and catalysts for others. An engaged employee tends to be contagious—their enthusiasm, dedication, and curiosity spread to peers, creating a positive feedback loop for the team or even the whole company.

Below, in Table 5.1 we have summarized the specific PACT behaviors discussed in this chapter, and which employees can focus on to improve their engagement through Passion, Accountability, Collaboration, and Transformation and personal development. The objective is not to be a comprehensive list of actions one can take to become more engaged, but rather to focus on some high-priority, specific things everyone can take to become more engaged, and take responsibility for their own engagement.

Table 5.1: Individual PACT actions to improve engagement.

P	A	C	T
PASSION	**ACCOUNTABILITY**	**COLLABORATION**	**TRANSFORMATION**
Identify Meaning * Align yourself with company mission, recognizing your role in fulfilling the mission.	**Take Ownership** * Be fully responsible for your own work.	**Communicate** * Listen to understand before you speak to be understood; prioritize regular, timely communication	**Own Your Future** * Take responsibility for your future. Develop a plan for your personal success.
Find Joy • Change aspect of your job that do not bring you joy and accept the things you cannot change.	**Be Trustworthy** *Act so that everyone can depend on your work and tour word.	**Value Diveristy** * Approach differences with respect, withouf judgement. Encourage unique ideas and learn from them.	**Develop New Skills** * Anticipate trends in work competencies. Learn something new every day.
Exceed Expectations *Continually strive to improve the quality of your work,;go the extra mile.	**Improve Continuously** * Llearn from your mistakes, look for root causes of problems and work to improve.	**Build Relationships** * Go out of your way to make new connections. "Any connection is better than no connection."	**Make Bold Goals** * Develpp a life vision, a *growth mindset*, and set SMART goals for yourself

Ultimately, the message is one of empowerment and choice. While not every day at work will be thrilling (there are always dull admin tasks and frustrating setbacks in any job), employees who take an active role in their engagement tend to navigate the lows better and capitalize on the highs more. They are the ones who, during tough times, will find strength in accountability and support in collaboration, and who, during good times, will push their passion into new projects and stretch their abilities further. They convert what could be a passive employment situation into an active, enriching career. It is sometimes said that "we can light all the fires we want as leaders, but ultimately each person must fuel their own flame." The four drivers discussed here are the fuel.

By cultivating passion, you fuel the heart of engagement—the emotional connection to your work. By embracing accountability, you fuel the will of engagement—the determination and ownership that propel you forward. Through collaboration, you fuel the spirit of engagement—the camaraderie and collective drive that uplift you. And via transformation and development, you fuel the mind of engagement—the continuous expansion and transformation of your capabilities and horizons. When the heart, will, spirit, and mind are all activated, work transforms from a tedious obligation into a meaningful endeavor to flame positive engagement.

It is important to note that while engagement is a personal choice, it is best realized in partnership with enlightened and engaging leadership. The onus is not solely on workers to keep themselves engaged regardless of circumstances. Rather, managers and organizations should recognize and encourage these four drivers, as will be discussed in the next chapter on leaders' and managers' responsibilities to create an engaging environment where employees choose to be engaged.

Key Questions
1. How could you help employees in your organization to accept personal responsibility for their own level of engagement?
2. What could you do to strengthen passion in your team and team members?
3. How can you increase employee accountability in your organization?
4. What specific stems or actions will improve positive collaboration in your organization, within and between teams?
5. How does your organization currently help you personally to develop and transform yourself? What else could or should your organization do?

Chapter 6
Engaging Leaders with Impact
Leaders' Responsibility to Become Engaging Leaders

> "Train people well enough so they can leave. Treat them well enough so they do not want to."
> — Richard Branson, Founder of the Virgin Group

Even though ultimately employees are largely responsible for their own engagement, as noted in the previous chapter, research indicates that *leadership quality is the single biggest influence on engagement*—Gallup famously found that the manager alone accounts for 70% of the variance in team engagement (Gallup 2023).

This chapter will specifically focus on the leaders', managers', and supervisors' responsibilities and opportunities to create an environment where the team members choose to be engaged, and to be passionate, accountable, and collaborative and choose to continue to develop themselves. This chapter will focus on the same PACT principles discussed in the previous chapter, but from the leaders' perspective, adding two additional dimensions available for leaders: incentives and mutual respect, so leaders can become not only engaged but *engaging leaders.* As leaders focus on these behaviors, all members of the organization are able to improve their engagement across all the five forces of engagement, as noted in Figure 6.1.

The phenomena shown in Figure 6.2 are typical of the companies we have worked with. It shows that leaders and managers themselves are consistently more engaged than staff or factory workers across all the five forces. Gallup estimates that globally, 27% of managers are engaged, compared to 18% of individual workers as shown in Figure 6.3 (Gallup 2025). However, it is not enough for successful leaders to be engaged; they also need to be *engaging, so they create an environment where the employees choose and want to be engaged.*

Too often leaders, managers, and supervisors make three, often wrong, assumptions about employee engagement:
1. Leaders assume that their team members are as engaged as they are. Most of the time, this is a false assumption, and unless leaders create an environment where people want to be fully engaged, it is unlikely to happen.
2. Leaders assume that it is enough for them to be engaged, and to be good examples of engagement. However, it is not enough to be an engaged leader; one needs to be an ENGAGING leader by creating an environment where people choose and want to be engaged.
3. Leaders assume that people become engaged if they are micromanaged—or even ordered—to be engaged. As noted in Chapter 1, "employee engagement is the emotional commitment and enthusiasm employees have for their work," and it

will not show up through micromanagement or orders. It is an emotional choice employees make (or not). Positive employee engagement cannot be forced or simply mandated by policy. It arises when people *want* and choose to give their best at work.

Figure 6.1: Multidimensional representation of employee engagement with leaders' IMPACT opportunities.

In a recent *Harvard Business Review* article, Hitendra Wadhwa notes that managers "have an innate capacity for exemplary leadership far beyond what many realize" (*Harvard Business Review* 2024, p. 42). Leadership plays a pivotal role in fostering employee engagement by creating an environment where employees feel valued, heard, and inspired to contribute fully. Effective leaders understand engagement is deeply personal and sustained through genuine interactions, frequent recognition, and meaningful work (Kahn, 1990). Moreover, leaders enhance engagement by demonstrating personal authenticity, consistent communication, and a clear vision, effectively linking employees' individual roles to broader organizational goals.

To identify characteristics and behaviors leaders can—and should—develop, we have created the IMPACT framework, aligned with the PACT framework discussed in Chapter 5, to help leaders develop specific behaviors to create an environment where

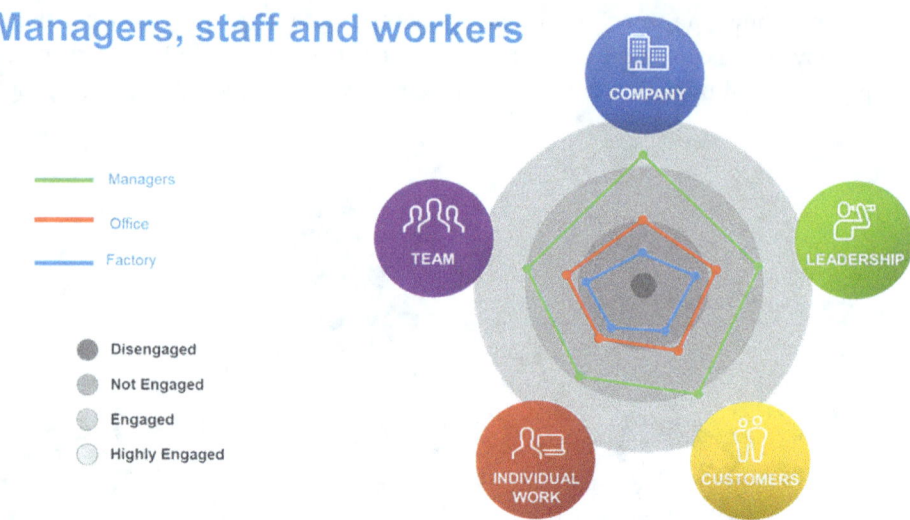

Figure 6.2: A typical example of engagement profiles for managers, office staff, and factory workers.

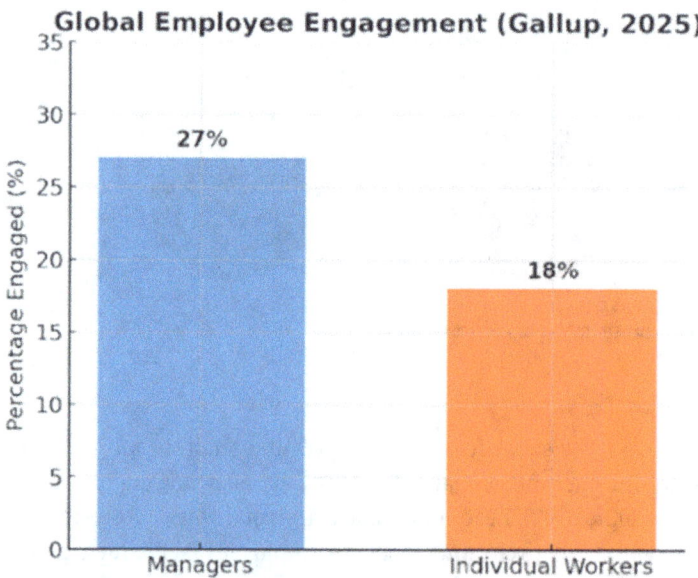

Figure 6.3: Managers vs. Individual Worker Engagement.
Source: *Gallup (2025)*

their associates and team members choose to be engaged and where employees are motivated to develop their own PACT (Passion, Accountability, Collaboration, and Transformation). The framework has been developed to mirror the PACT model, but from the leader's point of view, with two additional elements available for the leaders to help employee engagement: Incentives and Mutual Respect. This has created the IMPACT (*Incentives, Mutual Respect, Passion, Accountability, Collaboration, and Transformation*) framework to give leaders specific tools to develop themselves into more engaging leaders.

Incentives

Leaders can strategically use incentives to improve employee engagement by aligning rewards closely with behaviors that genuinely reflect organizational values and goals. However, incentives must be thoughtfully designed to reinforce intrinsic motivation rather than replace it. As Kohn (1993) cautioned in *Punished by Rewards*, poorly designed incentive systems risk undermining intrinsic motivation and genuine commitment, reducing work to a series of transactions rather than a source of meaning. Effective incentives should, therefore, emphasize meaningful recognition, foster a sense of achievement, and cultivate pride in contributing to shared objectives (Macey and Schneider, 2008). For example, companies like Google successfully engage employees by combining tangible rewards—such as bonuses tied to collaborative achievements—with intangible incentives like public acknowledgment and opportunities for personal growth.

Incentives, in both absolute and, maybe more importantly, relative terms, play an important part in having people fully engaged. Even though there is ample evidence that well-developed incentives may have a long-term positive effect on engagement, the opposite is also true. Incentives that are perceived to be unfair can kill motivation and engagement. In fact, we are convinced that perceived unfair incentives may often be the most important element for employees' disengagement. A strategic and fair use of work incentives has proven to be an important catalyst for employee engagement. Research shows that companies that use incentives to recognize and reward employees for their contributions and achievements report higher levels of employee engagement (89%), retention (87%), and loyalty (85%) compared to those that do not use incentives (Incentive Research Foundation 2018).

To utilize incentives to improve engagement, we have identified three behaviors every leader can choose to develop better, more motivating incentives. We have identified these three behaviors to help leaders, managers, and supervisors with concrete actions everyone can choose to take, and they are not meant to be all-inclusive, but are meant to be examples of what all leaders can do. The three behaviors to utilize incentives to improve engagement, each discussed below, are:
1. Be fair
2. Reward engagement
3. Set boundaries

Being Fair

Being fair may not be a sufficient condition, but it is *a necessary condition* in motivating people to be fully engaged. Leaders should continually evaluate if there are any incentives or incentive programs which communicate perceived unfairness to employees. It has been our experience that if employees perceive that employee treatment, rewards, or incentives are perceived to be unfair, it is very difficult to get employees engaged.

Financial incentives, such as salaries, performance bonuses, or profit-sharing, can boost engagement if they are perceived as fair and equitable, and if employees see a clear connection between their effort and the reward. For example, many organizations have implemented profit-sharing plans that distribute a portion of profits to employees, aiming to create an "ownership mentality." When done well, such programs can encourage employees to think and act like business owners, taking initiative to drive results. However, leaders must design these plans carefully. Research indicates that pay-for-performance systems—when poorly implemented or perceived as overly pressuring—can increase employee stress and reduce engagement, particularly where leader support is lacking (Park, Kong and Peng, 2024). To avoid this, the objectives tied to incentives should be achievable, transparent, and within the employee's sphere of control. Clarity is paramount—vague or unrealistic incentive goals will not motivate and may even demoralize staff. Managers should communicate how incentive metrics relate to team and company success, and ensure the metrics emphasize quality and collaboration—not just raw output at any cost.

In our research, the lowest scores are often given to the question: "I am fairly compensated for my work." So, it is not unusual for employees to feel this way. It is important that, in absolute and relative terms, the employee perception of the pay is transparent and fair if one wishes to keep employees engaged.

> Many years ago, I became the president of a company where the employees strongly felt that they were underpaid for their work, and the engagement, morale, and work satisfaction were very low. As management we felt that the pay was fair, and that the company benefits were comparatively good. However, we recognized that it really did not matter what we thought if the employee perception and the communication among the employees were that they were unfairly compensated. We decided to do two things: First we openly discussed the situation with the employees, and agreed with them that better information about relative pay would be useful, since we were a relatively small player in the area. Second, we monetarized all employee benefits and communicated annually to each employee what the monetary value of their company-paid employee benefits were. We found out from our research, and what was openly communicated to the employees, that the pay for most positions was at or above the average pay for the employees in similar positions in the area, and that the company paid benefits that significantly added to the value of the total incentives. If there were any unfair discrepancies, we corrected them immediately. Once we did the research and communicated the findings and our actions to the employees, the employees' attitudes about their pay quickly changed, and we heard very few complaints about the incentives after that, followed by improved employee engagement.

Being transparent and fair pays off. Feeling any sense of unfairness is often a significant source of disengagement for employees.

Rewarding Engagement

Importantly, extrinsic rewards alone are not sufficient to generate true engagement. Studies in behavioral science have long shown that if people focus solely on external rewards, their intrinsic motivation—the internal drive to do work because it's interesting or purposeful—can diminish. Thus, great leaders use incentives in a balanced way: recognize and reinforce great work, rather than just try to coerce performance. As *Harvard Business Review* has noted, the failure of many incentive programs is not due to a minor design flaw, but to the "inadequacy of psychological assumptions"—i.e., neglecting how complex human motivation really is (Kohn 1993, p. 54). People want to be paid fairly, but beyond that, engagement is fueled more by intangible factors like purpose, growth, and feeling valued. As one regional manager at a global retail chain describes her experience with bonuses, when she realized that cash bonus alone wasn't sparking commitment. It wasn't until they paired bonuses with public recognition and tied them to employees' core value of customer service excellence that the company saw employees light up and *want* to go the extra mile. In her experience, the bonus gave a tangible reward, but the recognition tapped into pride and meaning. Recognition-based incentives deserve special emphasis. Kahn (1990) argued that engagement is deeply personal, arising when employees experience works as meaningful and feel safe to invest themselves through genuine interpersonal interactions. Later research has also shown that frequent recognition helps sustain these conditions of engagement. Recognition is a low-cost, high-impact driver of engagement, and it can be delivered in many forms—from a sincere thank-you note or a shout-out in a meeting, to formal awards. A study by Achievers found that employee recognition is one of the top drivers of engagement worldwide (Achievers Workforce Institute 2020). When employees feel their work is seen and appreciated, their connection to the organization grows. Crucially, the recognition must be authentic, personal, and consistent. *One of the fastest ways to create disengaged employees is to teach them that you don't care about them as people.* On the flip side, when employees frequently receive acknowledgment for their engagement and contributions, they feel valued and motivated to continue to be engaged, performing at a high level. Achievers' research indicates that the most important factor in effective recognition is alignment with company values—employees should be praised for behaviors that exemplify the organization's mission and values. Respondents whose personal values were *very well aligned* with their company's values were five times more likely to report being engaged than those whose values were not aligned at all—highlighting that values alignment is a powerful predictor of engagement (Achievers Workforce Institute 2020).

The second factor is frequency: recognition is most powerful when it's frequent and timely, not saved only for annual award ceremonies. In fact, data from Achievers Workforce Institute shows a correlation between recent recognition and engagement—about half of employees who were recognized in the past week describe themselves as "highly engaged," compared to only 16% of those who have not been recognized in over a year (Achievers Workforce Institute 2020). This is a compelling argument for making recognition for engagement and performance a regular leadership habit.

The lesson for managers is that incentives to be effective in improving engagement must be part of a broader strategy to engage, not just a standalone solution. Leaders should regularly ask themselves: *Do our reward systems reinforce engagement, the behaviors, and the culture we want?* For instance, if collaboration is desired, is there a team-based bonus or acknowledgment of collaborative efforts? If innovation is valued, do employees get rewarded (or at least not punished) for experimenting and learning from failures? Strategic incentives are as much about removing disincentives as providing rewards—e.g., eliminating policies that unintentionally discourage risk-taking or information sharing. Ultimately, the most impactful incentives are those that make employees feel valued, appreciated, and connected. A public thank-you from a CEO can sometimes do more for engagement than a nominal gift card, because it resonates on an emotional level. In summary, fair pay and benefits may keep people on the job, but it is meaningful recognition and aligned rewards that inspire them to engage deeply with that job. Used wisely, incentives can catalyze an engaged workforce.

Setting Boundaries

Setting clear and respectful boundaries in the workplace significantly contributes to employee engagement by fostering an environment of trust, psychological safety, and balanced, equitable expectations. When leaders articulate explicit guidelines regarding values, workload, working hours, and availability, employees feel incentivized and empowered to manage their responsibilities effectively without risking burnout or excessive stress. As Delizonna (2017) highlights, psychological safety is fundamental for high-performing teams, enabling employees to engage fully, voice concerns openly, and collaborate authentically. Leaders can foster this safety by setting clear norms and modeling openness. Macey and Schneider (2008) argue that when employees perceive their organization as valuing their well-being and treating them with fairness and respect, they are more likely to demonstrate loyalty and engagement. Clear boundaries can reinforce this respect by signaling organizational support.

Setting boundaries is also a question of fairness. Once everyone knows that boundaries are clear and applied to everyone, employees see treatment as fair and transparent.

Setting clear boundaries in the workplace promotes mutual respect by establishing fair and transparent expectations around roles, responsibilities, and personal limits. Delizonna (2017) highlights that psychological safety depends on fairness and respect. Extending this idea, when leaders and employees define and honor common boundaries, it can reinforce that respect and support healthier collaboration.

Mutual Respect

The second element in our IMPACT model, following Incentives, is Mutual Respect. If incentives are the spark for engagement, a culture of mutual respect and trust is the oxygen that allows that spark to catch fire and sustain itself. Leaders who cultivate respect up and down the hierarchy create the fertile ground in which engagement grows. Mutual respect means that leaders treat employees as trustworthy, capable adults—and employees, in turn, respect each other, leaders, and organizational values. This mutual street of respect builds the foundation of trust, psychological safety, and positive relationships.

Mutual respect in the workplace lets all employees know that they are valued for their achievements, abilities, and qualities. Being valued and treated respectfully helps to promote a positive work culture in which employees feel fairly treated, and are fulfilled, loyal, engaged, and motivated to perform at their very best.

To promote mutual respect, we have identified three behaviors every leader can choose to improve the sense of mutual respect in their organizations. We have identified these three behaviors to help leaders with concrete actions they can choose to take, and they are not meant to be all-inclusive, but are meant to be examples of what leaders, managers, and supervisors can do. The three behaviors to promote mutual respect, each discussed below, are:
1. Create psychological safety
2. Encourage balance
3. Personalize rewards

Creating Psychological Safety

Psychological safety—the belief that one can be themselves, and speak openly without fear of negative consequences—is foundational to mutual respect and sustained engagement in the workplace. Employees who feel psychologically safe are more willing to share innovative ideas, openly discuss mistakes, and contribute authentically to team discussions, creating an environment of mutual respect where everyone's voice is valued (Delizonna, 2017). For example, Google's Project Aristotle revealed that psychological safety was the most critical factor distinguishing high-performing teams from their less effective counterparts, underscoring the profound link between safety, respect, and team effectiveness (Delizonna, 2017).

Furthermore, psychological safety deepens engagement by fostering trust and openness among colleagues, encouraging active participation and collaborative problem-solving. Edmondson (1999) found that when employees feel psychologically safe to express themselves, they are more willing to take risks, share ideas, and learn from mistakes. These behaviors enhance team performance and innovation, and when connected with engagement research, suggest a pathway to greater discretionary effort. Macey and Schneider (2008) argue that engaged employees invest discretionary effort, leading to stronger organizational outcomes. Companies such as Pixar illustrate this principle in practice: by cultivating an environment where employees at every level are encouraged to challenge ideas constructively, they sustain high engagement and continuous creative breakthroughs (Catmull and Wallace, 2014). Thus, promoting psychological safety not only enhances mutual respect but also creates a fertile ground for lasting employee engagement and organizational success.

According to HiPeople (2023), psychological safety "creates a supportive work atmosphere where all employees are treated with respect, embraced for their individuality, and appreciated for their contributions"—fostering genuineness, engagement, innovation, and commitment. Such a culture also boosts morale, productivity, and belonging.

The sense of psychological safety and engagement is not only common sense, but has well been established in popular and academic research. Employees who experience and perceive psychological safety are more likely to bring themselves fully to work and to exhibit and promote work engagement (Ge 2020). Research shows that the relationship between humble leadership and employee engagement is fully mediated by psychological safety. By acknowledging their own limitations and mistakes, recognizing followers' strengths and contributions, and modeling teachability, leaders foster a climate in which employees feel safe to act without fear of negative consequences and are therefore able to fully engage in their work (Walters and Diab, 2016).

A key task for leaders is to create an environment of psychological safety where everyone can show up as individuals and want to be fully engaged with the organization and their leaders, as well as their coworkers.

Encouraging Balance

Encouraging life balance in the workplace underscores an organization's respect for its employees as whole individuals with personal as well as professional aspirations. When leaders proactively foster an environment where employees can harmonize their work responsibilities with personal lives, it sends a clear message that employee well-being is valued—not merely as a means to productivity but as a fundamental aspect of respectful organizational culture. Hirsch (2023) argues that organizations promoting work-life integration foster greater employee engagement and satisfaction, which can reduce burnout and support retention. Patagonia, renowned for its progressive workplace policies, exemplifies this practice by strictly maintaining flexible working arrangements and offering extensive family and personal leave options, such as on-site child care, flexible working arrangements, and generous family leaves, resulting in notably high employee satisfaction and sustained engagement (Chouinard 2016). Gallup research shows that when employees believe their organization cares about their overall well-being, they are far less likely to job hunt and up to three times more likely to be engaged, suggesting that organizational support for balanced lifestyles can enhance both retention intent and engagement (Gallup, 2023).

Moreover, a workplace that actively supports balanced living encourages employees to reciprocate this respect through greater loyalty, discretionary effort, and commitment to organizational goals. For example, Google's employee-centric approach includes generous parental leave, extensive wellness programs, and flexible scheduling, practices that illustrate organizational respect for employees' life commitments beyond work, reinforcing mutual trust and engagement. Ultimately, promoting life balance not only enhances personal well-being but also strengthens the mutual respect vital for fostering a deeply engaged workforce.

Leaders can, and should, encourage people to have balance in their lives, and learn to integrate their life and work. It is good to remind our teams to keep in mind the comment attributed to Dolly Parton: "Never get so busy making a living that you forget to make a life." People want, and deserve to be seen and treated as more than just workers.

Personalizing Rewards

Personalizing incentives and rewards in the workplace significantly enhances employee engagement by demonstrating genuine recognition of individual preferences and contributions. Rather than using only standardized reward systems, leaders, managers, and supervisors who are able and willing to tailor recognition to match employees' unique motivations and aspirations reinforce the message that each individual's efforts and values are genuinely respected (Kohn, 1993). Macey and Schneider (2008) argue that engagement flourishes when employees feel supported and empowered by organizational practices. Google illustrates this principle in practice through customized perks—such as professional development courses, flexible work hours, and opportunities for charitable giving—that contribute to consistently high levels of engagement and employee satisfaction (Bock, 2015).

Employees want and deserve to be seen and treated as individuals, and not only as employees.

Furthermore, treating employees as individuals will also help them to feel more valued, and to be more engaged. Knowing people well enough to be able to personalize their rewards is important if we want to help people choose to be fully engaged in their work. Some employees are highly motivated by small financial rewards, whereas others may be more motivated by appreciation, or even one-on-one time with the manager. We are all different, and will be more engaged if our rewards meet our wants and needs. A good reminder of this is the 8-year-old who deliberately spelled a word wrong in the last round of the school spelling bee because "if you lose you get a piece of candy, but if you win you just get a boring medal." Know your team members well enough to personalize their rewards. Leaders and managers who invest in work design, rewards, and recognition are more effective at boosting employee engagement, research shows.

> To show mutual respect employees are individuals, and want to feel *valued*. There has been much discussion lately about the value of appreciation and employee recognition programs in boosting employee engagement. There is no question that these ways of showing appreciation are important ways to boost engagement. However, in our work we have found that appreciation is a necessary, but not sufficient to really empower engagement. People want to be appreciated, no question. But even more importantly people want to be value. And there is a difference between feeling *appreciated* and being *valued*.
>
> A few years ago, one of my children called me and expressed her dissatisfaction in their work because they did not feel *valued*. They had just received many forms of recognition for their work from top leaders, coworkers, and their team members. They were highly compensated, and yet they did not feel valued. And they have sense left the company for places where they are not only appreciated, but valued as an important member of their team and the company.

We must show sincere appreciation through our words, actions, and even recognition programs. We must learn and remember to thank people for their contribution often. As John F. Kennedy has said: "We must find time to stop and thank people who make a difference in our lives." However, in addition to sincere appreciation, we also must show that we *value* our team members, truly recognizing their contributions by listening to their ideas, by getting to know our employees' personal situations, and by asking them frequently how they are really doing. People must feel that we value them enough to be interested in them as people, not just workers, and that they in fact matter (*Harvard Business Review* 2025).

Enlightening Passion

Having passion and enthusiasm for one's work is an important element of individual engagement, and leaders play a critical role in facilitating an environment where people can experience this excitement and passion.

There are at least three important elements for leaders to promote passion for employees:

1. Establish an inspiring vision.
2. Align people's strengths with job requirements.
3. Bring joy and fun to the workplace.

Establishing Vision

Commonly attributed quote to Helen Keller (source unverified): "The only thing worse than being blind is having sight, but no vision."

Employees are likely more engaged when there is a clear and inspiring vision and purpose for their work. Leaders have a unique opportunity to ignite that fire by establishing an inspiring vision, and connecting employees to a deeper "why" behind their roles. Indeed, people hunger for purpose and meaning from their work—*this drives employee engagement.*

Leaders who articulate a compelling and clear vision for the organization ignite passion by aligning employees' everyday tasks with a broader sense of purpose and meaning. Employees become deeply motivated when their individual contributions visibly support meaningful organizational goals (Macey and Schneider, 2008). For instance, Steve Jobs famously inspired Apple's workforce by emphasizing their role in challenging the status quo and creating products that change lives—translating daily responsibilities into a visionary mission.

Crucially, effective vision-setting involves more than inspirational speeches; it requires leaders to embody their message authentically and consistently reinforce the vision through actions and decisions. Howard Schultz's leadership at Starbucks exemplifies this principle. By embedding the vision of creating a "third place"—an inviting space between home and work—into company practices, Schultz successfully generated passion among employees, driving remarkable customer engagement and organizational growth. When employees see leaders genuinely living their articulated vision, and the purpose for their work, it deepens loyalty and empowers individuals to engage in meaningful work passionately and purposefully.

> While serving as a CEO, one of the division heads used to collect pictures and stories of the best company projects into books, where our products were clearly displayed, and give them to the factory workers and staff to take home, so that they can proudly show their families and significant others what the end result of their work was. This allowed them to be proud of their work, and be part of the vision and purpose of the company. It worked! People were proud of their work, and they understood why the quality of their work and engagement mattered.

Aligning Strengths

One of the first phrases I learned as I was learning English many years ago was the statement: "People are down on things they are not up on." And it is definitely true.

Leaders who deliberately align employees' roles and responsibilities with their strengths significantly enhance passion and drive deeper engagement. Research consistently demonstrates that when individuals are placed in roles that leverage their personal talents and interests, they experience increased intrinsic motivation, productivity, and job satisfaction. For instance, at Facebook (Meta), leaders actively identify employees' core strengths through comprehensive feedback tools, subsequently tailoring job assignments and projects to amplify each individual's unique capabilities. This targeted approach not only fuels passion but also cultivates an environment where employees feel deeply valued and empowered to excel.

Moreover, effective alignment of strengths requires ongoing communication and mentorship from leaders who proactively nurture and encourage employees' skills and talents. Companies such as Adobe exemplify this approach by implementing regular "Check-In" conversations, enabling managers to continuously recalibrate roles and tasks based on individual strengths and career aspirations (Delizonna, 2017). By intentionally matching employees' duties with their strengths, leaders create an organizational culture marked by passion, commitment, and high performance, ultimately driving sustained engagement and organizational success.

> After finishing my MBA, my first business job was with Procter & Gamble in brand management. It was a great job for training, and a great opportunity. However, as part of every brand management trainee there was a requirement to spend a certain time in sales, so you could understand how our marketing actions impacted sales. Again, a great opportunity, and a good training. But I was a bad salesperson. There were so many things I did not like about the job, and I literally was no good at selling. I was not engaged in sales, and it may have been one of the reasons I did not continue my career with P&G. I knew I had a good analytical mind, and I had succeeded in school and work. But I could not sell. I was self-aware that I could work harder and longer hours than anyone, but my skills with people were not suitable for sales (at least that is what I kept telling myself). So, I would win all the sales competitions that had to do with activity (such as number of visits), and miserably lost all those that had to do with achieving sales volume goals. I very much enjoyed my job in brand management, and I think I was very engaged in my work. But once I was put in a job where success did not depend on my strengths, my engagement level immediately plummeted. And I think this is a common occurrence. People in general do not find passion, or do not engage in jobs they are not suited for, and will be much more excited and engaged in jobs where they can use their strengths.

The key for leaders to increase engagement and passion is to know the *people* and the *jobs* well enough to be able to match people's strengths with the job requirements. It is not an easy task, but a necessary one if we want people to have passion and engagement in their work.

Making Work More Fun

Another thing leaders can do to foster passion and a culture of engagement is to bring more joy and fun to work. As noted in a recent *Time* article: "When we are . . .. emotionally upset, we tend to underperform. Conversely, when we are "centered"—calm, attuned and open—"we're more likely to achieve high performance" (*Time* 2024).

Even though the objective of work is not to just have fun, and leaders' primary job is not to make work fun, there is much that leaders can do to make the work environment more enjoyable and joyful, so people want to be there, and want to perform well in their tasks.

Leaders who intentionally make work enjoyable foster a culture where passion and engagement flourish, directly impacting both morale and productivity. Injecting fun into the workplace isn't merely about occasional celebrations or perks; it's about consistently creating an environment where employees feel positive, energized, and connected to their colleagues (Macey and Schneider, 2008). For example, Southwest Airlines famously prioritizes humor and camaraderie within its teams, empowering employees to inject their personalities into customer interactions and daily tasks. This approach has not only boosted employee engagement—evidenced by consistently high employee satisfaction scores—but has also translated into exceptional customer loyalty and business performance.

Furthermore, cultivating a fun work environment requires leaders to model the behaviors they wish to see, demonstrating authenticity, openness, and approachability. Google's playful culture, with creative workspaces, team-building activities, and quirky internal traditions, stems directly from leadership decisions to embrace humor and creativity as core aspects of organizational life. By showing genuine enthusiasm and incorporating fun into everyday routines, leaders create a workplace that fuels passion, fosters meaningful connections, and sustainably elevates employee engagement.

Encouraging Accountability

While passion connects to the *why* of engagement, accountability connects to the *how*. An environment of accountability means employees understand what is expected of them, take ownership of their results, and feel a sense of responsibility for their own as well as their team's success. Far from being a punitive concept, true accountability is empowering—it gives employees agency and pride in their work. Leaders who cultivate accountability effectively are essentially saying to their people: "We trust you to own this, and we believe in your capability to deliver." This vote of confidence, coupled with clear expectations, can significantly boost engagement.

Wilson Learning Worldwide finds that when employees are clear about what's expected of them and know they will be held accountable, they tend to hold themselves accountable—and this personal accountability strongly drives engagement. People rise to the occasion when they know the bar is high *and* that their leaders trust them to meet it.

Three principles that can help leaders instill accountability in their employees and teams are:
1. Encourage autonomy
2. Set clear targets
3. Give meaningful feedback

Encouraging Autonomy

Our experience globally has been that people do not want, or even need, to be micromanaged. Most of the time more independence increases engagement. When people are accountable and take responsibility for their work, they are more engaged, and more responsible for the end results. People want to know what they need to do, but if they have the necessary skills and resources, most of the time, they do not want to be told how the work should be done.

Encouraging autonomy enhances employee accountability and drives engagement by empowering individuals to take ownership of their tasks and decisions. Employees who experience autonomy feel trusted and respected, motivating them to be more accountable for the end result, and more committed to their roles (Macey and Schneider, 2008). Netflix exemplifies this approach, fostering an environment of radical autonomy where leaders clearly communicate expectations and provide the freedom for employees to choose how best to achieve outcomes. This approach has not only heightened accountability but has also led to exceptional levels of employee engagement and innovation, underpinning Netflix's continued growth and success.

Leaders can effectively encourage autonomy by setting clear objectives, establishing open channels for feedback, and reducing unnecessary oversight. Providing employees with a sense of control over their work and decisions boosts intrinsic motivation, enhancing accountability and deepening their engagement (Deci and Ryan, 2000). At Spotify, leaders apply this principle by organizing teams into autonomous "squads," each empowered to set their own workflows, solve problems independently, and directly influence product innovation. The autonomy granted to these teams fosters heightened accountability, collaboration, and engagement, and has helped Spotify to maintain its innovative edge in a highly competitive market.

Setting Clear Targets

Setting clear and measurable targets significantly enhances accountability in the workplace by providing employees with precise expectations and a clear sense of direction. Clear targets not only help individuals understand what success looks like, but also promote engagement by offering tangible goals that employees can pursue and track (Locke and Latham, 2002). Google exemplifies this approach through its rigorous objective and key results (OKR) framework, where specific, ambitious targets are transparently set and consistently revisited. This method has proven effective at enhancing accountability, aligning teams, and dramatically increasing employee engagement by giving employees clear ownership of their objectives. A primary task for any leader, then, is to ensure clarity of expectations.

> One of the least engaging and most discouraging experiences I can remember took place more than 50 years ago when I was serving in the military. I was serving in the anti-tank force in the Finnish military, and after a long, and somewhat enjoyable, day of target shooting with bazookas, our task was to find the missed ammunition in the sand banks behind the target tanks. They were deep in the sand, hard to find, and we had no idea how many of them were hidden in the sand. We were given a target to find ten bullets. It took some time, but we found them, as directed. After we had accomplished the task, we were told to find five more, then five more, and still five more once the earlier target had been met. The moving and total unclear target was so demoralizing that I can still remember the total discouragement from the experience, more than 50 years later. Clear, well-communicated, and steady targets can be engaging and encouraging, whereas unclear, poorly communicated, and moving targets will likely discourage even the more engaged employees.

Leaders can further amplify the benefits of clear target setting by encouraging autonomy in how employees achieve their clearly defined goals. As noted above, autonomy on how to reach the well-defined goals fosters intrinsic motivation and creativity, empowering employees to take initiative, innovate, and be proactive in their pursuit of these objectives. For example, 3M famously embraces this approach through its "15% time" policy, encouraging employees to spend a portion of their workweek on self-chosen projects aligned with well-defined broader organizational targets. This has not only heightened accountability, as individuals take greater ownership of their projects, but also dramatically increased employee engagement and innovation, resulting in products such as Post-it Notes.

Giving Feedback

Clear targets followed up with good feedback are a great way for everyone to know how they are doing. Meaningful feedback is a critical element in encouraging engagement. People crave feedback. Both positive, and corrective, or even critical. It is important that we establish a system for regular and expected feedback through periodic, regular employee reviews. However, it is also important to have the "small talk" with employees, when issues are still "small." It is too often a mistake we make when we allow small issues to escalate into bigger issues before giving feedback, which they often do when we are unwilling to deal with issues when they are still small and easier to deal with. However, dealing with the issues when they are small requires our willingness and ability to give feedback regularly.

Even though people crave and deserve positive feedback (which should be given often), they also deserve the respect of corrective or critical feedback when it is needed. However, it is a skill to be able to give corrective or critical feedback, so that we give corrective feedback on issues, not people. And as is well known, positive feedback can be given in public, and corrective or critical feedback should always and only be given in private. Positive feedback can praise the person as well as the work, but corrective feedback is given to tasks, not directed to people. We too often forget this. Also, it is important to remember that once corrective or critical feedback is given, we learn to forgive and forget. Hanging on to old mistakes is demoralizing, and will not engage or accomplish anything positive.

And as we give corrective or critical feedback, it may be useful to remember that, as noted in the research by Laure Eskreis-Winkler, people often know what they should do, but they are just not doing it (Eskreis-Winkler et al 2016). In her work she found that people were much more likely to succeed to change their behavior when they were able to *give* advice, rather than *receiving* it. So, we may be more effective managers if we ask people to give advice on how they would deal with the problem at hand, rather than giving them advice on what they should be doing. For example, people who wanted to lose weight were more likely to succeed if they give weight loss advice than if they were paired with the nutritional expert from the Mayo Clinic. Often, when we are thinking about management, we are thinking about the situation as if we were in school, where we are the teacher, giving information, and our employees are students, receiving advice. However, if people are not doing their job, or are not engaged, the problem more often than not is that they are not lacking information or advice. They often know what they are supposed to be doing; they are just not doing it. It is not a lack of information; it is a lack of confidence and discipline. Asking people for advice, and if possible, setting people as mentors giving advice is likely going to be a much more effective course to change behavior than merely giving advice or negative feedback.

When corrective or critical feedback is necessary, how the feedback is framed is likely to have a significant impact on how it will be received, and what impact it will have on future behavior. A research study on giving effective feedback to high school students showed that students who were given severe criticism with a note that they were given severe feedback because the teacher believed in their potential, accepted the criticism significantly better, and were motivated by the criticism more than those students who were merely given a plain note that there is feedback on their work (Walton and Cohen 2023).

Effective feedback from leaders significantly bolsters accountability, which in turn enhances employee engagement by providing clarity, reinforcing expectations, and demonstrating genuine investment in employees' growth. Research shows that timely and constructive feedback clarifies goals, builds confidence, and motivates improvement, making it a powerful driver of performance and engagement (Hattie and Timperley, 2007). For instance, Adobe's implementation of frequent, informal "Check-In" conversations replaced traditional performance reviews with continuous feedback, reducing voluntary turnover by 30% and boosting employee engagement and accountability through ongoing communication and development (Cappelli and Tavis, 2016).

Encourage Collaboration

Leaders who actively foster collaboration significantly enhance employee engagement by building environments where teamwork, mutual trust, and shared purpose flourish. Research shows that effective collaboration encourages individuals to share ideas, support colleagues, and innovate collectively, thereby strengthening both personal commitment and organizational loyalty (Cross, Rebele and Grant, 2016). Pixar exemplifies this principle by structuring creative projects around collaborative teams that freely exchange feedback and ideas. This collaborative approach not only strengthens employee engagement but also consistently drives innovative storytelling and exceptional creative outcomes.

The three principles leaders can apply to their work to foster better collaboration are:
1. Be present
2. Encourage connections
3. Seek input

Being Present

It is important for employees that management is visible and accessible, if possible, in employees' own workspace. Managers and leaders can be engaging by prioritizing time with employees. The principle of "management by walking around" first emphasized by Tom Peters and Robert Waterman Jr. in their 1982 book, *In Search of Excellence: Lessons from America's Best-Run Companies*, continues to be a great principle for any manager who wishes to create an engaging environment and wants to be an engaging manager or leader. Communicating frequently and transparently as well as connecting personally with people we work with often means more to people than managers often think. My late father-in-law, Gary Egan, a former successful plant manager at Hewlett-Packard, taught me one of the important leadership principles: "Be present and treat others so that they always feel better having been with you." Great advice for anyone, especially for any manager. Being truly present and meeting people in their space is a great way to make sure that leadership is not a one-time achievement — it's something to be earned and re-earned every day. Be present.

> One of the best examples of leadership being present is the Chairman and major owner of Halton Group Ltd., Mika Halttunen. I worked with Mika for more than 13 years as the CEO of the company, and almost every year, Mika made sure he visited all the operations of the company in more than 30 countries and almost 2000 employees. Each visit naturally included the required management review, but an important part of each visit was Mika's visit to the staff and the factory workers. Mika would meet, greet, and listen to every member of each team, and he was present for each encounter. And when employees were asked what motivated them to be engaged, Mika and his presence would invariably come up as one of the main reasons for their strong engagement. Mika's visits and presence were always a highlight for the employees and an example to leaders to be present for the employees.

Encouraging Connections

Leaders who intentionally encourage interpersonal connections in the workplace foster environments where collaboration thrives, significantly enhancing employee engagement. By creating structured opportunities for informal interactions—such as coffee chats, team-building exercises, or cross-departmental events—leaders cultivate relationships built on trust, mutual respect, and genuine camaraderie. LumApps (2023) emphasizes that connected workspaces—especially those enabling interactive knowledge sharing and real-time engagement—enhance collaboration, employee motivation, and productivity. For example, Google's emphasis on creating social spaces and opportunities for spontaneous interactions has been central to fostering an innovative culture, resulting in employees consistently reporting high levels of engagement and satisfaction.

Feeling connected in the workplace is an important part of business. Social connections at work are important to people, and leaders can create regular opportunities for social interactions both in and out of work settings. Managers should encourage employees to become engaged with their peers, as well as with their work. Coffee breaks and lunch meetings are a good way to encourage good interactions and connections between peers. Celebrating individual and team successes provides uniting opportunities for leaders, as do any team activities. As leaders, we are more likely to create an engaging environment for employees if we encourage and enable communication between team members in and out of the workplace.

> Years ago, at one of our European facilities, management installed a foosball game in a well-accessible place in the office. It quickly became the central focus of breaks and lunch hour where management and workers at all levels met as equals, leaning to know each other, and appreciate the game skills regardless of the position. As a visiting company CEO I lost most of the games to more skilled office and factory workers, still connecting with them in ways not possible in any formal setting. At the foosball game we connected as people, even when at times language barrier often prevented more formal business connections.

Especially in the "workplace" where more and more work is being done remotely, it is often increasingly difficult to keep people connected, and to keep up a connected workplace culture (see Chapter 11 for a more detailed discussion on remote work and engagement). And it is so much more important that leaders make a diligent effort to help people stay connected, and to stay connected beyond technology (even though technology without question plays a critical role in a connected workplace). Whether an employee is in an office, at their home office, traveling for work, or away from their desk, a connected workspace means employees have their digital headquarters in their hands. A centralized tool that provides a connected experience for opportunities of collaboration, knowledge sharing, and engaging with colleagues. In her article, Kaplan (2025) outlines 13 effective ways to create a more connected workplace. Among these are taking steps to get to know employees, creating peer mentorship programs, keeping communication flowing across the company, hosting regular social events, and using integrations with collaboration suites to build stronger connectivity.

By using technology, we are able to integrate all collaborative tools to help maximize productivity while collaborating with each other, and being well informed by management and by the company.

When people feel connected in the workplace, they choose to be more engaged with their team mates, and also with the management, the company, their own work, and even with the customers. For many, being connected with others is a key motivation at work, and as we will see when we talk about teams (Chapter 7), a well-functioning team is a key driver for engagement. It is critical that leaders recognize this need and encourage these connections. "Divide and conquer" is not a great leadership strategy, but "connect and engage" is much more likely to bring out the best in people and in their teams. And as Steve Jobs said, "Great things are never done by one person. They are done by a team of people."

Seeking input

At times we meet managers who have the illusion that they already know everything, and that they do not need input from anyone, and that seeking input is a sign of weakness. Most of those managers or leaders are not very effective, and generally have rather short leadership careers. In fact, leaders who are open and willing to listen tend to be the more engaging leaders, and people working with them choose to be more engaged because they feel more empowered, and more valued. Also, leaders are more informed and get real input from all levels of the organization.

It is critical to seek input from all levels of the organization. People generally know more than we think.

Leaders who actively seek input from their teams foster an inclusive environment that dramatically enhances both engagement and collaboration. Soliciting feedback demonstrates genuine respect for employees' perspectives, instills a sense of ownership in shared outcomes, and encourages individuals to proactively contribute their best ideas (Delizonna, 2017). At Pixar, leaders routinely gather input from team members at all levels during "Braintrust" meetings, where candid feedback is not only invited but expected. This practice has not only elevated employee engagement but has been pivotal in creating groundbreaking, innovative storytelling (Cross, Rebele and Grant, 2016).

> Years ago, I was the president of a division of a retail equipment company, and we were facing a major technical difficulty in one of our key markets in Europe. Our research people had tried to solve the problem for some time, and we had engaged some university resources to solve it, but had not been able to solve it in any cost-effective way. While traveling and meeting with employees at our offices in Europe, I mentioned this problem to one of our service technicians at one of our offices. They looked at me a bit puzzled, and said that the challenge we saw was so insurmountable that it was not a problem at all, and that we already had most of the components in our products to solve the problem. He knew our products inside out, and understood the market certainly better than I or even our technical experts did. After evaluating the service technician's suggestion, it was in fact the solution implemented in our products with only minor modifications, and that one change made our product significantly more appealing in one of our major markets, and in fact increased the company value and our competitiveness significantly. I did not have that information, and neither did any other manager or expert, but it came from the service technician in one of our company backrooms. I always try to remember this experience when I am facing major problems I cannot solve.

Someone else always knows more than I do. As Bill Nye, the host of the Science Education television show, has well stated: "Everyone you will ever meet knows something you do not know." Seeking input from others in the workplace makes us wiser, and them more engaged.

Transformation

Most of us work in rapidly moving businesses, which offers us both challenges and opportunities. The challenge is to find ways for people to stay current, and on the other hand, rapid movement offers development opportunities for most employees. This is not always easy. Employees, especially the younger ones, both appreciate and even demand development opportunities for themselves in order to even consider career opportunities with any company. In fact, many consider development opportunities more important than pay. Development is one of the key elements that engages people in their own work, as well as in the company that provides these opportunities for them. "Making employee development a key part of company culture ensure workers stay up to date on industry bast practices and learn new skills. This, in turn, boosts employee engagement and attracts top talent" (Heinz (2023)).

Leaders play an important role in providing a work environment where people are able to learn and to develop. As leaders encourage innovation, even embrace mistakes as learning opportunities, employees are more likely to want to develop themselves, and to be more engaged in their work.

Leaders can encourage development and transformation for the employees through three behaviors:
1. Encourage innovation
2. Embrace mistakes
3. Promote development

Encouraging Innovation

Whenever possible, giving employees protected time and resources for creative work both engages people, and helps employees to take ownership of their work. Recognizing such development *efforts* helps people develop a "growth mindset," when they recognize that by putting forth more effort, they can and will learn, and that such development is recognized also by the leaders. Thus, it is often useful to recognize the effort as well as the outcome, as we want people to be more motivated and engaged in the development of their careers as well as the development of the company.

Companies that successfully encourage innovation typically foster environments characterized by openness, experimentation, and psychological safety. Google, for instance, is renowned for its "20% time" policy, allowing employees to dedicate one-fifth of their workweek to pursuing creative ideas outside their immediate job descriptions. This approach has led directly to groundbreaking products like Gmail and Google Maps, demonstrating how autonomy and space to experiment can drive substantial innovation.

Similarly, Amazon employs a method known as "working backwards," where teams begin by writing the future press release of a new product, clearly envisioning its impact on customers before development even begins. This method cultivates deep customer empathy and creative problem-solving, which have become hallmarks of Amazon's continuous innovation culture. Additionally, as already noted, 3M famously encourages innovation through its "15% rule," empowering employees to spend a portion of their time exploring self-directed projects. This policy notably led to the invention of Post-it Notes, highlighting the value of providing structured freedom for employee-driven innovation (Cross, Rebele and Grant, 2016).

Embracing Mistakes

Albert Einstein has been quoted as saying: "Anyone who has never made a mistake has never tried anything new."

As team members are encouraged to develop and innovate new things, mistakes happen. And mistakes happen even in all of our normal work. That is part of being engaged for all of us. It is critical that we deal with mistakes carefully if we want people to continue to be engaged, to develop, and to innovate. It is critical that when we see mistakes that we identify and correct the root causes, and do not look for someone to blame.

We can learn lessons from the airline industry's voluntary disclosure programs (VDPs), which encourages the reporting of safety-related incidents by offering frontline reporters immunity from disciplinary measures. For example, if a pilot in the United States accidentally violates a regulation or makes a mistake, and then reports the incident immediately, the pilot will not be penalized. As long as the incident was not intentional or seriously negligent, the Federal Aviation Administration (FAA) will not suspend or revoke the pilot's license. This practice has been extremely successful and helps gather important safety information. "Voluntary reporting of small mistakes can lead to a pool of important information from which patterns emerge," says Guenther Matschnig, IATA Senior Vice President, Safety, Operations, and Infrastructure. "This can result in changes being made to operational procedures, with significant safety benefits." For example, such a change in Danish law in 2001 to a nonpunitive stance resulted in the number of air traffic control safety reports rising from 15 a year to over 900, according to Navair, Denmark's air traffic provider (Matsching, 2025, n.p.).

Leaders who frame mistakes as learning opportunities foster psychological safety, which enables transparency, innovation, and continuous improvement in teams (Edmondson, 199). For instance, the former CEO of Ford, Alan Mulally, famously promoted a culture of candor by openly discussing challenges and setbacks during weekly meetings. By consistently demonstrating that errors were opportunities to learn rather than failures to hide, Mulally transformed Ford's culture, dramatically boosting employee engagement, accountability, and ultimately, the company's performance.

Organizations that normalize mistakes as part of learning foster psychological safety, encouraging employees to take calculated risks and innovate more boldly (Delizonna, 2017). At Pixar, for example, mistakes and failed experiments are celebrated as integral parts of the creative process. Leaders like Ed Catmull explicitly encourage team members to openly discuss failures in regular postmortem meetings, reinforcing the idea that creativity and improvement thrive in environments where failure is accepted and understood as part of success. By intentionally embracing and learning from mistakes, leaders build resilient, engaged teams committed to continuous growth and innovation.

To improve employee engagement and encourage employee development, we should learn from mistakes, regardless of who made them, and our objective should be to correct the error, and not to punish those who made the mistakes.

As leaders, we should also own and admit our own mistakes, which also allows others to admit their mistakes in a manner that retains their psychological safety. And if appropriate, approaching mistakes with a bit of humor can take a bit of the sting away, and help the organization and people to move forward to correct the mistakes, remember them, and yet not repeat them.

Promoting Development

Leaders can themselves be examples of continuous development by educating and developing themselves, and by making development an organizational priority. TalentGuard (2023) observes that in many organizations, employee development often takes a back seat to immediate operational demands and the pressure of "just getting things done." This short-sightedness seems to be a sure way to decrease the engagement of the best people. People want to develop, and want the leaders and organization they work for to support their development.

In our work with companies and teams, when people are given opportunities to choose what actions they think would most likely increase their engagement, two of the most common choices are to develop new skills and to set bold goals (see Chapter 5). People want to develop, and when leaders are able to promote development, they also create an environment where people want to move forward and be engaged.

Leaders who prioritize and visibly promote employee development not only enhance skillsets but also drive meaningful transformation and sustained engagement across their teams. Effective development goes beyond occasional training sessions or compliance-based exercises, embedding continuous learning and growth into the core organizational culture. By consistently signaling that employee growth matters, leaders foster intrinsic motivation, strengthen organizational commitment, and elevate performance (Deci and Ryan, 2000; TalentGuard, 2023). For instance, Deloitte famously implemented a comprehensive approach to employee development called the "Career Customization" framework, enabling individuals to shape their growth paths proactively. This structured commitment to personal and professional growth increased employee engagement, satisfaction, and ultimately, performance outcomes.

In Table 6.1 we have summarized the specific actions proposed in this chapter on how leaders can create an environment where people want and choose to be engaged.

Leaders, managers, and supervisors play a critical part in supporting people to be more engaged. In general, leaders' own engagement and enthusiasm serve as examples for everyone and, in itself, is an engagement motivator to others. However, it is not enough. Leaders need to create an *impactful* environment where people want to and choose to be engaged by using appropriate *incentives*, developing an environment of *mutual respect*, creating *passion* and *accountability*, as well as promoting *collaboration* and *transformation* and development.

Table 6.1: Leaders' actions supporting stronger employee engagement.

I	M	P	A	C	T
INCENTIVES	**MUTUAL RESPECT**	**PASSION**	**ACCOUNTABILITY**	**COLLABORATION**	**TRANSFORMATION**
Be Fair * Be equitable, unbiased, and just. Give credit when due – never take credit for other's work.	**Create Psychological Safety** * Never belittle anyone, even joking! Create a culture of trust.	**Establish Vision** * Create a vision that inspires you and aligns with others values. Communicate it with enthusiasm.	**Encourage Autonomy** * Do not micromanage. Tell people what to do, not how to do it.	**Be Present** * Be visible. Visit employees in *their* workspace. Be transparent.	**Encourage Innovation** * Budget resources for innovation. Give time for creativity.
Reward Engagement * Reward behavior you want. Manage expectations to avoid disappointments.	**Encourage Balance** * Know people personally. Give people adequate resources.	**Align Strengths** * Work to align tasks with employees strengths. Compensate for weaknesses.	**Set Clear Targets** * Communicate expectations clearly. Make goals challenging, but achievable.	**Encourage Connections** * Encourage and enable communication. Celebrate successes together.	**Embrace Mistakes** * Admit your own mistakes. See mistakes as life's lessons and learn from them.
Set Boundaries *State non-acceptable behaviors. Equitably enforce consequences.	**Personalize Rewards** * Be sincere, give recognition you know people want.	**Make Work Fun** * Surprise people in positive ways. Celebrate successes. Laugh, especially at yourself.	**Give Feedback** * Give positive feedback in public. Negative feedback in private. Forgive and forget.	**Seek Input** * Engage and get buy-in for decisions. Listen to truly understand what is being said.	**Promote Development** * Make development a priority. Be an example.

> **Key Questions**
> 1. How can you, as a leader, create incentive structures that are perceived to be fair?
> 2. As a leader, how can you personalize rewards, and how can that improve mutual respect in your organization?
> 3. What is your vision for your organization, and what part of that vision is inspiring for the team members?
> 4. How are you, or can you, encourage autonomy in your organization? What impact can that have on engagement?
> 5. What specific actions are you taking to encourage individuals to develop in your team or organization?

Chapter 7
Engaging Teams
Building Well-Functioning Teams Through Trust, Empathy, Appreciation, Mutual Agreements, and Synergy

> "Teamwork is the ultimate competitive advantage, both because it is so powerful and rare."
> — *Patrick Lencioni, an American business author, speaker, and consultant*

After working on improving employee engagement with companies around the world for the past several years, focusing on individual engagement and building more engaging leaders, we soon learned how critical well-functioning teams are for strong employee engagement. Also, substantial research confirms that well-functioning teams significantly enhance employee engagement. Gallup's 2023 engagement data underscore that teams with higher employee engagement—often those with strong collaboration and cohesion—are linked to greater productivity, commitment, and organizational outcomes. Gallup highlights that highly engaged teams consistently outperform their disengaged counterparts in performance and retention (Gallup, 2023). The underlying mechanism here is psychological safety—a hallmark of well-functioning teams—where employees feel secure enough to voice opinions, admit mistakes, and collaborate authentically without fear of negative repercussions (Edmondson, 1999; Frazier et al., 2017; Newman, Donohue and Eva, 2017).

This chapter specifically focuses on how teams can improve, so team members want to and choose to be more engaged. We have identified five critical elements of well-functioning teams, namely Trust, Empathy, Appreciation, Mutual agreements, and Synergy (TEAMS). Well-functioning teams thrive when built on the foundation of these five critical TEAMS elements. As teams improve these characteristics, the team members are able to increase their engagement across all the five forces of engagement, as noted in Figure 7.1.

Trust establishes psychological safety, enabling team members to engage authentically and take necessary risks without fear of judgment or reprisal (Edmondson, 1999). Empathy fosters deeper connections, allowing individuals to understand each other's perspectives and motivations, leading to more effective collaboration (Delizonna, 2017). Appreciation reinforces positive behaviors and contributes to heightened morale, ensuring individuals feel valued and motivated to contribute their best efforts (Gallup, 2023). Clearly defined mutual agreements set expectations and shared responsibilities, facilitating accountability and reducing conflicts through clarity and transparency (Costa, Roe and Taillieu, 2001). Finally, synergy emerges when these elements align, amplifying collective strengths and driving teams to achieve outcomes greater than the sum of individual contributions, thus creating sustained engagement and exceptional performance (Cross, Rebele and Grant, 2016). In the rest of the chap-

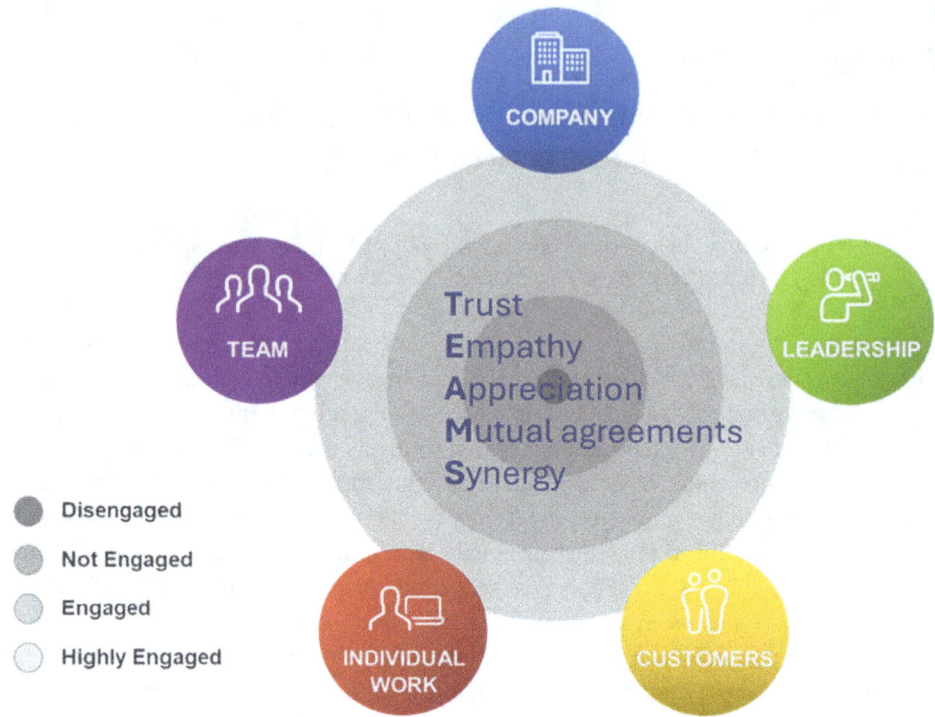

Figure 7.1: Multidimensional representation of employee engagement, focused on TEAMS responsibilities.

ter, we will explore each of these characteristics and present specific behaviors teams can foster to increase team engagement.

Trust

Trust fundamentally underpins effective teamwork by establishing psychological safety, which enables open communication, collaboration, and collective innovation (Edmondson, 1999).

> Pixar's success is often attributed to its high-trust culture, especially within its "Braintrust" meetings. These sessions allow creators to give and receive candid feedback without fear of personal attack. Because trust is the norm, teams are more willing to take risks, iterate creatively, and build stronger solutions together.

Specifically, team members build trust through consistently *delivering results*, demonstrating competence, reliability, and accountability. When individuals regularly meet or exceed their commitments, colleagues develop confidence in their abilities, fostering stronger interpersonal bonds. Additionally, *integrity*—demonstrated through honesty, transparency, and ethical behavior—reinforces trust by signaling reliability and respect within the team (Costa, Roe and Taillieu, 2001). For example, leaders at Netflix have famously emphasized integrity and performance as foundational team values, cultivating a trust-rich culture where employees collaborate freely, secure in the knowledge that colleagues will reliably and ethically fulfill their responsibilities.

The two things we think teams can agree to do to bolster trust are:
1. Deliver results
2. Have integrity

Delivering Results

Delivering consistent, promised, and reliable results is critical for establishing trust, a fundamental component of high-performing teams. When team members regularly fulfill their commitments, they signal dependability, reinforcing colleagues' confidence in their abilities and intentions (Costa, Roe and Taillieu, 2001). For example, Amazon emphasizes a results-driven culture through its Leadership Principles, explicitly highlighting "Deliver Results" as a core expectation. By setting clear standards and holding employees accountable for outcomes, Amazon reinforces a culture where trust is grounded in demonstrated capability—a foundation that supports strong, effective teams (Costa 2003). Furthermore, consistently delivering results enhances team psychological safety—where members feel secure enough to take interpersonal risks, knowing they can rely on each other's promises, competencies, and integrity.

Having Integrity

Integrity, characterized by honesty, consistency, and adherence to ethical principles, is foundational for building well-functioning teams. When leaders and team members consistently demonstrate integrity, they create an environment where individuals can confidently rely on each other's words and actions, thereby enhancing psychological safety and collaboration (Edmondson, 1999). At Netflix, integrity is deeply embedded in its organizational culture; the company famously promotes integrity, transparency, and candid feedback, ensuring that decisions and behaviors align closely with stated values. This deliberate alignment fosters trust among team members, enabling them to engage openly, innovate fearlessly, and perform effectively.

Moreover, integrity builds trust by signaling consistency and reliability, which fosters predictability and enables team members to collaborate without fear of hidden agendas or erratic behavior (Costa, Roe and Taillieu, 2001). Patagonia's unwavering commitment to ethical business practices and environmental sustainability exemplifies how principled leadership fosters trust. Employees observe consistent decisions aligned with core values, which strengthens engagement and builds cohesive teams united by shared purpose and accountability. Ultimately, integrity is more than a moral imperative; it is a strategic asset critical to trust, team cohesion, employee engagement, and ultimately organizational success.

Empathy

Harvard Business Review (2025) notes that many leaders dismiss empathy as a "touchy-feely" skill—yet neglecting it can seriously harm morale, retention, and open communication.

> Empathy is a non-negotiable for leaders, and the stakes are high for a leader who fails to embrace and model it. Dismissing empathy can result in negative consequences, including a toxic workplace, low morale, poor retention, and burnout. For leaders, it can result in failure to connect, inability to gather information, or being perceived as inaccessible. (Neale 2025)

Empathy—the ability to understand and genuinely relate to the experiences and perspectives of others—is critical for building cohesive, high-performing teams. Teams which demonstrate empathy actively foster psychological safety, enabling team members to communicate openly, share vulnerabilities, and collaborate authentically (Edmondson, 1999). For instance, Satya Nadella significantly transformed Microsoft's culture by placing empathy at its core—encouraging leaders to genuinely listen and understand employees' experiences. This shift fostered a more engaged, collaborative, and innovative workforce (Nadella, 2017; *Business Insider*, 2024; *Wired*, 2017).

Moreover, empathy enhances team effectiveness by promoting deeper interpersonal connections, reducing conflict, and fostering a collective sense of trust and support—a dynamic also reinforced by research showing that trust, grounded in benevolence and integrity, is central to team performance (Costa, Roe and Taillieu, 2001; Kock et al., 2019).

In addition, empathy-driven leadership practices create resilient, united teams better equipped to navigate complex challenges and innovate collaboratively. Ultimately, empathy is not merely a soft skill but a strategic imperative, driving sustained engagement and team performance.

Choosing to bypass empathy can feel like an efficient shortcut, but it is essential to connection, communication, and collaboration. Seeking to understand and showing genuine concern are essential practices that build empathy in teams by fostering deeper interpersonal connections and emotional awareness.

Two things teams can do to encourage empathy within their teams, and to strengthen team engagement are:
1. Seek to understand
2. Show concern

Seeking to Understand

When team members actively listen and strive to understand their colleagues' experiences, challenges, and perspectives, it validates those experiences and creates emotional resonance within the team. For example, leaders who regularly hold empathetic team conversations as well as one-on-one check-ins where employees can openly discuss personal or professional concerns—create environments where empathy naturally flourishes, increasing psychological safety and collaborative spirit.

Well-functioning teams prioritize mutual understanding by cultivating opportunities for open communication and actively practicing empathy. Team members engage in intentional listening, seeking to genuinely comprehend each other's perspectives and experiences. By proactively clarifying assumptions, addressing misunderstandings promptly, and creating a safe space for transparent dialogue, teams foster stronger interpersonal connections. This deeper understanding increases empathy, enhances collaboration, reduces conflicts, and boosts collective engagement, ultimately contributing to superior team performance and organizational success.

Showing Concern

Showing genuine concern further amplifies empathy by signaling to team members that their well-being is valued beyond mere task accomplishment. Demonstrating concern involves actions such as providing support during stressful periods, recognizing emotional cues, and proactively addressing issues before they escalate. At LinkedIn, leaders are trained explicitly to approach interactions with curiosity and compassion, cultivating an empathetic culture that strengthens team cohesion and mutual trust. By consistently modeling these behaviors, teams not only become more empathetic but also significantly enhance collaboration, morale, overall engagement, and demonstrate appreciation for other team members.

In high-performing teams, concern for colleagues is expressed not through grand gestures but through consistent, everyday actions. Team members build trust and cohesion when they listen attentively, check in on one another, and offer help before being asked. Acts such as acknowledging personal milestones, respecting boundaries, and celebrating professional wins create a sense of belonging that extends beyond individual tasks. Just as important are the smaller signals of care—validating frustrations, sharing knowledge, or simply ensuring that everyone's voice is heard in a meeting.

Appreciation

Appreciation fundamentally strengthens teams by fostering an environment of mutual respect and recognition, enabling team members to feel genuinely valued and motivated to contribute their best efforts. Specifically, actively *valuing diversity*—acknowledging and respecting individual differences in perspectives, experiences, and backgrounds—amplifies appreciation by signaling that each team member's unique attributes enhance collective success. Similarly, genuine listening demonstrates respect and interest, deepening interpersonal connections and making appreciation feel authentic rather than superficial. Research shows that inclusive practices require employees to feel their perspectives are valued (Roberson, 2006), and listening attentively is a primary way leaders and colleagues convey that respect and strengthen workplace relationships (Brownell, 1990).

For example, Salesforce exemplifies these practices by intentionally promoting inclusive behaviors, creating platforms for diverse voices, and establishing dedicated listening sessions to ensure employees feel heard and valued. Such initiatives have been linked to stronger morale and are widely recognized as drivers of trust, collaboration, and engagement, which in turn support high-performing teams.

Two things teams can do to show appreciation within their teams, and to strengthen team engagement are:
1. Value diversity
2. Listen

Valuing Diversity

Valuing diversity significantly enhances team strength by fostering a culture of appreciation and respect, where every member feels acknowledged for their unique perspectives and contributions. When teams embrace diversity—not just demographic differences, but varied experiences, skills, and viewpoints—they become more innovative and adept at solving complex problems. For example, Procter & Gamble has long championed diversity as essential to its success, leveraging diverse employee backgrounds to better understand global customers and drive breakthrough innovations. By openly recognizing and appreciating each individual's distinct talents and viewpoints, P&G reinforces an inclusive culture that deepens collaboration and boosts employee engagement.

Valuing diversity is not a political buzzword, but when sincerely practiced, it does show genuine appreciation and psychological safety for every individual on a team, regardless of their background, experiences, and opinions. Actively valuing diversity cultivates appreciation within teams by demonstrating a genuine interest in listening to and learning from different voices. Teams that actively solicit and consider diverse perspectives foster psychological safety, which enables members to learn from one another, show mutual respect, and collaborate more effectively (Edmondson, 1999).

Listening

George Barnard Shaw has been quoted as saying: "The single biggest problem in communication is the illusion that it has taken place." We often talk much, and listen little, and yet assume we have communicated.

Active listening significantly improves teamwork by creating an environment of open communication, an essential element of high-performing teams. When team members and leaders genuinely listen—showing attentiveness, withholding judgment, and asking thoughtful questions—they send a clear signal that each person's perspective is valued, directly fostering a sense of appreciation and psychological safety.

> At IDEO, active listening is embedded in design-thinking practices; during collaborative sessions, employees are encouraged to listen deeply so that diverse voices and ideas are fully considered. This not only fuels creative problem-solving but also builds the trust and respect essential for teamwork (Brown, 2009). Similarly, Google's internal study of team effectiveness, Project Aristotle, revealed that psychological safety—the strongest predictor of team success—was fostered through behaviors such as equal conversational turn-taking and attentive listening. Team members who felt genuinely heard were more willing to contribute ideas and take risks, resulting in stronger collaboration and innovation (Rozovsky, 2015).

Active and sincere listening demonstrates appreciation within teams by validating members' contributions and experiences, ultimately enhancing engagement and motivation. Leaders and team members who actively listen convey that everyone's opinions and feelings genuinely matter, which boosts morale and team cohesion.

Mutual Agreement

Mutual agreement significantly contributes to well-functioning teams by establishing clear, mutually agreed-upon rules of conduct, expectations, and common goals, enhancing accountability and reducing potential conflicts within the team or between team members. When team members clearly define and agree on roles, responsibilities, and goals, they build a shared mental model of success. This clarity strengthens coordination and provides a foundation of trust that supports effective collaboration (Costa, Roe and Taillieu, 2001). Companies such as Toyota exemplify this principle through structured consensus-building processes that ensure mutual agreement among team members before moving forward on critical decisions. Such deliberate alignments foster collective ownership and engagement, creating an environment where team members are mutually committed to achieving common objectives collaboratively and efficiently.

Two specific things teams can do to have mutual agreements within their teams to strengthen team engagement are:
1. Clarify roles
2. Have common goals

Clarifying Roles

Effective, well-functioning teams know the overall task to be accomplished by the team. The team is able to divide the total objective into smaller, nonoverlapping tasks, and is able to clarify the team members' roles, so the overall task is accomplished effectively. Such clearly defined team roles are essential for effective teamwork, facilitating mutual agreements and fostering stronger collaboration by minimizing ambiguity and conflict. When team members understand exactly what is expected of them and how their individual contributions align with shared objectives, they are more likely to collaborate proactively and cohesively.

Moreover, clearly articulated roles establish a foundation for mutual agreements, as team members can confidently hold each other accountable, knowing precisely who is responsible for specific outcomes. This clarity reduces overlaps and gaps in responsibilities, creating a harmonious and cooperative environment where team members willingly support one another. Ultimately, teams that actively clarify roles build a shared commitment to collective success, underpinning a collaborative culture that consistently delivers exceptional performance.

Having Common Goals

Teams that have simpatico for goals within and between teams are important for strong collaboration within and between teams. However, we often find ourselves in situations where there are specific conflicting objectives for different teams. A good concrete example of this, which we have often seen in our work, is between sales and production. Sales has a goal to reach high sales with less concern for the potential tailoring or development needs for what they sell, and production has a goal of running an efficient operation, with as little tailoring as possible. When such conflict exists, we see situations where this conflict erodes trust, collaboration, and eventually even personal relationships. Companies with such conflicting goals often cause irreparable damage to collaboration between teams and ultimately to the whole organization.

Having clearly defined, well-defined, and well-understood *common* goals enhances teamwork by providing team members with a unified sense of purpose and direction, enabling greater cohesion and collaboration. Shared objectives align individual efforts, reducing conflicts and focusing energy on collective outcomes, which facilitates mutual agreement and effective cooperation among team members. For instance, Google's rigorous use of objectives and key results (OKRs) creates clarity and unity around specific, ambitious goals, leading employees across different teams and departments to collaborate seamlessly. This goal-driven unity fosters deep engagement, empowering individuals to connect their daily tasks directly to organizational outcomes.

Also, common goals boost employee engagement by instilling a shared sense of ownership and collective accountability for team success. When team members co-create goals and agree on desired outcomes, they become emotionally invested, thus driving intrinsic motivation and sustained effort. Salesforce, for example, explicitly involves employees in goal-setting through its collaborative "V2MOM" (Vision, Values, Methods, Obstacles, Measures) process. This inclusive practice fosters agreement and collective commitment, strengthening engagement and delivering consistently high performance. Ultimately, teams that rally around shared goals cultivate a collaborative environment where mutual agreement, employee engagement, and collective success flourish.

Synergy

Synergy occurs when team members collaborate effectively, combining their individual strengths and perspectives to produce results far superior to what they could achieve independently. This dynamic interaction, driven by a win-win attitude, fosters a collective commitment among team members to mutual success, amplifying creativity, efficiency, and innovation. When teams embrace synergy, they prioritize collaboration, openly share resources and information, and support one another, ensuring that each individual's success enhances the collective outcome. Companies like Apple, through its integrated teams spanning design, engineering, and marketing, embody synergy, consistently achieving breakthrough products through collective collaboration, mutual trust, and unified commitment toward shared goals.

Two things teams can do to develop a strong sense of synergy within their teams and to strengthen team engagement are:
1. Act with a win-win attitude
2. Commit to succeed

Acting with a Win-Win Attitude

A win-win attitude is a belief that success is not a zero-sum game; one person's success does not require another's failure. Instead, the best outcomes come when all parties feel respected, heard, and satisfied with the result.

A win-win attitude among employees fosters synergy by aligning individual objectives with collective goals, creating a collaborative atmosphere that enhances overall team effectiveness. When team members approach tasks with such mutual benefit in mind, collaboration improves, and they tend to engage more openly, share ideas freely, and support each other's contributions. Covey (2004) emphasizes in *The 7 Habits of Highly Effective People* that adopting a win-win mindset encourages members to seek mutually beneficial outcomes rather than competing against one another. This collaborative dynamic reduces internal friction, builds trust, and leads to innovative solutions that individual members alone might not achieve.

Moreover, a win-win orientation enhances motivation and accountability within teams, as members recognize their success is interconnected with other team members, and also between teams. For instance, as noted, Google's renowned Project Aristotle discovered that psychological safety—a core component of win-win attitudes—was fundamental to high-performing teams, where members felt secure enough to contribute openly without fear of negative consequences (Duhigg, 2016). Consequently, teams exhibiting a win-win culture not only achieve stronger performance outcomes but also sustain higher levels of engagement and commitment.

Committing to Succeed

Employees' personal commitment to succeed acts as a foundational pillar for creating well-functioning teams. When employees genuinely invest in achieving collective goals, their determination fosters resilience, enhances cooperation, and aligns individual efforts with organizational objectives. A committed team member actively participates in collaborative problem-solving, contributes proactively, and willingly supports colleagues. Such behaviors reduce friction and increase team cohesion, creating an environment where members feel supported and motivated (Katzenbach and Smith, 2015).

Employees' common commitment to success significantly elevates engagement by cultivating a shared sense of purpose and ownership. Committed individuals perceive their roles as meaningful, not merely transactional tasks, which fosters intrinsic motivation, engagement, and deeper emotional investment in outcomes. This dedication stimulates consistent effort, resilience in facing setbacks, and a proactive attitude toward continuous improvement. Companies like Southwest Airlines exemplify this principle: high levels of employee commitment and relational coordination are directly linked to increased customer satisfaction and organizational performance, reflecting a culture grounded in shared success (Gittell, 2003).

Table 7.1 below summarizes the actions dicussed in this chapter on how teams can improve team members' and teams engagement.

Table 7.1: Actions supporting stronger teams for engagement.

T	E	A	M	S
TRUST	**EMPATHY**	**APPRECIATION**	**MUTUAL AGREEMENT**	**SYNERGY**
Deliver Results * Know expectations, make things happen and follow through	**Seek to Understand** * Assume everyone is doing their best, learn more about others	**Value Diversity** * Treat everyone with respect, encourage differences and unique ideas	**Have Common Goals** *Develop and communicate common understanding of goals	**Act Win-Win** * Behave like you are on the same team, always seek to win together.
Have Integrity * Tell the truth, take responsibility and be true to your word	**Show Concern** * Show personal interest, connect and celebrate others' successes	**Listen** * Be authetically interested, ask questions to ensure understanding, keep an open mind	**Clarify Roles** * Know your responsibilities and how you impact others	**Commit to Succeed** * Embrace challenges, win together, take action.

Positive teamwork forms the backbone of sustainable employee engagement by fostering strong personal relationships and environments of trust, empathy, mutual agreements, and respect, as well as shared purpose and goals. Teams that collaborate effectively not only drive productivity but also cultivate a sense of belonging, significantly enhancing individual motivation, job satisfaction, and engagement. Leaders who prioritize teamwork empower their employees to succeed, creating a virtuous cycle of engagement where passion, accountability, collaboration, and growth become the norm. Ultimately, organizations that invest in positive teamwork reap the long-term benefits of heightened innovation, improved morale, and increased resilience, positioning themselves to excel in an ever-evolving business landscape.

Key Questions
1. How does higher trust improve teamwork in your organization?
2. How can celebrating successes improve team spirit and work? Can you think of any examples?
3. How do you see the difference between being appreciated and valued in your own career? How have others made you feel valued?
4. How does having well-understood goals between teams improve teamwork in all the teams?
5. What have you specifically done to create a win-win attitude in your team? What else can you do?

Chapter 8
Strong Engagement to Company
Aligning with the Brand, Values, and Policies

> "When you're surrounded by people who share a passionate commitment around a common purpose, anything is possible."
> — *Howard Schultz, Former CEO of Starbucks*

In our "Five Forces of Engagement" framework, and in our practical work, *the company* plays a primary and significant role in determining the engagement level of employees and teams (Figure 8.1).

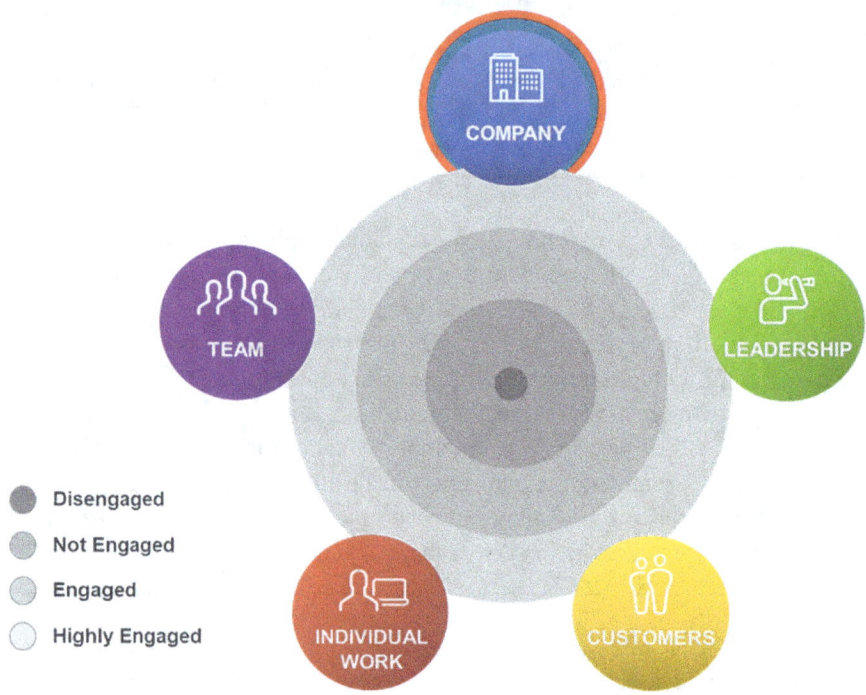

Figure 8.1: The five forces of engagement, with an emphasis on the company.

In this chapter we examine what elements in the company engage employees and teams and how leaders can improve engagement to the company.

New employees joining the company often join because they know of the company and are impressed by the brand they know, even though they may know very little about the company itself. This type of brand loyalty will engage employees for a short period at best, unless the company behavior and characteristics match and meet the new employees' expectations.

As a business school professor, I saw this so often, when students joined companies with the best-known brands, only to be disappointed by the company behavior. Thus, in order to have the COMPANY as a strong, lasting engagement force for the employees, the leadership behavior and values are significantly more important than the brand!

Companies that keep employees engaged tend to share specific organizational characteristics that foster trust, motivation, growth, and a sense of purpose. Based on research from Gallup, *Harvard Business Review,* and academic literature, following are the seven key company characteristics that drive employee engagement and which need to be focused on by company leadership

Purpose-Driven Culture

A purpose-driven culture is one of the most powerful drivers of employee engagement because it connects individual effort to a larger, meaningful mission. When employees understand how their work contributes to something greater than themselves, their motivation shifts from compliance to commitment. Research consistently confirms that purpose is not a luxury—it is a strategic necessity. According to a McKinsey study (Dhingra et al., 2021), 70 percent of employees say their sense of purpose is defined by their work; those whose sense of purpose is aligned with their company's mission report higher engagement, greater loyalty, and a stronger likelihood of remaining with the organization. Purpose-driven companies foster emotional attachment, which enhances resilience, discretionary effort, and team cohesion.

Practical examples highlight this dynamic. Unilever encourages employees to develop individualized purpose statements and share their aspirations via a talent marketplace—a practice designed to align personal values with organizational goals (Bersin, 2019; Unilever, 2019). Similarly, at Patagonia, the company's environmental activism mission fosters deep alignment with employee values, leading to strong internal culture and low turnover. As Rosso et al. (2010) argue, meaningful work emerges when individuals perceive a connection between their tasks and a broader social or ethical contribution. In this way, a purpose-driven culture doesn't just boost engagement—it creates workplaces where people are energized to contribute their best, not because they have to, but because they want to. Purpose gives meaning to tasks, increasing motivation, engagement, and emotional investment.

In a detailed case referenced by Pepperdine University, Vail Resorts undertook initiatives to help its 24,000 employees identify how their individual sense of purpose connected with the broader mission of delivering memorable mountain experiences. By engaging employees in workshops, storytelling sessions, and operational debriefs that connected their daily roles—from lift operators to guest services—to guest satisfaction and environmental stewardship, the company saw measurable increases in

> employee engagement and staff tenure. Elevating purpose from corporate mission to daily action ensured that employees felt their contributions mattered—boosting both morale and performance.
> Gasta, Mark R., Driving employee engagement through greater purpose (2016).

Strong, Trustworthy Leadership

In our work we have found out that often employees associate the "company" with the top leadership, and their level of engagement with the company is highly associated with their perception of the top company leadership. The same principles discussed in Chapter 6 are also relevant for the executive leadership, but it is also important to recognize that the executives represent not only their own leadership, but also the whole company culture and brand.

Trustworthy leadership is a cornerstone of employee engagement. When leaders act with integrity, communicate transparently, and show genuine care for their teams, employees are more likely to feel safe, valued, and committed. Leaders who are competent, consistent, fair, and supportive foster trust—a psychological foundation that allows employees to contribute more fully without fear of blame or exclusion. This environment encourages open dialogue, innovation, and accountability, all of which are critical for engagement. As a quote commonly attributed to Stephen R. Covey puts it, "Trust is the glue of life. It's the most essential ingredient in effective communication. It's the foundational principle that holds all relationships." (Covey, attributed)

There are numerous good examples of leaders standing for foundational company principles, and likely improving the engagement of employees. At Microsoft, CEO Satya Nadella's empathetic and transparent leadership style has been credited with revitalizing the company's culture and increasing employee engagement across global teams. Similarly, Doug Conant, former CEO of Campbell Soup Company, famously wrote over 30,000 handwritten notes to employees to recognize their contributions—building a culture of respect and connection that boosted both engagement and performance. As Jack Welch once noted, "You can't manage people without integrity. It's the basis for everything else." When employees trust their leaders, they are not just more engaged—they are more loyal, more resilient, and more willing to go the extra mile not only for the leaders, but also for the company. Trust in leadership boosts morale, commitment, and resilience.

Opportunities for Growth and Development

Opportunities for growth and development are among the most powerful drivers of employee engagement, as they signal to employees that their future in the company is valued and invested in. When organizations provide clear paths for skill enhancement, career progression, and personal development, employees are more likely to stay motivated, committed, and connected to their work. According to the *Workplace Learning Report* (LinkedIn, 2023), 94% of employees say they would stay longer at a company that invests in their learning and development. This investment enhances not only retention but also engagement, as individuals feel a stronger sense of purpose and potential. As Bersin (2014) emphasizes, high-impact learning cultures are closely linked to higher levels of engagement, innovation, and performance.

Companies that prioritize employee development reap measurable benefits. Adobe, for example, replaced its annual reviews with the "Check-In" system—regular growth conversations focused on feedback and alignment. This shift not only reduced voluntary turnover by nearly 30 percent but also increased engagement and performance transparency (Cappelli and Tavis, 2016; Harvard Business Review, 2017). Similarly, Google's internal CareerGuru program connects employees across functions with trained senior "Gurus" who coach them using the GROW framework through one-on-one sessions. Since its launch, over 900 Googlers have participated, citing the program as critical to both cross-functional learning and greater alignment with the company's strategic mission. These examples demonstrate that when employees are given the tools and support to grow, they are more likely to see their future within the organization and invest their energy accordingly. The quote, "The best way to predict the future is to create it," is widely attributed to Peter Drucker—a maxim that organizations embracing development clearly understand. Growth opportunities also foster commitment and engagement, and reduce turnover.

Fairness and Equity

Fairness and equity are fundamental to building a culture of trust and engagement in any organization. When employees perceive that the company treats them equitably—regardless of gender, race, tenure, or role—they are more likely to feel valued, respected, and committed to the organization. Organizational justice theory posits that perceptions of fairness in processes, treatment, and outcomes significantly influence employee attitudes and behaviors (Colquitt et al., 2001). Conversely, when inequities persist—whether in promotions, pay, or access to opportunities—engagement declines, and cynicism and disengagement rise. Research indicates that employees who perceive their workplaces as equitable tend to report higher engagement and stronger loyalty metrics (Colquitt et al. 2001).

Leading organizations are embedding equity into the fabric of their culture and systems. Salesforce, for example, conducts regular pay audits and has spent millions correcting pay inequities globally, reinforcing its commitment to fairness (Salesforce, 2022). Similarly, Accenture publicly reports diversity and inclusion metrics, holding leadership accountable for equitable representation and advancement. These practices not only increase transparency but also demonstrate that the company values fairness as a strategic imperative. The distinction between equality and equity is often summarized as, "Fairness is not giving everyone the same thing, but giving everyone what they need to succeed"—a phrase often widely attributed to Rosabeth Moss Kanter. When fairness becomes operationalized, engagement is no longer aspirational—it becomes cultural. Perceived fairness also influences trust, loyalty, motivation, and engagement.

Recognition and Appreciation

Recognition and appreciation are among the most effective—and often underutilized—drivers of employee engagement. When leaders acknowledge the contributions and efforts of employees in meaningful and timely ways, it signals that their work is seen, valued, and impactful. This fosters a deeper emotional connection to the organization and strengthens motivation. According to research by Gallup (2023), employees who receive regular recognition are more engaged, more productive, and less likely to leave the company. The effect is amplified when appreciation is specific, authentic, and linked to organizational values. As Amabile and Kramer (2011) observed in their research on inner work life, the single most important factor in boosting engagement is making progress in meaningful work—and having that progress recognized.

Leading organizations have embedded recognition into their cultures with measurable practices and visible outcomes. The UN's Office of Human Resources (DMSPC, 2023) provides concrete examples—ranging from Secretary-General Awards and peer "thank-you" initiatives to tailored recognition programs—that exemplify how institutions can build fairness and engagement through intentional recognition strategies.

Cisco implemented a social recognition platform that allows managers and peers to highlight achievements in real time, resulting in higher engagement scores across teams. These examples show that recognition is not just a morale booster—it is a strategic tool for reinforcing purpose, improving performance, and retaining talent (Workhuman 2018).

As Ken Blanchard famously said, "Catch people doing something right." The return on that simple act is powerful. Recognition meets psychological needs and reinforces strong engagement.

> Google set out to address this issue of recognition and appreciation with a multifaceted approach. The company offered rewards that reflect what matters to employees. It gave them a choice. They made the reward experience something employees wanted and not something determined by a few people. Furthermore, Google has embedded recognition into its culture by ensuring that rewards are meaningful, inclusive, and aligned with what employees value most. As Laszlo Bock, Google's former SVP of People Operations, explains, the company learned early on that large cash prizes—even as high as $1 million—created jealousy and resentment rather than motivation. Instead, experiential rewards

> such as travel, meals, or technology proved far more memorable and engaging, triggering a positive emotional response that cash alone could not deliver.
>
> To scale recognition, Google institutionalized programs such as spot bonuses (small awards given by managers for exceptional contributions), peer bonuses (where employees nominate one another for recognition), and team awards that celebrate group achievements. At the same time, peer-to-peer appreciation is encouraged through simple practices like thank-you notes, reinforcing everyday acknowledgment. These efforts demonstrate that recognition is not just a morale booster, but a strategic lever that fuels collaboration, engagement, and sustained performance (Bock 2015).

Inclusive and Collaborative Environment

Even in our current political environment, creating an inclusive and collaborative environment is important for fostering employee engagement, as it builds psychological safety, trust, and a sense of belonging. When employees feel included—regardless of their background, identity, or role—they are more likely to contribute ideas, support team members, and invest emotionally in their work. Research by Deloitte (2017) found that inclusive organizations are six times more likely to be innovative and twice as likely to meet or exceed financial targets. Furthermore, collaboration thrives in inclusive cultures where diverse perspectives are actively invited and respected, reinforcing engagement through mutual respect and shared purpose.

Leading companies have embraced inclusion as a strategic engagement driver. For example, Microsoft's inclusive hiring initiatives—such as their Autism Hiring Program—have enhanced both workplace diversity and employee engagement by valuing diverse talent and fostering team collaboration. Similarly, Accenture publicly tracks diversity metrics and links leadership performance bonuses to inclusion outcomes, aligning accountability with engagement goals (Accenture, 2022). These initiatives demonstrate that when organizations cultivate inclusive and collaborative cultures, employees not only feel heard and valued, but they are also more motivated to contribute, collaborate, and grow within the company. Many commentators argue that diversity only delivers business value when combined with genuine inclusion that unlocks people's potential (Bourke and Dillon, 2018). Inclusion fuels psychological safety and team synergy.

Effective Communication

Over the years, as we have conducted development seminars globally, we generally ask what employees see as the largest barriers to their engagement in their work. Almost without fail, one of the significant barriers identified is poor communication.

Effective communication is a foundational pillar of employee engagement. When organizations communicate clearly, consistently, and transparently, employees are more likely to understand their roles, align with company goals, and feel a sense of inclusion and trust. According to Towers Watson's *Communication ROI Study* (2014), companies with highly effective communication practices were more than 3.5 times more likely to outperform their peers in terms of engagement and financial performance. Effective communication not only reduces confusion and stress but also fosters alignment, clarity of purpose, and emotional connection to the organization's mission.

Industry leaders have leveraged communication to strengthen engagement across global teams. For instance, at IBM, leadership town halls and two-way digital platforms like "Think Academy" enable employees to share ideas and receive real-time updates, reinforcing transparency and mutual respect (IBM, 2020). Similarly, Salesforce uses its internal platform, "Chatter," to democratize communication across teams, enhancing collaboration and ensuring voices are heard across all levels of the company (Salesforce, 2021). These examples demonstrate that communication is not just about conveying information—it is about creating a culture where people feel informed, involved, and inspired to contribute. As noted earlier, George Bernard Shaw once stated, "The single biggest problem in communication is the illusion that it has taken place." Overcoming that illusion is essential to cultivating engagement. Effective communication reduces confusion, builds trust, and allows alignment of goals and processes.

> **Good Employer and Employee Communication: The Gold Standard**
>
> Let's first talk about what makes communication between employers and employees really work. It's not just about sending messages back and forth—it's about making sure both sides understand each other clearly (no room for second-guessing!) and can act on what they've learned. So, what does "good communication" in the workplace look like? Here are some key ingredients:
>
> 1. **Relevance and Timeliness**
>   Ever been bombarded with info that doesn't matter to you? It's the worst. Great communication means sharing what's actually relevant to employees' roles—and doing it fast. No one likes to feel left out of the loop.
> 2. **Employee-Centric Approach**
>   Think about this: when's the last time you felt like a company's message really *spoke* to you? Tailoring communications to employees' needs and preferences shows you're paying attention. It's like saying, "Hey, we see you."
> 3. **Two-Way Conversations**
>   Nobody wants to feel like they're shouting into the void. A solid communication strategy gives employees a way to share their thoughts—anonymously if needed—whether it's feedback, suggestions, or even venting.
> 4. **Positive Reinforcement**
>   Here's a fun one: catching people doing something *right*. Highlighting employees' wins and hard work isn't just nice—it builds a positive vibe that can ripple across the workplace.
> 5. **Transparency and Honesty**
>   This one's a biggie. Trust is built on being upfront about what's going on—good or bad. Employees appreciate it when leadership shares expectations, challenges, and decisions openly. It shows respect and fosters trust.
>
> theEMPLOYEEapp (2025)

The company or organization is one of the primary and key forces impacting employee engagement. The company brand or name is not enough to carry long-term employee engagement. Leaders are responsible that employees feel that the company cares about them as individuals! Employee engagement increases as employees feel that the company has a purpose-driven culture, strong and trustworthy leadership, there is an opportunity for their development and appreciation, the company is fair, and communicates effectively. The seven behaviors covered in this chapter are some the cornerstones to build a strong commitment and engagement to the company.

Key Questions
1. What elements in your organization have the greatest positive impact on employee engagement?
2. What elements in your organization could or should be improved for employees to be more engaged with, and committed to your company?
3. What could your company do to increase the sense of purpose for the employees?
4. What can you or your company do to promote growth and development for your teams and/or employees?
5. How could you improve the effective communication within your own organization?

Chapter 9
Employee Engagement and the Customer
Putting Customer First Needs an Engaged Workforce

> "Take care of the customers, and they will come back. Take care of the products, and they won't come back."
> — Eero Kinnunen, CEO Kesko Retailing Company

Customer-centric business is based on the ability to understand customer needs and create value for customers through close interaction with customers. This kind of activity cannot be done without a highly committed staff—a staff that is clearly dedicated and committed to the customers works proactively, is solution-oriented, and listens to the customer. This chapter focuses on customer orientation, and on what can be done to improve engagement for the customer (see Figure 9.1)

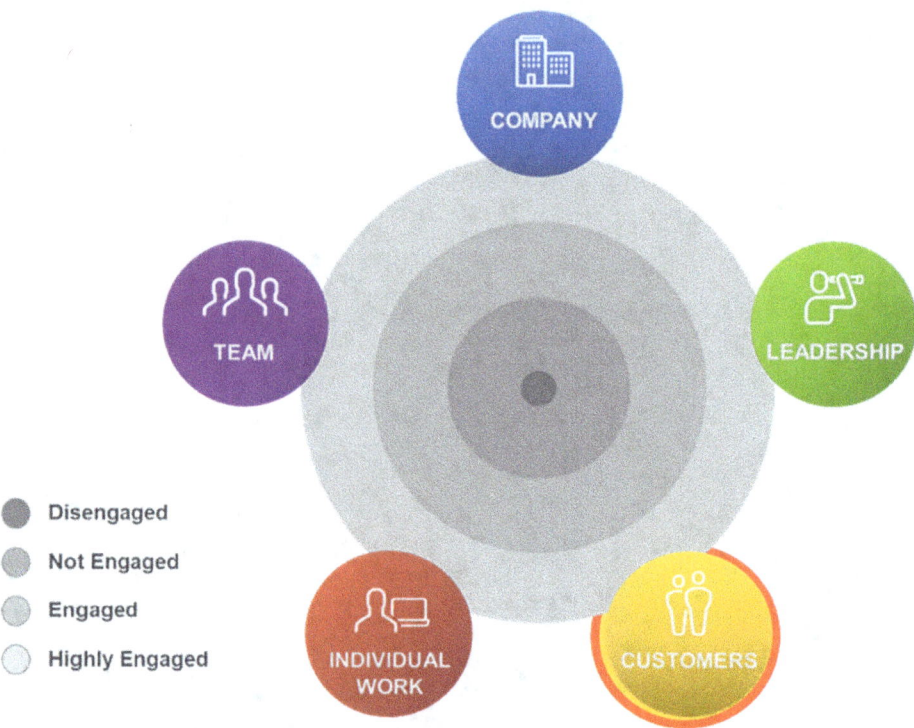

Figure 9.1: The five forces of engagement with emphasis on the customer.

What does customer orientation really mean? It does not mean pleasing customers or outsourcing decision-making to them. As a mindset, it means that the entire operation is guided by customer insight—a deep understanding of what customers truly think, how they behave, and what is important or less important to them.

Customer insight refers to the systematic identification and utilization of customer needs and expectations. This kind of customer-centric thinking is based on a strategic foundation: customer relationships and customer understanding are chosen as the guiding principles for the entire business.

Why is the importance of customer-centricity increasing? One key reason is the growing number of choices available to customers. They now have more options to choose from—services, products, and solutions that best suit their own operations.

Customers also increasingly expect personalized treatment and service. Even though there are many customers, each one should be treated individually, based on their own perspectives and needs. Competition for customers has intensified, especially due to multichannel environments, the opening of global markets, e-commerce, and digital service platforms. Customers are also increasingly networking with other customers and trusting their recommendations when choosing various products and services.

At the same time, competition in efficiency and impact is growing. Companies must find new ways to improve their operations and develop revenue models—and what better way to do that than together with customers? A new trend has emerged: even through mass customization, it is possible to offer customers better, more personalized solutions that are still produced economically and efficiently. These new tools have also been adopted in public organizations.

An Engaged Employee Creates the Basis for Customer Engagement

Studies have extensively identified how employees who are committed to their work and organizations create high customer satisfaction, customer experience, and broad customer engagement. Denise Lee Yohn (2023) has stated that employee experience (EX) has a direct impact on customer experience (CX). According to him, companies that invest in both employee and customer experience can charge up to 16% more for their products and services.

It has also been recognized that customer-centricity and employee engagement are mutually reinforcing factors. Pavithra et al. (2018) emphasize that employee engagement is key to building a customer-centric culture, especially in the IT and service industries. Customer-centricity and employee engagement affect a company's financial performance. Mittal et al. (2018) have found that a high level of engagement among both customers and employees is positively correlated with productivity and profitability.

The role of information technology and knowledge-based management in employee engagement and its positive impact on customer success should also not be forgotten. Alabi et al. (2024) have found that data analytics can strengthen engagement and improve customer service. In their research, they have found that employee- and data-driven HR strategies can improve employee engagement and thus customer satisfaction.

Committed Staff Ensures Customer Engagement

The customer-centric approach is based on four key elements, in all of which a highly committed staff plays a key role. These factors are creating customer value, delivering on customer promises, creating customer relationships, and strengthening a positive customer experience. Operations do not arise by themselves, but they require leadership and interaction with the personnel. Studies have found clear differences in client performance between committed and poorly committed organizations and individuals (Matsuda, 2025, Yohn, 2023 and Gallup, 2020).

Committed Staff Creates Value for Customers

Customer value refers to the benefit, value, or significance that the customer feels they get from a product, service, or customer relationship. Value is a relative thing, which is affected by the expected benefit and the sacrifices involved in obtaining the benefit. Value is created not only through a product's features or price, but also through the holistic experience that encompasses the customer's needs, expectations, and user journey (Rintamäki, 2016). Customer value is not created by itself, but creating and making it visible requires committed and competent staff. According to Rintamäki, the financial, functional, emotional, and symbolic dimensions are closely linked to customer value. The key to economic value is what the product or service costs and what its value is to the customer. Functional value focuses on the functionality of the product or service and how it helps the customer in their everyday life. Emotional value reflects the customer's experience and how customer service in its various forms has fulfilled the promises made. Symbolic value reflects key norms and principles that are very valuable to the customer, such as the responsibility and ethics of operations. Ultimately, customer value is concretized in all the results of the personnel's work that customers enjoy. Therefore, it is not insignificant how employees act.

Poor results are Often the Result of Less Engaged Employees

The values must be reflected visibly and experientially in the organization's customer promise.

A customer promise is a clearly and understandably defined expression of what a company or organization offers to its customers. It is very important that the customer promise is meaningful to the customer and that the customer feels that it produces value for them. It is clear that a customer promise also raises expectations in the customer, and it is precisely these expectations that the organization must be able to meet (Lindblom and Mitronen, 2025).

The customer promise must be based on the organization's unique expertise and ability to deliver on the promise made. Otherwise, the promise is just empty talk and can only cause strong disappointment among customers. So, on the one hand, a customer promise should be based on the needs, wishes, and values of the customers, but at the same time, it is something that is built on the internal strengths of the organization. In the end, the customer promise is concretized as the engagement of the staff in how well the promise is fulfilled in all everyday activities with customers.

Committed Employee Lays the Foundation for a Long-term Customer Relationship and Loyalty

Customer Relationships represents one of the most significant areas of customer-centric business and one of the key factors influencing customer engagement within an organization. This means that the customer is no longer merely a target but an active partner. Operations begin with the customer's needs, and the goal is to find solutions to those needs. The core idea is co-creating value with the customer—not just offering a product promise, but a customer promise: What value does the product or service bring to the customer? How does it make their operations easier, reduce costs, or improve their experience?

One of the key goals of customer relationship management is to build long-term, even lifelong, customer relationships. When employees perceive customers as "their own," genuine engagement and better service naturally follow. CRM aims to foster engagement not only from customers but also from the entire staff. Finally, it's essential to remember that customer promises are fulfilled in customer encounters—for example, in stores, service situations, and digital channels.

Positive Customer Experiences Depend on Engaged Employees

Customer experience is an internal and subjective reaction that arises from a customer's direct or indirect interaction with a company. A direct experience typically occurs during a purchase or while using a service. An indirect experience may result from feedback, advertisements, reviews, or recommendations. These issues help organizations understand how to create positive, lasting impressions and build loyalty.

Customer experience includes preexperience expectations (e.g., marketing, word-of-mouth), experience during service (e.g., purchasing, using the product or service), and postexperience reflections (e.g., customer service in case of problems).

Engaged Employees Drive Excellent Customer Engagement

A committed employee is worth their weight in gold to their organization. Through their own actions, the employee decides how the organization and the employee create value for customers, deliver on the customer promise, and strengthen profitable and long-term customer relationships. An engaged employee can gain customer trust in many ways and create a foundation for customer-centric operations—the differences are evident in how the employee thinks and acts (e.g., Yohn, 2023; Mittal et al., 2018; and Pavithra et al, 2018). The following five ways illustrate how engaged employees promote customer engagement:

1. **Emotional Engagement Leads to Better Service**
   Engaged employees are emotionally invested in their roles, which translates into empathetic and personalized customer interactions. They take ownership of customer outcomes and proactively solve problems, leading to improved satisfaction and loyalty. A committed employee works actively, listens to the customer, and strives to solve problems quickly and efficiently. They exceed expectations, which increases the value and satisfaction experienced by the customer.
2. **Positive Energy and Attitude Strengthens the Customer Relationship**
   High morale among engaged employees creates a positive atmosphere that customers notice. These employees are more likely to go the extra mile and contribute to a welcoming environment that enhances brand perception. Empathetic and personal interaction describes a committed employee well. It is important that the customer feels that they have been heard and appreciated, which strengthens the customer relationship. This creates emotional value that can be crucial in customer loyalty.
3. **Feedback and Innovation Improve Service and Product Quality**
   Engaged employees actively share customer insights with management and suggest improvements to processes or products. Their participation in continuous learning helps elevate service quality and responsiveness. A committed employee is innovative and actively produces development proposals for their customers and organizations. Engaged employees bring up ideas that improve products, services, or processes—often from the customer's perspective. This can lead to tangible improvements in the organization's operations and customer value creation.

4. **Consistency and Reliability Strengthen Operational Flexibility and Reliability**
   With an engaged employee, speed and flexibility are emphasized. An engaged employee acts on their own initiative and reacts quickly to changing customer needs. This inevitably increases the functional and emotional value for the customer. Employees who are engaged tend to remain with the organization longer and perform more consistently. This stability results in fewer errors, stronger relationships with repeat customers, and trust-building through dependable service.
5. **Alignment with Brand Values Helps to Deliver on the Customer Promise**
   Employees who are aligned with the company's mission, values, and customer promise represent the brand authentically. They deliver consistent messaging and tone, strengthening the customer-brand connection and fostering loyalty. A committed employee succeeds in creating long-term and confidential customer relationships. When an employee is committed, they build trust and continuity—the customer feels that the relationship is stable and valuable. In such a relationship, the problems and annoyances that always happen in between do not destroy the relationship, but when handled well, they strengthen trust and long-term profitable operations on both sides.

Companies and Organizations Drive Excellent Employee and Customer Engagement

Employee engagement has emerged as a critical factor in driving customer satisfaction and operational excellence. Companies across various industries have leveraged employee-centric strategies to improve service delivery, reduce costs, and enhance customer experiences (Matsuda 2025).

In customer-centric thinking, a crucial target group is the organization's own engaged personnel. While the organization must make customer promises, it is equally important to ensure that employees are empowered to fulfill those promises. This is known as internal marketing: how the organization communicates with its staff, justifies customer-related decisions, and builds the capacity to understand the company's strategy and the value it aims to deliver to customers.

Employee engagement is a critical factor in delivering exceptional customer experiences. When employees are emotionally committed to their work and aligned with organizational goals, they are more likely to provide high-quality service, foster customer loyalty, and contribute to business success.

Companies that effectively manage their workforce to foster engagement can achieve higher customer satisfaction, loyalty, and advocacy. This article explores key strategies organizations can use to manage employees in ways that enhance customer engagement. Research by Gallup indicates that companies with high employee engagement outperform competitors by 147% in earnings per share. Engaged employees are 87% less likely to leave, reducing turnover-related service disruptions. Organizations with engaged employees also see 10% higher customer ratings.

Engagement Management Requires Leadership and Management

It is important to know how one's own team, individual working methods, and attitudes toward customers are decisive – what customers truly mean to the organization—just as Peter Drucker emphasized that the purpose of business is to create and keep a customer (Drucker, 2001). Building on this principle, effective engagement management requires five leadership practices:

1. **Training and Development Must Be at the Heart of Leadership**
   Providing employees with comprehensive training equips them with the skills and knowledge needed to deliver exceptional customer service. Ongoing development programs ensure that employees stay updated with best practices and evolving customer expectations. Training also boosts employee confidence and competence, which directly impacts customer interactions.
2. **Empowerment Requires a Confidential Management Approach From Supervisors**
   Empowering employees to make decisions and solve problems independently fosters a sense of ownership and accountability. When employees feel trusted and supported, they are more likely to take initiative and go the extra mile for customers. Empowerment leads to faster resolution of customer issues and more personalized service.
3. **Management Must Give Recognition and Reward for Good Work**
   Recognizing and rewarding employees for their contributions to customer engagement reinforces positive behaviors. Incentive programs, public acknowledgment, and performance bonuses motivate employees to maintain high standards of service. Recognition also enhances job satisfaction and retention, which contributes to consistent customer experiences.
4. **Communication and Feedback Must Be at the Core of Leadership**
   Open and transparent communication between management and employees fosters trust and collaboration. Regular feedback helps employees understand their performance and areas for improvement. Listening to employee insights about customer needs can lead to valuable innovations and service enhancements.
5. **Alignment with Customer Values and Promises Provide Guidelines for Action**
   Ensuring that employees understand and align with the company's mission and customer-centric values strengthens brand representation. Employees who share the organization's engagement to customer satisfaction are more likely to deliver authentic and meaningful experiences. Cultural alignment enhances employee engagement and customer loyalty.

Case Examples of Employee Engagement as a Driver of Customer Excellence in Action:

CVS Caremark implemented self-service scheduling through NICE's Employee Engagement Manager (EEM), resulting in 39.9% increase in positive employee sentiment, 17.9% improvement in scheduling efficiency, and higher retention and improved customer service delivery. Employees cited scheduling flexibility as a key reason for staying, which translated into more consistent and empathetic customer interactions.

Lowe's used NICE's WFM and EEM tools to process 434,000 hours of schedule changes. Save $1 million in operational costs and improve employee autonomy and engagement. This resulted in better customer coverage during peak hours and enhanced service quality.

TD Bank optimized scheduling for 15,000 contact center agents, achieving 88 million minutes reduction in customer wait times, 11% increase in calls handled, and millions in annual savings. Flexible scheduling empowered agents to deliver more responsive and personalized customer service.

Travel + Leisure Co. with a 98% remote workforce, adopted mobile-first scheduling tools, resulting in 86% agent adoption rate, stabilized attrition rates, and improved service quality. Remote employees felt more empowered, leading to better customer interactions.

Designing Employee Engagement by Customer Processes

In managing employee engagement, it is essential to open up and internalize the internal and external service mindset. The key question becomes: how do supervisors, teams, and each employee perceive their role in serving customers? It is essential to reflect on what employee and customer engagement can offer to your organization. How do you improve leadership, teamwork, and your own engagement? It is very important to shift the focus from organization-centered thinking to supporting the customer's operations.

The goal is to understand the customer's processes and ask:
– How can we enhance the employees and customer's operations?
– How can we reduce their costs, effort, or frustration?
– What can we do on behalf of the employees and customers?
– What can we do together with the employees and customers?
– What do we expect from the employees and customers to ensure business goals and success?

This collaborative thinking is especially important in situations where the customer also serves their own customers—for example, a restaurant purchasing goods from a wholesaler. In such cases, it's essential to understand the needs of the end customer as well.

Checklist for Leaders: How to Manage Employee Engagement as a Tool for Customer Engagement:
1. Find out who are the key customers, what do they expect, and how they can be served in different channels.
2. Identify what your organization's core customer promise is and what value you are creating for customers.

3. Summarize what the customer promise means to the staff and what is expected of them in their dealings with customers.
4. Determine how you will lead the staff and create a natural opportunity for staff engagement.
5. Identify weaknesses that need to be improved and strengths that need to be strengthened in staff engagement.

Key Questions
1. Why is employee engagement important for customers?
2. What personal experiences have you seen where employee engagement wither adds or distracts from customer loyalty?
3. Why are engaged employees more likely to build customer loyalty?
4. How can leadership support employee engagement and customer loyalty simultaneously ?
5. How can you support you own team to be more customer oriented?

Part 3: **Emerging Themes in Engagement**

Chapter 10
Dealing with the Disengaged
Meeting the Challenge of the Disengaged

> "One highly disengaged or toxic employee can spread discontent like a virus, undoing the positive efforts of several engaged colleagues."
> — *Daniel Goleman (2000), author of* Working with Emotional Intelligence

One of the greatest challenges leaders, managers, and supervisors face with employees is knowing how to deal with the actively disengaged. In our work around the globe in different industries, almost every company has some actively disengaged employees, and unfortunately, everyone (often even the disengaged themselves) knows who those people are, and how destructive they are for the teams and the company. Our greatest successes, and our greatest failures were often dealing with thee disengaged. It seldom took much time to identify who they were, but dealing with them was often a challenge.

Employee disengagement is a pervasive and costly problem in today's workplace. Global surveys indicate that only about 23% of employees are engaged at work, leaving the majority either not engaged or actively disengaged. In the United States, Gallup found that just 31% of employees were engaged in 2024, while 17% were actively disengaged—a level of discontent not seen in a decade.

This chapter focuses on the specific topic of how leaders can deal with the actively disengaged. In addition to individual responsibility (Chapter 5), leadership opportunities (Chapter 6), and team focus (Chapter 7), a key way to improve the culture of engagement in an organization is to effectively deal with the challenge of the actively disengaged. Even though it may seem easy to just eliminate the disengaged, it may often not be possible, or even the best approach. In many cultures, especially internationally it is not possible to let go of the disengaged, and even when it is legally possible, merely "firing the problem cases" can create a sense of insecurity and unfairness among other employees, and reduce psychological safety. In many situations it is a challenge to know how to deal with the disengaged while they still continue to be part of the team.

Actively disengaged employees are not only unhappy at work; they are "disgruntled and disloyal"—their unmet needs manifest in negativity that can spread to coworkers (Harter, 2022). For organizations, the stakes are high: actively disengaged workers drive absenteeism, turnover, and even sabotage performance. Leaders, managers, and supervisors cannot afford to ignore this issue. This chapter provides examples and specific comments on how (and how not to) to effectively deal with actively disengaged employees. We will explore how to recognize the signs of active disengagement, address root causes, communicate and coach effectively, establish accountability, and implement evidence-based strategies to turn disengagement around.

Successes and Failures

In our work globally, the most common failures, and most significant successes have come from dealing with the actively disengaged. Most companies have some disengaged employees, and everyone seems to know who those people are, and also how destructive they are for the organization.

We also recognize that when we have met a disengaged employee, we have met ONE disengaged person. Each case of disengagement is unique, and even though there are many things leaders can do to help them, understanding the underlying causes of each case becomes paramount. Often there is no one-size-fits-all solution, but the solutions tend to be "one-size-fits-one."

However, as a generalization our experience has been that the most common failures to help the disengaged are due to their own reluctance to accept the premise that they have any responsibility for their disengagement and/or lack of engagement. And unfortunately, there are many such cases. Here in the boxes below are just a few representative examples; three clear failures, and two successes. (The names and some specifics have been changed to retain anonymity, without diminishing the content).

> **Sam**
> Sam was a customer relations manager we worked with for some time. Sam was committed to his work, to the customers, and to his OWN team, but totally actively disengaged with the company, leaders, and any teams that were not his. His individual profile would likely be represented with a figure like that in Figure 10.1.
> Even though Sam was committed to his work, customers, and his own team, other teams and leaders had a very difficult time dealing with Sam, and no company initiatives or strategies were accepted by Sam. (It is important to note that if there were no multidimensional representation of Sam's engagement profile, he would likely be classified as an engaged individual.) Over time, many managers worked with Sam with little success, and finally full confrontation caused Sam to become totally disengaged from the company, and eventually Sam recognized that this was not the best place for him, and departed.
>
> **Mary**
> Mary worked in a small customer service team and had been working in the same role for over twenty years. She was ready to retire in a few years, but was very actively disengaged, making any teamwork with Mary almost impossible. She was disengaged in all dimensions, including her team, her own work, as well as the customers. She was a negative, and vocal, critic of leadership, the company, and the teammates. People in the team did not want to come to work when she was there, and her negativity was known in the whole company. No amount of work we did with her helped, and even though she recognized her negativity, she was not willing to take any responsibility for her actions. She blamed everyone else for her disengagement and was not willing to make any changes. We completely failed to make any difference; we failed Mary, her team, and the company. And looking back, we failed to initiate a sincere dialogue to understand Mary's issues and her side of the story. We were too quick to judge her behavior.

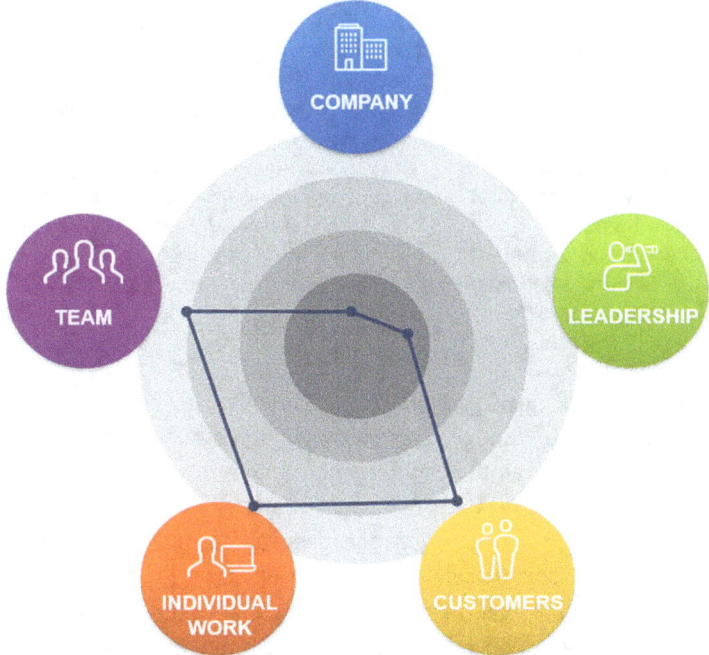

Figure 10.1: A representation of Sam's engagement profile.

Tom
Tom also worked in a relatively small service team, but unlike Mary, he was very committed to the customers, even when he was extremely negative about all the other engagement forces (company, leaders, team, and even his own work). And he was totally unaware of his negativity, and how others saw him. Initially, we were very hopeful that we could improve Tom's level of engagement by helping him understand how his negativity influenced his team. However, Tom's lack of self-awareness and his unwillingness to accept any personal responsibility made it difficult to help him make any positive improvements. In fact, any attempt we made to help him only made things worse, and he became suspicious of any efforts we, or the company, made to help him. And he became even more negative on all dimensions (except the customers). Despite all the effort, we were not able to give Tom feedback that would have helped him make a change for the positive.

Anna
On the positive side is Anna. Anna was a long-time employee in a sales organization, and had been negative and disengaged for some time. Anna had experienced some personal hardships, had clearly checked out of her work, and took out her negativity on others in her team. After working with Anna's team for some time, Anna totally changed. She became a positive force for her team and teammates, and everyone in the organization wondered what had happened to Anna. On one of our follow-up visits, Anna told us that in one of the development seminars, she chose "finding joy" as one of her primary goals for work and for life, and she had realized that only she is able to change her attitude and behavior. So, every morning she made daily goals to find something positive in her work and in her teammates. Interestingly, the whole team atmosphere improved once Anna's negativity was eliminated, again illustrating how destructive even one person's negativity can be on the whole team.

> **John**
> John worked in a relatively small technical team. Our surveys showed that the team was one of the most engaged teams in the unit, except for one person, John. However, on our follow-up surveys the team had improved significantly, because John had changed and had become the most engaged person in the already highly engaged team.
> Of course, John's manager was excited, since John had been a thorn in his side for years. In the next team meeting John told how, after our initial meeting, he had realized what negative impact he had had on the team, and how his disengagement had impacted his personal and even his family life. He also noted that it was the first time he realized he is responsible, and he is the only person who can change, so he made a specific plan to become more accountable and collaborative. His personal change and transformation visibly changed the team for the positive.

These are just a few negative and positive examples of how the disengaged impact others, and how, if they are able to change, they can have a positive impact on the workplace. There are many other examples, and as mentioned, the common theme seems to be that the disengaged can and will only change if and when they are able to take personal responsibility for their negativity and disengagement. In our experience, continuing to blame others merely deepens the disengagement.

However, in order to make a change, there are ways for management to identify disengagement, find the root causes of disengagement, and help the disengaged.

Identifying the Disengaged

It is important to note that difficult does not equal disengaged. Yes, it is possible for some employees to be difficult, but this does not always mean they are disengaged. Dealing with the difficult may be very different from dealing with the actively disengaged.

Actively disengaged employees often exhibit common behaviors long before their performance hits rock bottom. The first step for any leader is to identify these individuals early. Common warning signs include:

- Withdrawal and Isolation: Disengaged employees often withdraw: they stop volunteering ideas, avoid teamwork, skip optional meetings or social events, and limit interactions with colleagues (15Five, 2024; WebMD, 2025).
- Declining Performance: Look for a drop in work quality or productivity. Disengaged employees often do the bare minimum—meeting basic requirements but missing deadlines or delivering lower-quality work. They may appear to be on autopilot, performing just enough to get by" (CultureMonkey, 2025; Teramind, 2024).
- Negativity and Resistance to Change: Disengaged employees often openly express cynicism toward new ideas and company initiatives. They'll resist change, prefer to 'stick with what they know,' and can erode team morale with negativity or criticism"(SHMR, 2024)

- Absenteeism and Tardiness: Disengagement often correlates with increased absenteeism—frequent sick days, coming in late, or leaving early—as the employee's commitment wanes. High absence rates can be a red flag that someone has mentally checked out.
- Lack of Initiative or OwnershipDisengaged employees often show little curiosity or initiative beyond their narrow job tasks. They tend to avoid responsibility, do not seek feedback, and tend to contribute only the bare minimum, if that. (CultureMonkey 2025; PeopleHR 2024 However, not every difficult or quiet employee is disengaged—personality and other factors play a role—so managers should use judgment and context. However, if multiple red flags appear and performance or behavior is deteriorating, it's likely the person is actively disengaged. Identifying these individuals with data and observation is critical. As Wendy Hanson explains in SHRM (2024), disengaged employees may stop initiating work, become less communicative, and begin withdrawing from colleagues.Early recognition allows leaders to intervene before the disengagement spreads or leads to irreversible performance issues.

Causes of Disengagement

Once an actively disengaged employee has been identified, effective leaders should listen, and act like detectives to diagnose why the disengagement is occurring. Understanding the root causes is essential to formulating the right response. Disengagement rarely emerges from laziness or a poor work ethic; instead, it is typically rooted in unmet needs or workplace frustrations—from lack of feedback and support to unaddressed environmental shortcomings (Rastogi et al., 2018; CultureMonkey, 2025). Some common drivers include:
- Unclear Expectations and Purpose: A leading cause of disengagement is a lack of clarity about employees' roles or how their work connects to the organization's mission. Gallup surveys consistently find that a significant portion of workers do not know what is expected of them at work or do not see how their contributions matter. This ambiguity breeds disengagement.
- Lack of Autonomy and Control: Employees who feel they have no say in *how* they do their work—no flexibility or decision-making power—often become apathetic. A lack of job control (low autonomy) is strongly associated with lower engagement and morale (Rastogi *et al.*, 2018). Micromanagement or rigid bureaucratic rules can sap motivation.
- Insufficient Resources and Support: When people don't have the tools, training, or support to do their jobs well, frustration mounts. Lack of job resources—such as inadequate equipment, training, or staff—is a key factor that can lead to disengagement (Windon, 2023). Similarly, a perceived lack of support from manage-

- ment or colleagues (or feeling that "no one cares about me" at work) is often cited by disengaged employees (Alton, 2024).
- Limited Growth or Boredom: Monotonous, unchallenging work can turn even once-enthusiastic employees into disengaged ones. If a role provides no opportunity for learning, creativity, or advancement, employees may mentally check out. Literature reviews show that monotony and low job complexity—often experienced as boredom—are directly linked to disengagement, especially when high performers feel trapped in stifling roles lacking development opportunities.(Rastogi et al., 2018).
- Inequitable Rewards and Recognition: Disengagement often takes root when high performers see mediocre effort being rewarded equally. A culture that responds by giving more work to the competent—without commensurate recognition—can chip away at morale and motivation. This is especially true when pay and benefits fail to reflect what employees truly value. Industries and organizational psychology research warn that such practices can rapidly erode engagement (Peter Barron Stark Companies, 2024).
- Personal Stress and Burnout: Sometimes disengagement has roots outside the workplace or in personal well-being. The COVID-19 pandemic, for example, heightened burnout and mental health issues; many workers became disengaged due to exhaustion or external stressors. If an employee is dealing with heavy personal issues or burnout, they may withdraw and disengage as a coping mechanism. A mental health crisis or life change can trigger disengagement even in a previously engaged individual.

Importantly, disengagement often has multiple causes in play. A McKinsey study in 2023 identified six key drivers of employee dissatisfaction and disengagement: inadequate compensation, lack of meaningful work, limited workplace flexibility, few career advancement opportunities, unsupportive colleagues, and an unsafe (or unhealthy) work environment (De Smet *et al.*, 2023). Any combination of these factors can push an employee from mild discontent into active disengagement. Leaders should take a holistic view, examining organizational practices and the individual's situation to pinpoint why they have become "checked out," and potentially disruptive and even toxic in the workplace. By addressing root causes—whether it's clarifying expectations, adjusting a workload, improving management practices, or offering support—you treat the disease of disengagement, not just the symptoms.

Dealing with the Disengaged

Here are ten strategies for leaders and managers can use to address employee disengagement:

1. Initiate a Genuine Dialogue: Engage directly with disengaged employees through empathetic, one-on-one conversations. Listening actively and understanding personal challenges as well as listening to their concerns often reveals actionable insights to reignite motivation. Seek to understand, and not judge.
2. Clarify Expectations and Goals: Clearly articulate roles, responsibilities, and performance expectations. Ambiguity can breed disengagement, so aligning goals enhances employees' sense of purpose and direction.
3. Provide Constructive Feedback and Recognition: Regularly offer specific, actionable feedback and consistently recognize contributions. Recognition fosters self-worth and validates employee efforts, boosting morale and engagement.
4. Offer Opportunities for Growth and Development: Promote continuous learning and career advancement through training, mentoring, or stretch assignments. Employees who see clear opportunities to grow professionally become more invested in their roles.
5. Foster Team Collaboration and Social Connections: Encourage collaboration and team-building activities to strengthen interpersonal relationships. A sense of belonging reduces isolation and increases motivation to contribute meaningfully. Sometimes the disengaged will respond more positively to their team than they do to their leaders.
6. Address Work-Life Balance Issues: Actively identify and resolve work-life balance concerns. Excessive workloads and unrealistic deadlines can overwhelm employees, triggering disengagement and burnout.
7. Empower Autonomy and Decision-Making: Give employees greater autonomy and trust in decision-making. Empowered individuals often demonstrate higher engagement as they feel ownership and responsibility for their work.
8. Align Individual Values with Organizational Purpose: Connect an employee's tasks and roles explicitly to the broader organizational purpose and values. Employees aligned with organizational purpose experience increased motivation and commitment.
9. Regularly Evaluate and Adjust Workplace Conditions: Continuously monitor the work environment and proactively adjust conditions, such as ergonomic comforts, flexible work arrangements, or technology resources, ensuring a supportive atmosphere.
10. Lead by Example: Demonstrate consistent, visible engagement, commitment, and enthusiasm as a leader. Employees mirror leadership behaviors, so active engagement from management serves as a compelling model, influencing employees positively.

Effectively addressing disengagement begins with thoughtful identification, delves into genuinely understanding root causes, and concludes with targeted, supportive actions to restore engagement. Leaders who proactively recognize disengagement signs, commit to uncovering underlying issues—whether personal, managerial, or organizational—and consistently apply strategic interventions can transform disengaged employees into motivated, productive contributors. This deliberate process not only recovers lost potential but also fosters a culture where individuals feel valued, heard, and driven, ultimately positioning the organization for sustained growth and competitive advantage.

Key Questions
1. What has been your own experience with the actively disengaged?
2. What steps would you take to identify what the reasons are for active disengagement?
3. Have you had any unsuccessful experiences dealing with an actively disengaged employee? What happened?
4. Have you had any successful experiences dealing with an actively disengaged employee? What happened?
5. In the future, what actions would you take to deal with a potentially disengaged employee?

Chapter 11
Remote Work and Employee Engagement
Remote Work Sets New Requirements for the Management of Engaged Personnel

> "You have to have a level of empathy, especially at a leadership level, to show people that you care"
> — Rokhaya Ndiaye, CEO and founder of Ro&Partners

Remote work requires versatile engagement management. Remote work and doing it have become part of normal work and the operations of organizations around the world. Remote work includes full-time or full-week remote work and partial hybrid work, i.e., combinations of remote and workplace work.

According to Gallup's global survey, more than half of the global workforce works remotely or in a hybrid environment. The share of complete remote work is about 27% and 52% work on a hybrid model, i.e., partly in remote work and partly work is done at the workplace. It is estimated that by 2035, 60% of the global workforce will work remotely at least three days a month (Prezi, 2024). According to studies, on average, less than a day is spent on remote work per week, but in English-speaking countries, such as the United States, Canada, and the United Kingdom, about 1.4 days a week are spent on remote work (Gallup, 2025).

However, employees would be willing to work more remotely than at present. According to a global survey published in 2024, 91% would like to work fully or almost entirely remotely (Neat 2024). On the other hand, it is estimated that about 16% of companies in the world already operate completely remotely without a physical office (Forbes Advisor 2024).

According to a Gallup survey, while the share of remote work has increased, employee dissatisfaction and disengagement with the workplace have also increased. Only 31% of those who work fully remotely are engaged, which is of course more than those who work in a hybrid or in the office. At the same time, they experience more stress, loneliness, and emotional challenges.

The most worrying thing about this development is that the engagement of supervisors in particular has decreased, and the share of committed employees is now only 27% (Gallup, 2025). This very low level of engagement is naturally reflected both in the managers' own actions and results, and naturally in their teams and employees. In addition, it has been found that the more people work remotely, the more employees experience loneliness during the COVID-19 period (Fostervold et al, 2024).

Effects of Remote Work on Engagement

According to studies (Madjak, 2025), the manager's leadership approach plays a very important role in creating a sense of community and further affects engagement. The supervisor is expected to play the role of a coach, not the attitude of a supervisor, as engaging remote management is based on psychological safety and responsibility. The management of operations cannot be based on the physical supervision of the past, but on clear goals and mutual trust between teams and the entire work community.

Remote work has many strengths and benefits, also in terms of engagement. When done well, remote work strengthens employees' motivation and productivity. It is important that the support of supervisors and one's own team is available at work, that proper work tools are used, and that the organization's operating methods support the employee's individual and social needs.

Working remotely has many benefits in creating an engaged culture. The independent position of employees gives them the freedom to work as they see fit. It is not the use of time that is decisive, but the results of the work. Even if the work is done alone remotely at home or elsewhere, the employee must not be left alone.

Support and a sense of community must be available, and at the same time, active communication and feedback must be ensured. Remote work must also offer opportunities for development and career advancement, and most importantly, remote work must be able to combine work with the rest of life in a balanced way. Otherwise, there is a risk of employee burnout and increased disengagement (Forbes Advisor, 2024 and Madžak, 2025).

Employers and supervisors can strongly increase employee engagement through remote work. At best, work goes smoothly, and the set goals are achieved despite traditional control. With engagement, employee turnover and absences decrease, and well-being at work improves. Remote work emphasizes employees' ability to work independently and trust in their own competence, which in turn is reflected in engagement (FlexJobs, 2024, Owl Labs, 2024 and Day, 2025).

Remote Work and Engagement—Managing Engagement Requires Leadership

Successful management of remote work requires clear practices and a humane management approach to make work sensible and useful for both the employee and the employer. There are seven things which support engagement for remote workers:

1. In leadership, it is worth setting clear goals and building a relationship of trust
In the end, all leadership is action with the help of and through people. In practice, successful, engaging leadership requires that work goals and profit expectations are defined clearly and understandably. Even though the ideas and models of perfor-

mance management are behind it, employees must have the freedom to choose their working methods. The key is that results are achieved. Experts in their own work do not need "continuous micromanagement that looks over their shoulders," but operations must be based on trust in the employee, as trust increases motivation and engagement.

2. Constant communication and communication
In remote work, employees are detached from the normal work community and are alone with their own thoughts and problems. Alienation from the everyday life of the organization lurked everywhere, so it is very important to agree on regular monthly, weekly, or daily discussions. Some of these can be done remotely, and some can also be done at the workplace. Modern multichannel tools, such as Teams, Zoom, or Slack, can be used to help you keep in touch. All kinds of communication are always welcome, but it is worth remembering to distinguish between communication that includes operational management and social communication that takes care of the work community; both are very necessary.

3. Fostering a sense of community and culture
The work community, teams, and culture of operations must be nurtured in creating engagement and maintaining a high level. It is worth remembering that breaks and informal discussions create opportunities for innovation and new insights. At workplaces, coffee breaks and rest areas are important meeting places for people. When working remotely, everyone is working remotely, and at the same time, it must be ensured that they are really present, both physically and mentally. Therefore, it is worth arranging virtual coffee breaks and informal electronic team meetings, such as remote coffee or lunches. In addition to these, it is worth organizing and agreeing on regular supervisory meetings and joint days at the workplace, and, in addition to these, occasionally, recreational days for the whole family, for example.

The best feedback is usually obtained from colleagues. It is worth fostering a culture of trust and respect for others, where feedback is given and received from colleagues. Of course, we must not forget to rejoice in our shared successes and try to learn together from setbacks and failures. Mental well-being is an undeniable prerequisite for strong engagement.

4. Visible support and proper resources for remote work
In remote work, each employee is the master of their own situation and also surrounded by their own circumstances. At the workplace, the conditions are usually in order on behalf of the employer in terms of physical workers, equipment, and support. And if not, it is possible to react to them quickly. On the other hand, the situation is more difficult for the employee at home or in other remote workplaces. These remote conditions and tools must therefore be cherished to prevent nonengagement and avoid annoyance. Even a good team or interesting work cannot compensate for bad conditions.

Good working conditions create engagement, and correspondingly, bad factors flatten engagement. The employer should provide proper working equipment, such as PCs, remote connections, headphones, additional monitors, and, if possible, support in purchasing ergonomic desks and chairs. It is also essential to take care of information security and IT support and, of course, to offer support in dealing with any problems.

5. Work-life balance
When working remotely, managing work-life balance can sometimes be difficult. Poor engagement can cause underperformance and at the same time lead to susceptibility to changing employers or even be reflected in bad lifestyles. It is in everyone's interest that remote work allow for self-management and the opportunity to decide flexibly on working hours, but at the same time, there is an incentive to set one's own boundaries and rhythm of work and take breaks. On the other hand, supervisors must also act in an exemplary manner and avoid, for example, messaging late at night and demanding to always be available.

6. Giving feedback and supporting development
The management of remote work requires the presence of supervisors, which naturally differs from cooperation at the workplace. The problem may be that the supervisor remains invisible, is not interested in how their subordinates or team are doing, or what kind of problems or problems the subordinates are working on. In remote work, normal good people management practices are highlighted so that people commit to their own organization, tasks, and teams. It is therefore important to have regular goal, performance, and development discussions; agree on learning and competence goals; and discuss career opportunities.

7. The role of the leader and supervisor is to be a coach, not a supervisor
Managing remote work requires leadership. Good leadership requires real mental presence so that people can genuinely feel that they are valuable and valued employees. The feeling of worthlessness is quickly reflected in poor engagement, which in turn is reflected in poor results and even worse engagement—the negative spiral is complete. The supervisor must be accessible and, if necessary, help and support. Each employee is their own individual, which also requires individual leadership. Of course, it is worth remembering that remote work is not suitable for everyone, and not all work can be done remotely.

In remote work, an employee can contribute a lot to their own engagement. When working remotely, employees have more control than they might realize over their own engagement. The most effective starting point is to build intentional routines that create a sense of structure and momentum. Research consistently shows that engagement is strongly linked to daily progress toward meaningful goals (Amabile and Kramer, 2011). Remote employees can replicate this by setting clear priorities at the beginning of each day, breaking larger objectives into achievable steps, and celebrating small wins. This sense of progress not only builds motivation but also reduces the feeling of isolation that can accompany remote work. Equally important is the practice of proactive communication. Remote employees who wait passively for information often feel disconnected, while those who take ownership of their visibility—by updating colleagues, sharing insights, and contributing ideas—tend to feel more engaged and valued (Bloom et al., 2015). Engagement grows when employees make themselves part of the conversation, whether through regular video check-ins, quick chat updates, or sharing perspectives in digital collaboration tools. By doing so, they reinforce their presence and impact within the wider team.

Remote work can also blur boundaries, making it tempting to overwork or disconnect entirely. Employees who actively invest in well-being—through breaks, exercise, and clear start-and-stop times—tend to sustain higher levels of energy and focus (Deloitte, 2023). Engagement is not only about effort but about resilience: remote workers who protect their well-being create the conditions to show up consistently engaged, creative, and collaborative.

Finally, engagement is closely tied to meaning. Remote employees who intentionally connect their daily work to the larger mission of the organization report higher commitment and satisfaction (Kahn, 1990; Saks, 2006). This can be done by seeking out stories of customer impact, asking leaders for context, or reflecting personally on how their contributions support colleagues and clients. In other words, employees do not need to wait for engagement to be delivered from the outside—they can cultivate it by aligning their own routines, communication, well-being, and sense of purpose.

Remote work and its management can make or break engagement. Remote work has a lot of impact on engagement for both employers and employees. Remote work has good but also bad features. There are many factors in the organization and management of remote work that must be mastered in order for the work to be productive and interesting for employees and employers, and at the same time to enjoy the benefits of engagement. On the one hand, there is a risk that the possibility of remote work offers uncommitted employees the opportunity to underperform and hang out, but on the other hand, highly committed employees are at risk of overachievement and burnout. Therefore, engaging remote work management requires knowledge, skills, and competence.

Remote work is characterized by the absence of spontaneous encounters with other employees. You may feel lonely for long periods of time, so especially internal formal and informal communication must be consciously arranged. It is also clear that technical or ergonomic problems reduce efficiency and the smoothness of work. In remote work, the line between work and leisure time can easily become blurred, which can increase the employee's workload and cause a lack of engagement. An employee who works remotely may be left in the "shadows" if management communication is sporadic, feedback is not given, or the employee feels forgotten and their development opportunities are not believed (see *Bulletin of Business and Economics* 2024).

> Checklist for Leaders: Using Remote Work to Drive Engagement
> 1. The leader should be positive and interested in people: This increases alertness and engagement in remote work.
> 2. The leader must set an example and act with trust and respect: This supports employees' engagement and confidence in their own abilities.
> 3. Flexible formal and informal communication by the leader: Improves team spirit and social cohesion.
> 4. Monitoring the progress of remote work: Addressing problems and following good practices strengthens the shared engagement.
> 5. Remote work also requires joint meetings and physical presence from time to time: This creates faith in the power of collaboration and strengthens a successful corporate culture of engagement.

Engagement to Remote Work Requires Care

Engagement in remote work does not arise by itself, as remote work distances you from other people and the work community, the organization's customs and culture, and work and workplace routines. It is therefore important to identify and know how remote work and the related management and operational practices support better engagement. For example, daily virtual coffee and team meetings keep people engaged in everyday life.

In remote work, people are socially lonely, and they are expected to lead themselves. It has been observed that independent work in itself is very committed, but at the same time, job dissatisfaction can insidiously increase. However, not everyone is able to manage themselves, and there is a risk of under- or overperformance. In underperformance, work does not go smoothly, the results are modest and the employee may get used to the wrong lifestyle. Overachievement is never something that can be relaxed, and a strong autonomic self-sufficiency can cause stress and threaten burnout. The organization must ensure that working hours are clear, emphasize the importance of breaks, and, if necessary, create practices for managing digital working hours.

Maintaining engagement is facilitated by the supervisor's mental and visible care and empathetic leadership. The support of work teams and communities, clear work goals, and functional work tools are also important.

> Case Examples of Remote Work and Engagement in Action:
> Microsoft Viva: Empowering Engagement needs tools—Microsoft launched Microsoft Viva, an employee experience platform integrated into Microsoft Teams, to support engagement, well-being, learning, and connection in remote settings.
> Sweco Finland: Remote work increases well-being and efficiency by ensuring a sense of community in the organization.
> GitLab: A fully remote company and their documentation-first culture ensure clarity and alignment, which has led to high engagement and productivity.

Managing engagement in remote work requires leadership and a leadership approach in which there is knowledge about what is being led and how it is being managed. In the management of remote work, it is advisable to apply the so-called remote work method, in which the leader inspires, motivates, and develops their employees to exceed their own expectations and grow both as individuals and as part of the organization. It is not based on orders or control, but on trust, vision, and individual support (Bass and Avolio, 1990; and Northouse, 2021).

Key Questions
1. Has the organization clearly agreed on remote work and its ground rules?
2. How have supervisors been instructed and coached to manage remote work, and how have employees been trained to work remotely?
3. What kinds of methods are used in the management and regular communication of personnel in remote work, as well as in interaction while working remotely?
4. How to address problems or shortcomings caused by remote work and correct practices?
5. How systematically does the organization monitor the effects of remote work on employee engagement and well-being at work?

Chapter 12
AI and Employee Engagement
Humanizing Technology for a More Engaged Workforce

> "AI will not replace managers, but managers who use AI will replace those who don't."
> — Tomas Chamorro-Premuzic (2020)

AI Meets the Human Workplace

In recent years artificial intelligence (AI) has been changing the balance of work, reducing the need for task coordination and increasing autonomy across teams, and has become an everyday tool in many companies. It continues to expand exponentially! AI is no longer just a backend tool; it is increasingly embedded in everyday work—from predictive analytics and automated decision-making to virtual assistants and personalized learning platforms. As companies implement AI-driven systems to gain a competitive advantage, the question of employee engagement looms large. Will AI alienate employees by making them feel obsolete, or can it be harnessed to empower and engage?

The answer lies not in the technology itself, but in how leaders deploy it. For managers, this shift opens the door to new ways of working. But making the most of it requires a clear view of what to automate and who stands to gain. Like electricity in the industrial age, AI holds transformative potential—but only when applied with human-centered intent. This chapter explores the impact of AI on engagement and offers practical leadership strategies to maximize its benefits while minimizing risks.

The Double-Edged Sword: How AI Affects Engagement

Empowering Potential

When used thoughtfully, AI can enhance employee engagement in multiple ways. First, it automates mundane, repetitive tasks, allowing workers to focus on higher-value, creative, or interpersonal work that fosters meaning and satisfaction (Bessen, 2019). For instance, AI-enabled customer support platforms can handle routine queries, freeing up human agents for complex problem-solving and empathy-driven interactions.

Second, AI tools improve communication and inclusion. Natural language processing (NLP) systems can analyze internal chat data to surface team sentiment and highlight employees who may feel left out or underrecognized. These insights allow leaders to intervene constructively and promote a culture of belonging.

AI-driven platforms like Microsoft Viva and IBM's Watson have redefined internal communication and feedback mechanisms, ensuring employees feel heard and supported. For instance, IBM used its "Think Academy" platform to foster a culture of continuous learning and two-way communication, enabling employees to stay connected and engaged. Similarly, AI-powered pulse surveys and sentiment analysis tools can detect engagement levels in real-time, allowing leaders to intervene proactively and foster a more responsive and inclusive culture.

Third, AI can deliver personalized development experiences. Adaptive learning platforms analyze an employee's performance data and tailor content to individual skill gaps and career aspirations. This kind of just-in-time support fosters continuous learning and fuels a sense of growth—key drivers of engagement (Bakker and Demerouti, 2008).

Platforms like Workday and Eightfold AI use machine learning to suggest personalized learning paths and career growth opportunities, aligning employee aspirations with organizational goals. This not only drives motivation but also enhances retention by showing employees a future within the company. As Gallup (2023) notes, providing meaningful development opportunities is a key driver of engagement, and AI makes this scalable across large, diverse workforces. When leveraged ethically and transparently, AI becomes a strategic ally in creating an agile, responsive, and engaging workplace.

The Risk of Disengagement

On the other hand, poorly implemented AI can erode trust and engagement. The most immediate concern is job insecurity. Research from Frey and Osborne (2017) suggests that nearly half of current jobs are susceptible to automation. Even if jobs aren't eliminated, fear of redundancy can undermine psychological safety—a cornerstone of engagement (Kahn, 1990). When organizations fail to communicate a clear vision for how AI will support—not replace—workers, it fuels uncertainty and undermines engagement. For instance, research by Gartner (2020) found that nearly 70% of employees expressed concern about AI's impact on their jobs, yet only a fraction felt their employers were adequately preparing them for future roles. Engagement suffers when employees feel left behind or undervalued in a digital transformation.

AI implementation can also lead to unintended disengagement when the key concern is the erosion of human agency and autonomy. When AI systems are used to micromanage tasks or monitor employee performance excessively—such as through algorithmic management in gig platforms like Amazon or Uber—it can diminish trust and morale. Studies have shown that surveillance-driven environments increase stress and reduce motivation, leading employees to feel more like cogs in a machine than valued contributors (Mateescu and Nguyen, 2019). When decision-making is offloaded to algorithms without transparency or room for human judgment, employees may disengage due to a lack of control or understanding of how their work is being evaluated. AI-driven monitoring tools that track keystrokes, screen activity, or location data may lead to a culture of micromanagement and erode autonomy. When employees feel controlled rather than empowered, disengagement inevitably follows.

Furthermore, it is important that managers understand that biased algorithms or opaque systems often breed resentment. If employees believe that AI is used to make decisions without transparency or fairness—such as in promotions, performance reviews, or shift scheduling—trust in leadership declines.

Strategic Leadership Responses to AI's Impact

To ensure that the AI implementation improves rather than diminishes engagement, leaders should take into account the following four strategic key issues:
1. Clarify the role, use, and purpose of AI
   Helping everyone to understand honestly how AI can and will be used, and what the objectives are, will assist people to see how AI will impact their work. Having a clear, honest picture will help employees to see how they are impacted, and how they can benefit from the use of AI.
2. Framing AI as an Engagement Enabler
   An early step for leaders is to reframe the narrative. AI should be positioned not as a threat but as a copilot—augmenting human capability rather than replacing it. Leaders must communicate this vision consistently and transparently.

   At IBM, for example, the company rolled out its Watson AI platform alongside clear messaging that the goal was to assist, not eliminate, human roles. This framing helped employees embrace AI as a productivity partner, not a rival.
3. Building Trust in Technology
   Trust in AI starts with ethical design and transparent implementation. Leaders must ensure that employees are involved early in the development or selection of AI tools. Participatory design processes increase acceptance and reduce resistance.

   Moreover, organizations should audit AI systems regularly for bias and explainability. Employees need to understand how decisions are made. A "black box" approach—where algorithms are inscrutable—will alienate even the most tech-savvy teams.
4. Investing in Reskilling and Growth
   AI changes the skills landscape, but it also offers opportunities to redeploy talent. Rather than letting automation displace workers, forward-thinking leaders use it as a chance to upskill and re-skill.

   LinkedIn's 2024 *Workplace Learning Report* notes that companies investing in AI-driven upskilling programs experience higher retention rates. By equipping

employees to thrive in an AI-augmented environment, leaders demonstrate commitment to their future—one of the most powerful engagement levers.

Designing Engagement-Enhancing AI Systems

As the organization contemplates how AI will be used in the organization it is important to account for the human impact and design systems so that they increase rather than reduce employee engagement.

To harness the full potential of AI while protecting and promoting employee engagement, organizations must intentionally design AI systems that respect human needs, foster trust, and reinforce a sense of purpose. Rather than deploying AI solely to maximize efficiency or reduce headcount, leading companies are embedding AI into human-centric workflows that enhance autonomy, development, and collaboration. A human-centered approach to AI requires cross-functional collaboration between HR, IT, and business leaders to ensure that systems align with the values, capabilities, and aspirations of the workforce (Daugherty and Wilson, 2018).

One effective strategy is to use AI to augment, rather than replace, human capabilities. At Unilever, for instance, AI-powered recruitment tools are used to screen candidates and match them with roles based on their skills and potential. However, final hiring decisions remain with human managers, maintaining relational trust and accountability. This combination of AI efficiency and human empathy has led to faster hiring processes and increased candidate satisfaction (Bersin, 2019). Similarly, IBM's Think Academy uses AI to personalize learning experiences for employees, aligning development programs with individual career goals—thereby boosting engagement through visible growth opportunities (IBM, 2020).

Crucially, AI systems must be transparent and inclusive. When employees understand how AI systems work and are invited to provide feedback, engagement levels rise. Research from McKinsey (2021) shows that organizations involving employees in AI implementation decisions saw significantly higher adoption rates and workforce morale. Adobe's "Check-In" performance system, supported by AI-driven analytics, promotes frequent manager-employee conversations rather than annual reviews, helping employees feel more valued and empowered (Adobe, 2020). By designing AI systems that prioritize transparency, enable personal development, and maintain human oversight, organizations can use technology as a tool for amplifying—not diminishing—employee engagement.

Examples of Specific Systems Designed to Enhance Employee Engagement Include

1. Performance and Recognition Tools
   AI can revolutionize feedback. Platforms like Culture Amp and Lattice integrate machine learning to provide real-time feedback based on project performance and peer input. Employees receive timely recognition, which is a proven motivator.
2. Listening at Scale
   Conversational AI tools and sentiment analysis engines allow organizations to listen to employees more effectively. Instead of relying solely on annual engagement surveys, leaders can tap into ongoing data streams to understand team mood, stress levels, and motivation. These insights empower proactive engagement strategies.
3. Personalized Development Journeys
   AI-powered coaching systems like BetterUp AI Coach—a hybrid digital coaching platform designed to offer personalized, always-on development support while preserving human expertise. These types of systems offer support for leadership development, mental well-being, and career planning. These platforms help employees feel seen and supported, even in large, distributed organizations.

> Case Examples of AI in Action:
> - **IBM Watson Career Coach**: This AI tool helps employees map out internal mobility paths based on skills, goals, and available roles—enhancing clarity and engagement.
> - **Deloitte's Workforce Experience Platform**: Deloitte uses AI to monitor sentiment, well-being, and collaboration metrics across teams, enabling tailored interventions.
> - **Startup Use Case—Humaxa**: A small AI chatbot startup that uses real-time feedback to suggest peer shoutouts, training modules, or manager follow-ups—demonstrating that AI for engagement isn't just for enterprise giants.

Leadership Capabilities for the AI-Driven Future

Leading effective AI implementations requires more than technical competence—it demands a new kind of managerial agility rooted in empathy, adaptability, and strategic vision. As AI reshapes workflows and decision-making processes, managers must act as both translators and bridge-builders: translating technological potential into human value, while bridging the gap between data scientists, frontline employees, and organizational leadership. This requires strategic curiosity—a willingness to understand the capabilities and limitations of AI systems—and contextual intelligence, the ability to align AI tools with business goals and employee workflows (Daugherty and Wilson, 2018).

Equally important is empathetic change leadership. As already noted, AI initiatives can provoke fear, skepticism, or confusion, particularly when automation affects job roles. Effective managers foster psychological safety by involving employees early, communicating transparently, and co-creating implementation roadmaps. Research from McKinsey (2021) shows that organizations with inclusive change processes—where employees were engaged in AI design and rollout—saw significantly higher success rates and employee morale. Managers who acknowledge these concerns while positioning AI as a partner rather than a replacement can build trust and long-term engagement.

In addition, successful AI leadership requires a growth mindset and a commitment to continuous learning. Since AI capabilities evolve rapidly, managers must cultivate digital literacy—not to become technical experts, but to ask the right questions, challenge assumptions, and lead cross-functional teams effectively. For example, at DBS Bank in Singapore, managers underwent targeted digital training to understand AI's role in enhancing customer service and operational resilience. This enabled them to champion adoption across departments while preserving the bank's culture of innovation and human-centered service (Chui et al., 2018). In essence, managers who lead with empathy, clarity, and a commitment to upskilling are best positioned to deliver AI implementations that enhance both performance and engagement.

> Checklist for Leaders: Using AI to Drive Engagement
> 1. Clarify AI's Role: Communicate whether AI is replacing, supporting, or enhancing a task.
> 2. Co-Design with Employees: Involve users early in AI selection and rollout.
> 3. Ensure Transparency: Explain how AI systems work and why decisions are made.
> 4. Upskill Continuously: Provide resources for employees to learn and evolve.
> 5. Measure Sentiment: Use AI tools to listen and adapt to changing engagement levels.

Individual Opportunities in AI Adoption

Employees themselves can influence how AI will impact their own engagement and work. The following are some ideas that each individual can implement to improve the impact of AI in their organization:
1. Take an Active Role in AI Adoption
   - Experiment with AI tools relevant to your role and share feedback.
   - Volunteer for pilot programs or innovation initiatives involving AI.
   - Suggest ways AI could help automate repetitive tasks or improve workflows.
2. Invest in Learning and Skill Development
   - Attend 1. Take an Active Role in AI Adoption
   - Experiment with AI tools relevant to your role and share feedback.
   - Volunteer for pilot programs or innovation initiatives involving AI.
   - Suggest ways AI could help automate repetitive tasks or improve workflows.

3. Advocate for Ethical and Transparent Use
   - Ask questions about how AI is used in decision-making and data handling.
   - Encourage open dialogue about AI's impact on work culture and fairness.
   - Support policies that promote responsible and inclusive AI practices.
4. Use AI to Enhance Feedback and Well-being
   - Engage with AI tools that offer real-time feedback or help track well-being.
   - Use AI to manage workload, prioritize tasks, or improve time management.
   - Explore digital assistants or wellness apps that support mental health.
5. Collaborate with AI, Don't Compete
   - View AI as a partner that enhances your capabilities, not a threat.
   - Focus on tasks where human judgment, creativity, and empathy are essential.
   - Combine AI insights with your own expertise to make better decisions.

Improving Teamwork Through AI

AI can significantly enhance team engagement when applied thoughtfully and strategically. Here are key ways AI contributes to stronger, more connected teams:

1. Enhancing Collaboration in Meetings
   AI can transform team meetings by:
   - Preparing agendas and summarizing previous discussions ("AI sets the table").
   - Assisting facilitators with real-time insights ("AI at one seat").
   - Empowering all participants with AI tools during meetings ("AI at every seat").
   - Automating Routine Tasks
     AI reduces the burden of repetitive work, allowing team members to focus on creative and strategic tasks. This shift increases job satisfaction and engagement.
2. Personalized Communication and Updates
   AI tools can deliver curated, role-specific updates, reduce digital overload, and help employees feel more informed and connected.
3. Real-Time Feedback and Recognition
   AI can analyze performance data to identify top contributors and provide timely, personalized recognition, which boosts morale and motivation.
4. Smarter Scheduling and Workload Balancing
   AI-powered scheduling tools help teams manage availability, time-off, and workload, creating more balanced calendars and reducing burnout.
5. Personalized Learning and Development
   AI can assess skills, identify gaps, and recommend learning paths tailored to individual and team goals, fostering continuous growth and engagement.

6. Streamlined Onboarding and Support
   AI-enabled onboarding platforms and virtual assistants provide 24/7 support, helping new team members feel welcomed and empowered from day one.

The Human Side of the Machine

As organizations navigate the complexities of digital transformation, AI stands out not just as a tool for operational efficiency, but as a catalyst for deeper, more meaningful employee engagement. When designed and deployed thoughtfully, AI can personalize development pathways, streamline communication, and offer real-time support that empowers employees at every level. It enables managers to gain insights into engagement drivers, respond proactively to challenges, and create more agile and responsive work environments. But these benefits are only realized when AI is implemented through a human-centered lens—one that prioritizes trust, transparency, and inclusion.

Ultimately, AI should not replace the human touch; it should amplify it. The organizations that succeed in using AI to elevate engagement will be those that strike a balance between data and empathy, automation and autonomy. By engaging employees in the design process, offering opportunities for reskilling, and ensuring that AI reinforces rather than undermines human connection, leaders can build workplaces that are both technologically advanced and emotionally intelligent. In doing so, they won't just improve engagement—they'll cultivate a future-ready workforce equipped to thrive in a world where human potential and AI go hand in hand.

In the hands of visionary leaders, AI can deepen rather than diminish the human experience at work. The challenge is not to control the machine—but to use it to empower people.

Key Questions
1. What could be the greatest benefits for your organization from using AI?
2. What are the concerns of employees in your organization about implementing AI?
3. How can you reduce employees' concerns about AI in your organization?
4. How can you personally prepare for the future use of AI and support the success of AI in your organization?
5. What are the potential benefits of AI in your teams and organization?

Chapter 13
International Multiculturalism and Employee Engagement

Knowledge of Cultural Differences Lays the Foundations for Engaged Employees

> "You can dream, create, design, and build the greatest places in the world, but you need people to make your dreams come"
> — Walt Disney

As many companies and organizations expand globally, managing employee engagement in an international and multicultural organization is a challenge, and requires multicultural understanding. Even though engagement is critical in every company and country, there are differences management should be aware of as they strive to improve employee engagement globally in their organizations.

Employee engagement varies significantly across countries, shaped by cultural norms, economic conditions, leadership practices, and workplace expectations. Global surveys—particularly those conducted by Gallup (2023, 2025)—highlight these differences and suggest that engagement is not a universal constant but deeply contextual.

Several factors explain these cross-national differences:
- Cultural norms—Collectivist societies may prioritize harmony and group identity over personal expression at work, influencing how engagement is experienced and measured.
- Economic conditions—Where jobs are scarce, employees may remain in roles despite low engagement, while in competitive economies, disengagement often leads to mobility.
- Leadership and trust—Cross-cultural research shows that national culture and levels of institutional trust shape how employees connect and engage with leaders and with organizational purpose (Hofstede, 2001; Inglehart and Welzel, 2005)
- Workplace structures—Flexible work arrangements and autonomy, common in North America, correlate with higher engagement, whereas rigid hierarchies can suppress it.

For leaders managing global companies and teams, the lesson is clear: engagement strategies must be localized. A recognition program that resonates in the U.S. may not have the same impact in Germany or Japan. Instead, leaders should tailor measurements and approaches—emphasizing meaning and autonomy in North America, trust and transparency in Europe, and community and relational ties in Latin America. The universal truth is that employees everywhere seek purpose, respect, and growth, but the ways these drivers are expressed and reinforced differ markedly by culture and context.

Also, while companies, public institutions, and nonprofits operate in distinct contexts, the fundamentals of management share many commonalities. At the same time, their core tasks, stages of development, and operating environments differ in meaningful ways, which naturally shapes the requirements and expectations placed upon them. Effective leaders recognize these nuances and design management systems that are not one-size-fits-all, but instead tailored to the organization's mission, operational realities, and unique circumstances. For example, a multinational corporation like Unilever manages global supply chains with performance metrics and efficiency-driven systems, whereas a nonprofit such as Médecins Sans Frontières (Doctors Without Borders) emphasizes agility and mission alignment to deliver critical medical aid in unpredictable environments. Both organizations require disciplined management and engagement, but the methods and priorities they employ must reflect the unique demands of their respective contexts (Lawrence and Lorsch, 1967; Drucker, 1990; Bryson, Crosby and Bloomberg, 2014).

Ultimately, effective people management transcends organizational boundaries. What unites most modern organizations globally—whether corporate, public, or nonprofit—is that they are increasingly international, bringing together individuals from diverse cultural backgrounds. At the same time, it is essential to recognize that every culture and employee is unique, requiring leaders to pay attention to individual needs, motivations, and circumstances. Practices, norms, and values can vary widely, both across cultures and within teams, placing significant demands on leaders seeking to foster genuine engagement. In such environments, the collective value of people working together becomes immeasurable, reinforcing the critical role of leadership in shaping culture and connection (Schein, 2010; Sinek, 2019).

With internationalization, intercultural understanding has become a key part of effective leadership and cooperation. Cultural differences can cause conflict, but they also provide an opportunity for learning and innovation. Needless to say, cultural intelligence is a key competency in today's international organizations. Studies have shown that organizations that are able to adapt their management practices to the local culture are more successful in international markets (e.g., Sarfraz, Bhutta, and Ivascu, 2024; Leadership Reframed for Future, Harvard Business Publishing, Corporate Learning, 2023).

In this chapter, we explore the contrasts in corporate culture and management practices across Finland, the United States, Germany, Japan, China, and Brazil. These countries were selected because they represent striking cultural differences, and we draw on direct experiences from our work with organizations in each context. Our findings suggest that when it comes to managing engagement, the most critical differentiators lie in organizational structures, leadership styles, decision-making processes, and communication practices. We outline how engagement can be effectively fostered in international and multicultural environments—highlighting the roles of leaders, supervisors, teams, and individual employees in building inclusive, high-performing workplaces.

Geert Hofstede (2001) developed six useful cultural dimensions that can be used to analyze and understand national cultures and their impact on leadership and employee engagement.

These six dimensions developed by Geert Hofstede (2001) are: (1) Power Distance, (2) Individualism vs. Collectivism, (3) Masculinity vs. Femininity, (4) Uncertainly Avoidance, (5) Long-term vs. Short-term Orientation, and (6) Indulgence vs. Restraint.

Power Distance describes how much society accepts the unequal distribution of power. A large power distance means that hierarchies are clear and authorities are not questioned. A small power distance means that the distribution of power is evened out, and leaders can and are challenged.

Individualism vs. Collectivism describes whether the importance of the individual or the group is emphasized. According to individualism, independence and self-centeredness guide people's behavior, in which personal achievements and individual rights are at the center. According to the collectivist view, the interests of the group or work community always come first, in which case loyalty and community are more important than the individual's own goals.

Masculinity vs. Femininity describes what kind of values and norms are dominant in the culture. For a masculine consumer, competition, individual success, and performance-orientation are emphasized, while in a feminine community, mutual care, close cooperation, good quality of life, and equality are valued.

Uncertainty Avoidance describes how well individuals and communities tolerate uncertainty and risks. In cultures of avoiding high uncertainty, there is a great need for rules, clear organization, structures, and security. In cultures of avoiding low uncertainty, uncertainty is accepted as part of normal life, where flexibility is valued and where experiments and failures are treated with understanding and encouragement.

Long-Term Orientation describes how the culture relates to time and the future. In cultures that value the long term, frugality and perseverance are valued, and planning for the future plays an important role. In a culture that emphasizes the short term, respect for traditions is important, and the pursuit of quick results is key.

Indulgence vs. Restraint is the sixth dimension in Hofstede's classification is the degree of pleasure and restraint. This cultural dimension describes the extent to which a culture allows pleasure and the satisfaction or abstention of desires. Indulgence means the freedom to express emotions and enjoy life to the fullest, while restraint emphasizes the importance of social control and clear norms as limits and frameworks for behavior.

The characteristics of the corporate culture in different countries affect how employee engagement can be influenced.

Below we have described how Hofstede's (2001) six cultural dimensions may influence employee engagement:

Power Distance
In high power distance cultures, hierarchical structures are accepted and employees may expect top-down decision-making. Engagement in such environments often depends on strong, directive leadership and clear authority. In contrast, in low power distance cultures, employees are more engaged when leaders foster openness, inclusivity, and participatory decision-making. A manager in Finland, for example, might boost engagement by inviting dialogue, whereas in China, engagement may be reinforced by demonstrating authority and providing clear direction.

Individualism vs. Collectivism
In individualistic cultures, such as the United States, engagement grows when employees are recognized for personal achievements and given autonomy over their work. In collectivist cultures, such as China or Brazil, engagement is more closely tied to group cohesion, team success, and loyalty to the organization. Leaders who align recognition practices and incentives with cultural expectations—individual awards in the U.S., collective achievements in China and Brazil—can strengthen commitment.

Masculinity vs. Femininity
Masculine cultures, such as Japan or Germany, value competition, performance, and achievement. Engagement here is often linked to career advancement, measurable results, and high standards. Feminine cultures, such as Finland or the Netherlands, place more emphasis on quality of life, collaboration, and work-life balance. In these contexts, employees feel more engaged when workplaces prioritize well-being, inclusivity, and consensus-building.

Uncertainty Avoidance
In cultures with high uncertainty avoidance, such as Germany or Japan, employees are more engaged when leaders provide structure, clear policies, and detailed planning. In contrast, in cultures with low uncertainty avoidance, such as the U.S. or China, engagement flourishes when employees are encouraged to take risks, experiment, and innovate. Leaders who calibrate between clarity and flexibility can better sustain engagement across cultural contexts.

Long-Term vs. Short-Term Orientation
Long-term oriented cultures, such as China and Japan, emphasize perseverance, sustained investment, and future rewards. Engagement grows when leaders connect employees' work to long-term goals and development opportunities. Short-term oriented cultures, such as the U.S. and Mexico, often emphasize quick wins, immediate results, and traditions. Engagement in these settings is strengthened by celebrating short-term achievements while still linking them to a broader purpose.

Indulgence vs. Restraint
In indulgent cultures, such as Brazil or the U.S., engagement is enhanced when workplaces allow personal expression, enjoyment, and flexibility. Employees feel valued when organizations support a positive work atmosphere and celebrate successes. In restraint-oriented cultures, such as China or Japan, engagement may depend more on discipline, duty, and adherence to rules. Leaders in these settings build engagement by reinforcing shared responsibility and aligning work with social expectations.

Hofstede's six cultural dimensions remind leaders that *engagement is not universal*—it is filtered through cultural values. A recognition program, communication style, or leadership approach that energizes employees in one country may have little impact, or even backfire, in another. Effective global leaders tailor their engagement strategies to cultural contexts while anchoring them in universal drivers of purpose, respect, and growth.

Understanding the business culture in different countries is essential for successful employee engagement in international business. Differences between different cultures affect organizational behavior, leadership, communication, and decision-making. That is why it's good to see how cultural differences can be seen as an example in a few interesting countries, paraphrasing Hofstede and touching on our own experiences.

The Finnish business culture is known for its low hierarchy, the independence of the actors, and the operation based on trust. Decision-making is consensus-oriented and leadership is participatory. In Finnish culture, femininity, low power distance, and high avoidance of uncertainty are emphasized. Finnish working life is characterized by a low hierarchy, mutual trust, and a strong sense of community. Things are said as they are, without beating around the bush.

In the United States, the corporate culture emphasizes individualism, performance orientation, and competitiveness. Organizations are often results-oriented and management is direct and goal-oriented. Decision-making is fast and leader-centered, while communication is confident and expressive. Remuneration is mainly based on personal performance.

The German business culture is bureaucratic but rational. Punctuality, logical thinking, and quality are valued there. Management is formal and based on expertise. In Germany, a high level of avoidance of uncertainty and a moderate distance of power are typical.

In Japan, collectivity, loyalty and group harmony are emphasized. Decision-making is often slow and thoroughly considered, but then the final implementation is effective. Communication is indirect, contextual, and hierarchical, and negative things are avoided until the very end. Leadership is based on seniority and the common interest.

Chinese business culture is based on hierarchy, networks of relationships (guanxi), and keeping face (mianzi). Communication is very indirect and situation-specific. Leadership is authority-oriented, but loyalty to leadership and belonging to a group are key values.

In Brazil the corporate culture is emotional and relationship-based. Leaders are often charismatic and decision-making is concentrated at the top of the hierarchy, but informal networks have a strong impact. Communication is often indirect and emotional expression is common.

Leaders in a successful organization need to recognize the cornerstones of culture-based engagement. Management is constantly developing their professional knowledge and area of expertise, the mastery of which requires both theoretical understanding and practical application. In leadership, it is not enough to just work and work at the limits of one's strength, but the most important thing is to achieve results through and with the help of people in different cultures (Raikaslehto, T., Mansukoski, S., and Mitronen, L. 2024).

The first cornerstone of engagement management is the ability to read the situation clearly and form a well-grounded perspective. Leaders must assess whether the strategy requires adjustment, confirm that strategic choices remain valid, and ensure that the overall direction of operations is well defined and understood. A good example is Satya Nadella's early tenure at Microsoft, where he recognized that the company's long-standing strategy was stifling innovation and employee morale. By clarifying a new strategic direction—shifting toward cloud computing and a growth mindset culture—Nadella reenergized employees around a shared purpose, demonstrating how recalibrating strategy can directly strengthen engagement (Lohr, 2017).

Another cornerstone of engagement management is the careful selection and development of the leadership team. The composition of this core group should reflect both the current situation and the organization's future needs. In some cases, no structural changes are necessary, and existing leaders simply need the opportunity to demonstrate their value—often with new tools, perspectives, or support to help them face emerging challenges. The greater risk lies in making rapid personnel changes based on incomplete or superficial assessments, which can undermine stability and trust. At the same time, leaders must act decisively when certain individuals consistently damage morale. As one executive we interviewed put it: "Rotten eggs must be replaced as soon as possible, because they poison the atmosphere." Research supports this view: toxic employees can spread negativity, reduce team performance, and undermine engagement across the organization (Felps, Mitchell and Byington, 2006). Similarly, Jim Collins' work emphasizes that long-term success depends on "getting the right people on the bus" and ensuring alignment between leadership capabilities and strategic direction (Collins, 2001). Tolerating destructive behavior threatens engagement and must be addressed immediately. (See also Chapter 10 on Dealing with the Disengaged.)

The third cornerstone is the application of management practices, which also shape and reinforce a culture of leadership. While values tend to endure, practices and cultural norms evolve over time. One professor at a leading business school illustrated this point to a group of alumni who had graduated 50 years earlier. When shown the current economics exam, an alumnus remarked: "These are exactly the same questions you asked us fifty years ago." The professor replied: "Yes, but the correct answers are completely different today than they were then." The story highlights how management practices must adapt to changing contexts and cultures, even as core values remain constant. As Schein (2010) emphasizes, organizational culture is built on enduring assumptions and values, but leaders must continually update practices to respond to new realities and cultures. Similarly, Kotter (2012) argues that organizations that thrive are those able to preserve their core while embracing continuous changes in the world.

Understanding the impact of cultures is crucial for organizations operating internationally. Taking into account the similarities and differences between cultures promotes efficiency, engagement, collaboration, and employee well-being. It is equally clear that leadership is not just an individual's skill, but involves understanding and shaping the organization's culture and structures so that everyone's expertise and the organization's capital can be used as efficiently and fully as possible. In managing engagement in different cultures, it is important to have goals and measures as well as ways to improve engagement for individuals, leaders, and teams.

> Key cultural factors to consider for Strategy, Leadership, and the Individual
> Strategy
> - Long-term vs. short-term weighting
> - Risk-taking vs. prudence
> - Starting point of communication, value-based communication vs. outspokenness
> - Cultural constraints of market choices and partnerships
>
> Supervisory work
> - Leadership style (participatory vs. hierarchical)
> - Power distance and proximity to the Manager's role
> - Level of decentralization and concentration of decision-making
> - Feedback and motivation methods
>
> Teamwork
> - Communication, direct vs. indirect
> - Group harmony vs. individual expression
> - Conflict management
> - Division of roles and dynamics of cooperation
>
> Individual
> - Source of motivation, internal vs. external
> - Work-life balance
> - Cultural identity and adaptability
> - Receiving personal feedback and career development

High Demands for Multinational Leaders

Today's multinational leaders, managers, and supervisors are subject to many demands in different cultures. For example, business results, responsibility, openness, ethics, multiculturalism, and sustainable development have become key elements of effective leadership in recent years in most cultures. Without learning and implementing these globally in practice, a manager's career is likely to be short and rocky.

It seems that an individual leader will have to master a large number of different leadership styles, especially in an international setting, in order to succeed in managing the business as well as achieving high employee engagement.

In our work we have discovered that the basic IMPACT principles from Chapter 6 both resonate and are applicable in all cultures, but need to be wisely implemented by leaders. The role of incentives varies between cultures. As noted for incentives, in a country like the US, individual engagement grows when employees are recognized for personal achievements. On the other hand, in collectivist cultures, such as China or Brazil, engagement is more closely tied to group cohesion, team success, and incentives. Similarly, wise cultural implementation of the other IMPACT elements (Mutual respect, Passion, Accountability, Collaboration, and Transformation) is critical in leading a highly engaged workforce in different countries and cultures. Leading strong engagement in different cultures requires a high level of cultural awareness from the leaders.

When a new manager or supervisor steps into a multinational role, it is essential to first understand the scope of the task they are taking on. What expectations do business owners or decision-makers hold? Which problems require immediate attention, and what new opportunities might be leveraged? Leaders must also assess the capabilities of their supervisors and the readiness of different teams to execute the current strategy internationally—or determine whether the strategy itself requires cultural adjustments. Equally important is understanding the engagement and composition of the workforce and the true nature of its competencies, since the engagement, skills, and strengths of employees ultimately determine the organization's ability to deliver on its ambitions. Leading employee engagement in a multidimensional setting is both challenging and rewarding.

Teams Lay the Foundation for Good Cooperation

Even though teamwork may be seen differently in different cultures, in all the countries we have worked in, well-functioning teams, both within and across teams, play an important role in keeping employees fully engaged. Conflicts and lack of trust within or across teams erode engagement and success in all cultures. So, it is critical in all cultures to build well-functioning teams, and we have found that the TEAMS (Trust, Empathy, Appreciation, Mutual agreement, and Synergy) principles are universal, even if they are implemented somewhat differently in different cultures. (See Chapter 7.)

In today's dynamic operating environment, the ability of teams to adapt and reinvent themselves has become a critical success factor. High-performing teams with highly engaged team members are not only self-directed but also capable of managing change with agility, and able to respond flexibly to shifting demands. Just as importantly, engaged teams are better equipped to thrive in uncertainty—because engagement fosters trust, accountability, and collaboration in all cultures. When employees feel secure and connected to their work and to one another, they are more willing to share knowledge, take initiative, and support colleagues through turbulence. In this way, engagement transforms teams in all cultures from collections of individuals into resilient units that can sustain performance even amid constant change.

Each Employee is Responsible Everywhere

The one area in our work with companies where we have seen significant variation in different areas of the world is how employees see their own responsibility for their engagement. In individualistic countries, such as the US, employees accept more readily their own responsibility for engagement than in collectivistic countries such as the Nordic Countries, China, or Brazil.

However, across all cultures, one principle remains constant: every employee must take ownership of their own engagement, skills, and attitudes. In multicultural and international organizations, this means balancing confidence in one's own values with openness, tolerance, and genuine appreciation for others. Employees who actively engage in this way not only recognize their personal strengths and limitations but also contribute to a culture of trust, inclusivity, and shared optimism. By doing so, they reinforce engagement at both the individual and team level in all cultures—demonstrating that sustainable performance depends as much on personal accountability as it does on organizational systems everywhere. The PACT (Passion, Accountability, Collaboration, and Transformation) represents universal drivers of individual engagement, and can be implemented globally by individual employees (see Chapter 5).

Chapter 13 Key Issues

1. Global Engagement Is Contextual. Employee engagement is critical in every organization, but it varies significantly across countries and cultures.
2. Cultural Differences Matter. Drawing on Hofstede's six cultural dimensions—power distance, individualism vs. collectivism, masculinity vs. femininity, uncertainty avoidance, long-term vs. short-term orientation, and indulgence vs. restraint—the chapter illustrates how national culture influences engagement.
3. The three key leadership cornerstones in multicultural contexts:
   A. Strategic Clarity
   B. Selecting and Developing Right Leaders
   C. Evolving Management Practices
4. Multinational leaders face increasing demands: responsibility, ethics, multicultural competence, and sustainable development have become essential. They must master multiple leadership styles and apply the IMPACT framework (Incen-

tives, Mutual respect, Passion, Accountability, Collaboration, and Transformation) with cultural sensitivity.
5. Well-functioning teams are central to engagement everywhere. The TEAMS model (Trust, Empathy, Appreciation, Mutual agreement, and Synergy) offers a universal framework, though applied differently across contexts.
6. Across cultures, one principle is constant: each employee must take ownership of their engagement and apply culturally the PACT (Passion, Accountability, Collaboration, and Transformation) to improve their own engagement.

Key Questions
1. Why does international management of engagement require more from leadership?
2. How do cultural factors impacting differ for different cultures?
3. What personal experiences have you had in dealing with employee engagement in international settings?
4. How would you expect the multidimensional engagement profiles to differ in China and Scandinavia? Why?
5. If you wanted to influence engagement, how would your leadership style likely differ in the United States and Scandinavia?

Chapter 14
Making it Happen
Leading the Change for Higher Engagement

>"Change before you have to."
>— Jack Welch

At some level, the principles of individual engagement (PACT) in Chapter 5, the leadership principles creating an environment of engagement (IMPACT) in Chapter 6, and creating effective teams (TEAMS) in Chapter 7 are common sense, and known to most. However, the real challenge we all face is how to lead and make a lasting change in our own organizations. That is the difficult part. And unfortunately, there are few shortcuts, and it seems that there are no magic answers.

In many organizations, employee engagement is treated as an initiative—launched with enthusiasm, measured with surveys, and often forgotten once the next priority arises. But genuine, sustained engagement is not the result of isolated programs or perks; it is the outcome of a consistent and intentional culture built over time. It is the by-product of leadership behavior, structural alignment, and everyday actions that collectively make engagement the norm rather than the exception. Improving the culture of engagement is a "change initiative" and must be treated and led like any other major change in an organization: carefully and intentionally.

Our past experience with companies focusing on improving employee engagement has admittedly been mixed; some companies and teams have improved their engagement scores significantly, and others have not. Even though the results vary, generally the teams with a higher level of engagement tend to improve more than teams with lower engagement, which is always a concern for companies wanting to specifically improve the engagement of less effective teams and organizations.

On the positive note, we have seen significant improvements in individuals who have realized that their own engagement is their choice. In one of the relatively small teams we worked with, most of the team members were highly engaged, with one clearly disengaged individual. After we did our initial surveys and development processes, one individual realized that his negativity had a negative impact on the team, and as he stated during our follow-up session, "I realized that my negativity was selfish, and I wanted to change." In fact, during our follow-up sessions with the team, this individual was one of the most engaged and positive individuals, improving the total team effectiveness and engagement.

In another team, there was a person with a very difficult personal life situation which had impacted them, and the unfortunate negativity was brought into the workplace by active disengagement impacting the whole team. However, during our first encounter with the team, this individual chose as their task to find more joy in work, by focusing on the most enjoyable parts of their daily tasks, and doing something they loved every day. In our follow-up session they said, "I realized that my negativity impacts everyone, and I wanted to be a positive force to the team. By accepting things in my life I could not change, and changing those aspects of my work I can impact, I can speak and think in more positive terms." And everyone on the team and leadership had recognized, and supported, the positive change. They said that becoming more positively engaged in their work was a lifesaver for them in their life.

These kinds of positive individual and team changes are encouraging and have motivated us to continue the effort to improve employee engagement. However, unfortunately, this is not always the outcome. Sometimes, especially those with the most negative attitudes, and the highest level of dissatisfaction and active disengagement just do not want to change, and at times any effort to improve their outlook on work and life backfires. And that is when leadership must step in. To truly and permanently improve engagement, leaders and employees must shift their mindset from just fixing disengagement to empowering sustained commitment. This is a major change initiative.

Leadership is a people-oriented profession, where the leader must be sensitive in guiding both organizations and, especially, individuals in a way that best serves them. A leader cannot rely on just one leadership style, because organizations and their circumstances differ from one another, and people are also different. A leader must also be able to see the consequences of their own leadership—what works and what does not. In leadership, action alone is not enough; results must follow.

> Leading change is among the most demanding challenges for any leader. It can involve refining established processes through continuous improvement, or more radical shifts such as crisis restructuring or a full strategic reset. In every case, resistance to change is a predictable dynamic: some employees embrace it quickly, others adapt with support, and a few ultimately cannot make the transition.
> At one ICT company, a large-scale transformation of operating practices and IT architecture illustrated this pattern clearly. Roughly 20% of employees immediately embraced the new model, eager to implement it. The majority—about 60%—joined the effort once they received targeted coaching, training, and support through a structured change program. But the final 20% could not adapt to the new ways of working. Rather than forcing compliance, the company enabled those individuals to transition into other roles internally or move on externally.
> This experience underscores a critical insight for leaders: successful change requires both structural support and recognition that not everyone will come along. Preparing for these dynamics—champions, the movable middle, and resistors—enables leaders to guide organizations through disruption while maintaining morale and long-term engagement.

In any change leadership, employee commitment is absolutely central. In such a transformation, it is necessary to inspire not only the leadership but also managers, teams, and ultimately each individual employee to join in, and choose to be engaged. We have extensive research findings and practical experience showing that individual commitment and engagement play an exceptionally crucial role in the success of change.

An award-winning behavioral scientist, Katy Milkman's national bestseller book *How to Change* outlines some key principles from academic research which make change possible. In their final chapter on "Changing for Good," they make the statement:

> "Study after study (mine included) has shown that achieving transformative behavior change is more like treating a chronic disease than curing a rash. You can't just slap a little ointment on it and expect it to clear up forever . . . . They won't just go away once you have started 'treating' them. They're human nature and require constant vigilance." (Milkman 2021, p. 197)

This has also been our experience. Frequently, in our work with organizations, management wants "quick fixes" and jumps from one program to another, without consistent and persistent effort to improve organizational culture, leadership, and/or employee engagement. And disappointment too often follows these sporadic efforts without staying power. And management's belief in possible change often wanes and frustration grows.

But even in this complicated environment, there is a constant need for improvement for individuals and for organizations. And thankfully, we are convinced that with persistent and consistent effort, change is possible for individuals and for organizations.

In our experience, successful commitment to permanent change requires both a general understanding of change management and practical tools for leading the change. One such tool is the so-called Four Rooms of Change model, developed on the basis of research from Stockholm University Janssen (1996). See Figure 14.1.

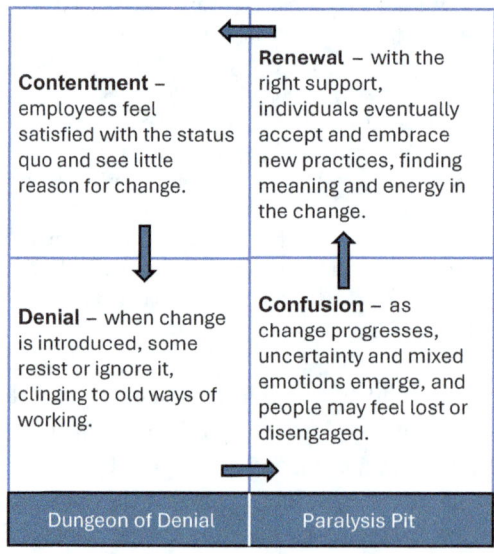

Figure 14.1: Four Rooms of change Model.

The model suggests that people typically move through four psychological "rooms" when confronted with change:
1. Contentment—employees feel satisfied with the status quo and see little reason for change.
2. Denial—when change is introduced, some resist or ignore it, clinging to old ways of working.
3. Confusion—as change progresses, uncertainty and mixed emotions emerge, and people may feel lost or disengaged.
4. Renewal—with the right support, individuals eventually accept and embrace new practices, finding meaning and energy in the change.

For leaders, the key insight is that not all employees move through these rooms at the same pace. Effective change leadership requires tools that help identify where all individuals and teams are on this journey and strategies to guide them forward. In practice, this might mean offering reassurance to those in denial, providing clarity to those in confusion, and celebrating progress for those entering renewal.

For those who participate in the engagement improvement process and change they arrive in the final room—so-called room of renewal, where change and improvement in the engagement culture is experienced as positive and energizing. People see that the new model works and celebrate successes. This enthusiastic phase lasts for a while, but the change is not permanent. Eventually, the cycle returns to the starting point—the room of contentment—waiting for the next change.

Leading this attempted change and improvement in engagement affects everyone in the organization—leaders, teams, and individual employees. To bring all of these groups on board, it is necessary to measure the current state of engagement and identify the areas and teams where the most important change is needed. This is where the multidimensional view of engagement model (Chapters 3 and 4) and the specific change concepts (Chapters 5, 6, 7, 8, and 9) become useful tools for the leaders and for the organization.

Even though in many aspects, permanently improving the engagement culture is like any major change initiative, there are specific principles to follow to make a positive shift in organizational engagement.

In the following section we outline eight interlocking pillars that, when embedded into a company's DNA, can manage this change process and transform engagement into a lasting cultural advantage. These principles are in line with the leadership principles discussed in Chapter 6, as well as other principles covered earlier in the book. However, these principles are so central to making a permanent change that we have decided to repeat them here, focusing on the permanent change:

1. Anchoring the Culture in Purpose
   Purpose-driven organizations consistently outperform others in engagement and loyalty. When employees see how their work contributes to a meaningful mission, they engage more deeply—not just with tasks, but with the company's success. Leaders must do more than craft a purpose statement. They must weave purpose into the daily rhythm of work—from goal setting to recognition and storytelling. Studies show that employees who understand their company's purpose are 2.5 times more likely to be engaged (PwC, 2016).

2. Leadership That Builds Trust
   According to Gallup (2023), **70% of the variance in employee engagement** can be attributed to the manager. Trustworthy, authentic leaders foster environments where people feel safe, valued, and motivated to contribute. This means being transparent in decisions, listening actively, and leading with empathy.
   The most enduring engagement cultures are not built on charismatic leadership alone, but on consistent managerial behaviors that cultivate belonging, autonomy, and trust.

3. Clarity of Goals with Autonomy in Execution
   Engagement thrives where there is clarity of direction and freedom of movement. Employees want to know what is expected—but also want the autonomy to figure out how to deliver.
   Amabile and Kramer (2011) argue that employees are most engaged when their work is clearly aligned with meaningful goals and when managers remove obstacles and avoid micromanagement. Effective organizations support this by ensuring roles and tasks contribute to progress that matters. Clarity and autonomy together create the conditions for that progress.

4. Feedback and Recognition as a Daily Practice
   Recognition is not a luxury—it is a powerful engagement lever. Organizations that embed continuous feedback and recognition into their culture enjoy better retention, productivity, and morale. Towers Watson (2014) found that companies with effective recognition programs had 31% lower voluntary turnover.
   Recognition should be both manager-led and peer-enabled, tailored to individual preferences, and linked to contributions that reflect company values and purpose.

5. Growth, Learning, and Career Momentum
   Few things disengage employees faster than feeling stuck. Growth-minded cultures offer both vertical and lateral development, promote from within, and empower people to take ownership of their career paths.
   At IBM, the Think Academy initiative promotes continuous learning and open communication across its global workforce, helping to strengthen alignment and employee connection (IBM, 2020). Growth isn't just about training—it's about opportunity, visibility, and challenge.

6. Team Cohesion and Psychological Safety
   People don't engage with companies; they engage with teams. Strong, inclusive, and collaborative teams foster higher performance and deeper emotional commitment. Google's Project Aristotle found that psychological safety—the belief that team members can speak up without fear—was the number one predictor of team effectiveness (Rozovsky, 2015).

   Well-functioning teams are built on mutual respect, clearly defined roles, and shared goals. Investing in team dynamics is investing in engagement.

7. Well-being and Flexibility
   Sustained engagement is impossible when employees are burnt out. Organizations must prioritize **mental, physical, and emotional well-being** as part of their core culture—not as an afterthought.

   Deloitte (2023) reports that well-being is now a top-three driver of both retention and engagement. Flexible work arrangements, wellness resources, and empathetic leadership are no longer optional—they are essential infrastructure for an engaged workforce.

8. Data-Driven and Employee-Led Improvement
   Sustaining engagement requires listening—and acting. Companies must measure engagement regularly, track trends over time, and involve employees in shaping the solutions. When employees see their feedback driving action, engagement becomes self-reinforcing.

The best organizations move beyond annual surveys to embrace real-time pulse checks, transparent reporting, and accountability at all leadership levels. Engagement metrics should be integrated into regular performance measurements and leadership evaluations.

Kate Milkman (2021) makes some key points on how to make changes happen and become permanent, and these basic principles are helpful for both individuals as well as for organizations. She points out that an ideal time to consider pursuing change is after a "fresh start." For individuals such starts can be a new year, a birthday, a new location, or a stage of life. Even though real "fresh starts" in organizations may not be so clear, new strategic initiatives, structural or ownership changes offer similar possibilities. However, such opportunities are often, unfortunately, not utilized to their fullest potential when they are not combined with initiatives and changes to improve employee motivation and engagement.

In one of our recent organizations, we worked with a customer service organization on a new initiative to provide a more fluent service offering, with a significant promise to the customer. To make the new initiative a reality, it was clear that employee engagement was paramount. Combining our "empowering engagement" initiative for individuals, leaders, and teams with the new significant organizational initiative made a significantly better platform for making a change for higher engagement, and for continuity for both initiatives. Timing of change does make a difference.

Final Thought: Engagement as a Way of Life

However, sustained engagement is not about programs—it is about principles, behaviors, and culture. It is about creating a workplace where people feel that their contribution matters, their growth is valued, and their voices are heard. Engagement is not a goal to be achieved, but a culture and relationship to be nurtured—between people, teams, leaders, customers, and the mission they serve together.

In the end, the organizations that win are not those with the biggest budgets or flashiest perks—but those that consistently and authentically create a place where people choose to give their best.

Key Questions
1. What has been your experience in attempting to make permanent changes in your own life?
2. What have been your experiences in trying to make permanent changes in your organization?
3. What principles have aided your personal and/or organizational changes to become permanent?
4. Why would it help combining programs to improve employee engagement with significant strategic company initiatives?
5. Overall, how important do you think improving employee engagement in your organization will be in the future?

References

Introduction

ActivTrak (2024). *Exploring the True Cost of Disengaged Employees*, July 4. https://www.activtrak.com/blog/cost-of-disengaged-employees/

Afrahi, B., Blenkinsopp, J., Fernandez de Arroyabe, J. C., & Karim, M. S. (2022). Work disengagement: A review of the literature. *Human Resource Management Review*, 32(2), 100822.

Gallup (2013). *State of the Global Workplace: Employee Engagement Insights for Business Leaders Worldwide*. Washington, DC: Gallup.

Gallup (2015). *State of the American Manager: Analytics and Advice for Leaders*. Washington, DC: Gallup Press.

Gallup (2020). *State of the Global Workplace Report*. Washington, DC: Gallup Press.

Gallup (2022). *State of the Global Workplace: 2022 Report*. Washington, DC: Gallup.

Gallup (2025) *State of the Global Workplace: 2025 Report*. Washington, DC: Gallup. Available at: https://www.gallup.com/workplace/349484/state-of-the-global-workplace.aspx

Harter, J.K., Schmidt, F.L. & Hayes, T.L. (2002). Business-unit-level relationship between employee satisfaction, employee engagement, and business outcomes: a meta-analysis. *Journal of Applied Psychology*, 87(2), 268–279.

Kahn, W.A. (1990). Psychological conditions of personal engagement and disengagement at work. *Academy of Management Journal*, 33(4), 692–724.

Klotz, A. (2021) cited in *Bloomberg* (2021). *Why the Great Resignation Is a "Great Renegotiation."* Bloomberg, 15 November.

Kruse, K. E. (2012) *Employee Engagement 2.0: How to Motivate Your Team for High Performance – A "Real-World" Guide for Busy Managers*. Richboro, PA: The Kruse Group.

Mvuyana,S., Nzimakwe, T. I. & Utete,R. (2025). Exploring the relationship between employee engagement and counterproductive work behaviour. *Frontiers in Psychology, 15:143450*

Pitonyak, J., DeSimone, R., Wigert, B. & Nelson, B. (2024). *How to Engage Frontline Managers*. Gallup. 2024.

Schaufeli, W.B., Bakker, A.B. & Salanova, M. (2006). The measurement of work engagement with a short questionnaire: A cross-national study. *Educational and Psychological Measurement*, 66(4), 701–716.

Chapter 1

Collins, J. (2001). *Good to Great: Why Some Companies Make the Leap . . . and Others Don't*. New York: Harper Business.

Conant, D.R. (n.d.). *The Campbell Soup Story*. Available at: https://conantleadership.com/the-campbell-soup-story/

Felps, W., Mitchell, T.R. & Byington, E. (2006). How, when, and why bad apples spoil the barrel: Negative group members and dysfunctional groups. *Research in Organizational Behavior*, 27, 175–222.

Gallup (2020). *The Relationship Between Engagement at Work and Organizational Outcomes: 2020 Q12 Meta-Analysis*. Gallup, Inc.

Gallup (2024). *U.S. Employee Engagement Stagnates at 32%*. Gallup Workplace Article, 22 January. Available at: https://www.gallup.com/workplace/608675/new-workplace-employee-engagement-stagnates.aspx.

Gallup (2024). *State of the Global Workplace: 2024 Report*. Gallup, Inc.

Gallup (2025a). *Global Employee Engagement Falls for Only the Second Time Since 2009*. Gallup Workplace, 6 February.

Gallup (2025b). *Indicator: Employee Retention & Attraction – Top Reasons for Leaving a Job*. Gallup Workplace.
Hadley, C.N. & Wright, S.L. (2024). We're still lonely at work. *Harvard Business Review*, November–December.
Joly, H. (2021). *The Heart of Business: Leadership Principles for the Next Era of Capitalism*. Boston: Harvard Business Review Press.
Kahn, W.A. (1990). Psychological conditions of personal engagement and disengagement at work. *Academy of Management Journal*, 33(4), 692–724.
Lohr, S. (2017). *Satya Nadella Rewrites Microsoft's Code. The New York Times*, 24 June.
PeopleThriver (2025). *The 2025 Engagement Retention Report*. PeopleThriver, Inc.
Piscioni, D.P. & Drean, J. (2025). *Employment Is Dead*. Boston: Harvard Business Review Press.
Robertson, I.T. & Cooper, C.L. (2010). Full engagement: the integration of employee engagement and psychological well-being. *Leadership & Organization Development Journal*, 31(4), 324–336.
Schein, E.H. (2010). *Organizational Culture and Leadership*. 4th edn. San Francisco: Jossey-Bass.
Steger, M.F., Dik, B.J. & Duffy, R.D. (2012). Measuring meaningful work: The Work and Meaning Inventory (WAMI). *Journal of Career Assessment*, 20(3), 322–337.

Chapter 2

Aon Hewitt (2018). *2018 Trends in Global Employee Engagement*. Aon Hewitt.
Conant Leadership (2015).Speaker Sheet, https://conantleadership.com/wp-content/uploads/2015/12/speaker_sheet_final1-2.pdf?utm_source=chatgpt.com
Gallup (n.d.) *Employee Engagement – What We Measure*. Available at: https://www.gallup.com/394373/indicator-employee-engagement.aspx
Gallup (2013) *State of the American Workplace: Employee Engagement Insights for U.S. Business Leaders*, Gallup.
Gallup (2014). "Why great managers are so rare." *Gallup Workplace News*, 13 March.
Gallup (2020). *State of the Global Workplace: 2020 Report*. Washington, DC: Gallup, Inc.
Gallup (2021). *State of the Global Workplace: 2021 Report*. Washington, DC: Gallup, Inc.
Gallup (2022). *State of the Global Workplace: 2022 Report*. Washington, DC: Gallup, Inc.
Gallup (2023). *Employee Engagement Strategies: How to Build a More Engaged Workforce*. Gallup, Inc.
Gallup (2024). *State of the Global Workplace: 2024 Report*. Washington, DC: Gallup, Inc.
Gallup (2024) 'Global Indicator: Employee Engagement', Gallup. Available at: https://www.gallup.com/394373/indicator-employee-engagement.aspx
Gallup (2025). *U.S. Employee Engagement Stagnates at 33%*. Gallup Workplace, 25 January.
InStride (2022). *The cost of employee disengagement*. InStride, 26 April.
Kruse, K. (2012). *Employee Engagement 2.0: How to Motivate Your Team for High Performance*. New York: The Kruse Group.
Saks, A.M. (2006). Antecedents and consequences of employee engagement. *Journal of Managerial Psychology*, 21(7), 600–619.
Sinek, S. (n.d.) *"When people are financially invested, they want a return. When people are emotionally invested, they want to contribute."* Available at: https://simonsinek.com/quotes/
Sinek, S. (2009). *Start with Why: How Great Leaders Inspire Everyone to Take Action*. New York: Portfolio/Penguin.
The Engagement Institute (2017). *The Cost of Disengaged Employees: Research Report*. The Engagement Institute (a collaboration of The Conference Board, Sirota, Deloitte, ROI, The Culture Works, and Consulting LLP).

Chapter 3

Bakker, A.B. & Demerouti, E. (2008). Towards a model of work engagement. *Career Development International*, 13(3), 209–223.

Harter, J.K., Schmidt, F.L. & Hayes, T.L. (2002). Business-unit-level relationship between employee satisfaction, employee engagement, and business outcomes: a meta-analysis. *Journal of Applied Psychology*, 87(2), 268–279.

Heskett, J.L., Jones, T.O., Loveman, G.W., Sasser, W.E. & Schlesinger, L.A. (1994). Putting the service-profit chain to work. *Harvard Business Review*, 72(2), 164–174.

Kahn, W.A. (1990). Psychological conditions of personal engagement and disengagement at work. *Academy of Management Journal*, 33(4), 692–724.

Markos, S. & Sridevi, M.S. (2010). Employee engagement: the key to improving performance. *International Journal of Business and Management*, 5(12), 89–96.

May, D.R., Gilson, R.L. & Harter, L.M. (2004). The psychological conditions of meaningfulness, safety and availability and the engagement of the human spirit at work, *Journal of Occupational and Organizational Psychology*, 77(1), 11–37.

Mazzetti, G., Vignoli, M., Schaufeli, W.B. & Guglielmi, D. (2022). A multilevel study on the relationships between engaging leadership, team resources, and work engagement: The mediating role of team resources. *PLoS ONE*, 17(6), 1–25

Rucci, A.J., Kirn, S.P. & Quinn, R.T. (1998). The employee-customer-profit chain at Sears. *Harvard Business Review*, 76(1), 82–97.

Saks, A.M. (2006). Antecedents and consequences of employee engagement. *Journal of Managerial Psychology*, 21(7), 600–619.

Salanova, M., Agut, S. & Peiró, J.M. (2005). Linking organizational resources and work engagement to employee performance and customer loyalty: the mediation of service climate. *Journal of Applied Psychology*, 90(6), 1217–1227.

Sinek, S. (2009). *Start with Why: How Great Leaders Inspire Everyone to Take Action*. New York: Portfolio/Penguin.

Xu, J. & Thomas, H.C. (2011). How can leaders achieve high employee engagement? *Leadership & Organization Development Journal*, 32(4), 399–416.

Chapter 5

Bakker, A.B. & Demerouti, E. (2008). Towards a model of work engagement. *Career Development International*, 13(3), 209–223.

Bailey, C. & Madden, A. (2016). *What makes work meaningful — or meaningless. MIT Sloan Management Review*, 57(4), 53–61.

Bandura, A. (1997). *Self-Efficacy: The Exercise of Control*. New York: W.H. Freeman.

Bernstein, E., Sandino, T., Minnaar, J. & Lobb, A. (2022). *Buurtzorg*. Harvard Business School Case, 122-101, June 2022 (revised January 2023).

Bredehorst, J., Krautter, K., Meuris, J. & Jachimowicz, J. M. (2024). *The Challenge of Maintaining Passion for Work Over Time: A Daily Perspective on Passion and Emotional Exhaustion*. Organization Science, 35(1), 364–386.

Cascio, W.F. (2019). *Managing Human Resources: Productivity, Quality of Work Life, Profits* (11th ed.). New York: McGraw-Hill Education.

Costa, A.C., Roe, R.A. & Taillieu, T. (2001). Trust within teams: The relation with performance effectiveness. *European Journal of Work and Organizational Psychology*, 10(3), 225–244.

Deci, E.L. & Ryan, R.M. (2000). The "what" and "why" of goal pursuits: Human needs and the self-determination of behavior. *Psychological Inquiry*, 11(4), 227–268.

Delizonna, L. (2017). "High-Performing Teams Need Psychological Safety: Here's How to Create It." *Harvard Business Review*, August 24, 2017.

Dweck, C.S. (2006). *Mindset: The New Psychology of Success*. New York: Random House.

Edmondson, A.C. (1999). Psychological safety and learning behavior in work teams. *Administrative Science Quarterly*, 44(2), 350–383.

Gallup (2020). *State of the Global Workplace Report*. Washington, DC: Gallup Press.

Kahn, W.A. (1990). Psychological conditions of personal engagement and disengagement at work. *Academy of Management Journal*, 33(4), 692–724.

Kerr, J.M. (2025). Use psychological ownership to gain better staff engagement. *Psychology Today*, June 28, 2024.

Latham, G.P. (2004). The motivational benefits of goal-setting. *Academy of Management Executive*, 18(4), 126–129.

Locke, E.A. & Latham, G.P. (2002). Building a practically useful theory of goal setting and task motivation: A 35-year odyssey. *American Psychologist*, 57(9), 705–717.

London, M. & Smither, J.W. (1999). Empowered self-development and continuous learning. *Human Resource Management*, 38(1), 3–15.

Lysova, E. I., Fletcher, L. & El Baroudi, S. (2023). What makes work meaningful? *Harvard Business Review*, 12 July. Available at: https://hbr.org/2023/07/what-makes-work-meaningful

Macey, W.H. & Schneider, B. (2008). The meaning of employee engagement. *Industrial and Organizational Psychology*, 1(1), 3–30.

Moreira, A., Encarnação, T., Viseu, J. & Sousa, M.J. (2022). Job crafting and job performance: The mediating effect of engagement. *Sustainability*, 14(22), 14909.

Perna, M. (2023). Why Younger Employees Will Switch Jobs for an Employer Who Invests in Them. *Forbes*, February 14.

Roberson, Q.M. (2006). Disentangling the meanings of diversity and inclusion in organizations. *Group & Organization Management*, 31(2), 212–236.

Rosso, B.D., Dekas, K.H. & Wrzesniewski, A. (2010). On the meaning of work: A theoretical integration and review. *Research in Organizational Behavior*, 30, 91–127.

Saks, A.M. (2006). Antecedents and consequences of employee engagement. *Journal of Managerial Psychology*, 21(7), 600–619.

Shore, L.M., Cleveland, J.N. & Sanchez, D. (2011). Inclusive workplaces: A review and model. *Human Resource Management Review*, 21(4), 311–326.

Training Magazine (2022). How Learning and Development Can Help Keep Younger Employees Engaged.

Whitener, E.M., Brodt, S.E., Korsgaard, M.A. & Werner, J.M. (1998). Managers as initiators of trust: An exchange relationship framework for understanding managerial trustworthy behavior. *Academy of Management Review*, 23(3), 513–530.

Wrzesniewski, A. & Dutton, J. E. (2001). *Crafting a job: Revisioning employees as active crafters of their work*. Academy of Management Review, 26(2), 179–201.

Wrzesniewski, A., Dutton, J. E. & Debebe, G. (2003). *Interpersonal sensemaking and the meaning of work*. In K. S. Cameron, J. E. Dutton & R. E. Quinn (eds.), *Positive Organizational Scholarship* (pp. 93–112). San Francisco: Berrett-Koehler.

Chapter 6

Achievers Workforce Institute. (2020). *2020 Culture Report: Culture Continuity and Employee Engagement During COVID-19*. Achievers.

Bock, L. (2015). *Work Rules!: Insights from Inside Google That Will Transform How You Live and Lead*. New York: Twelve.

Cappelli, P. & Tavis, A. (2016). "The performance management revolution." *Harvard Business Review*, 94(10), pp. 58–67.

Catmull, E. & Wallace, A. (2014). *Creativity, Inc.: Overcoming the Unseen Forces That Stand in the Way of True Inspiration*. New York: Random House.

Chouinard, Y. (2016). *Let My People Go Surfing: The Education of a Reluctant Businessman*. Revised and expanded ed. New York: Penguin.

Cross, R., Rebele, R. & Grant, A. (2016) 'Collaborative Overload', *Harvard Business Review*, 94(1/2), pp. 74–79.

Deci, E.L. & Ryan, R.M. (2000) 'The "What" and "Why" of Goal Pursuits: Human Needs and the Self-Determination of Behavior', *Psychological Inquiry*, 11(4), pp. 227–268.

Delizonna, L. (2017). High-Performing Teams Need Psychological Safety: Here's How to Create It. *Harvard Business Review*, 1 August.

Edmondson, A.C. (1999) 'Psychological Safety and Learning Behavior in Work Teams', *Administrative Science Quarterly*, 44(2), pp. 350–383.

Eskreis-Winkler, L., Milkman, K.L., Gromet, D.M., & Duckworth, A.L. (2016). 'Knowing what to do, but failing to do it: Self-control and the brain–behavior gap', *Psychological Science*, 27(7), pp. 995–1006

Gallup. (2023) *How to improve employee engagement in the workplace*.

Gallup (2025) *Global employee engagement falls for only the second time since 2009*. Gallup Workplace, 6 February.

Ge, Y. (2020). *Psychological safety, employee voice, and work engagement. Social Behavior and Personality: an international journal*, 48(3), 1–7.

Harvard Business Review (2024). 'Managers have an innate capacity for exemplary leadership', *Harvard Business Review*, 15 March.

Harvard Business Review (2025). 'Empathy is a core leadership skill', *Harvard Business Review*, 5 May.

Hattie, J. & Timperley, H. (2007). *The power of feedback*. Review of Educational Research, 77(1), pp. 81–112.

Heinz, K. (2023) '6 Reasons Why Employee Development Is Key', *Built In*. Available at: https://builtin.com/company-culture/employee-development.

HiPeople. (2023) 'What is Company Culture? Strategies, Examples', *HiPeople*.

Hirsch, A.S. (2023) 'From Work/Life Balance to Work/Life Integration', *SHRM*, 4 May.

Incentive Research Foundation (2018) *The impact of tangible employee rewards*. St. Louis, MO: Incentive Research Foundation.

Kahn, W.A. (1990). 'Psychological Conditions of Personal Engagement and Disengagement at Work', *Academy of Management Journal*, 33(4), pp. 692–724.

Kaplan (2025) *'13 Effective Ways to Create a More Connected Workplace'*. LumApps Insights. Available at: https://www.lumapps.com/digital-workplace/how-to-create-a-connected-workplace.

Katzenbach, J.R. & Smith, D.K. (2015). *The Wisdom of Teams: Creating the High-Performance Organization*. Boston: Harvard Business Review Press.

Kohn, A. (1993). *Why incentive plans cannot work. Harvard Business Review*, 71(5), 54–63.

Locke, E.A. & Latham, G.P. (2002) 'Building a practically useful theory of goal setting and task motivation: A 35-year odyssey', *American Psychologist*, 57(9), pp. 705–717.

LumApps (2023). 'Improve knowledge sharing: The key to employee productivity', *LumApps*.

Macey, W.H. & Schneider, B. (2008) 'The Meaning of Employee Engagement', *Industrial and Organizational Psychology*, 1(1), pp. 3–30.

Matschnig, G. (2025) *Statement on voluntary reporting and safety data*, International Air Transport Association (IATA).
Park, S., Kong, D.T. & Peng, J. (2024) 'Pay-for-performance doesn't have to stress workers out', *Harvard Business Review*, 17 October.
Roberson, Q.M. (2006). 'Disentangling the meanings of diversity and inclusion in organizations', *Group & Organization Management*, 31(2), pp. 212–236.
alentGuard (2023). 'Why employee development often takes a back seat to operations', *TalentGuard Blog*.
Time (2024) 'Time to Take a Breathing Break at Work', *Time*, 8 July.
Wadhwa, H. (2024). *Leading in the Flow of Work. Harvard Business Review*, 102(1), 74–81.
Walters, K. N., & Diab, D. L. (2016). *Humble Leadership: Implications for Psychological Safety and Follower Engagement. Journal of Leadership Studies*, 10(2), 7–18.
Walton, G. M., & Cohen, G. L. (2023, August 17). *3 Ways Teachers Can Instill Belonging in Students*. Time Magazine.

Chapter 7

Brown, T. (2009). *Change by Design: How Design Thinking Creates New Alternatives for Business and Society*. New York: Harper Business.
Brownell, J. (1990). *Perceptions of effective listeners: A management study. Journal of Business Communication*, 27(4), 401–415.
Business Insider (2024). How Satya Nadella turned Microsoft into a powerhouse by investing early in AI and backing OpenAI. *Business Insider*, 27 July.
Costa, A.C. (2003). Work team trust and effectiveness. *Personnel Review*, 32(5), 605–622.
Costa, A.C., Roe, R.A. & Taillieu, T. (2001). Trust within teams: The relation with performance effectiveness. *European Journal of Work and Organizational Psychology*, 10(3), 225–244.
Covey, S.R. (2004). *The 7 Habits of Highly Effective People: Powerful Lessons in Personal Change*. Simon & Schuster.
Cross, R., Rebele, R. & Grant, A. (2016). Collaborative overload. *Harvard Business Review*, 94(1), 74–79.
Delizonna, L. (2017). High-performing teams need psychological safety. Here's how to create it. *Harvard Business Review*, 24 August.
Duhigg, C. (2016). What Google Learned From Its Quest to Build the Perfect Team. *The New York Times Magazine*, February 25.
Edmondson, A.C. (1999). Psychological safety and learning behavior in work teams. *Administrative Science Quarterly*, 44(2), 350–383.
Frazier, M.L., Fainshmidt, S., Klinger, R.L., Pezeshkan, A. & Vracheva, V. (2017). Psychological safety: A meta-analytic review and extension. *Personnel Psychology*, 70(1), 113–165.
Gallup (2023). *State of the Global Workplace: 2023 Report*. Washington, DC: Gallup.
Gittell, J.H. (2003). *The Southwest Airlines Way: Using the Power of Relationships to Achieve High Performance*. McGraw-Hill Education.
Harvard Business Review (2025). Empathy Is a Core Leadership Skill. *Harvard Business Review*, 5 May.
Katzenbach, J.R. & Smith, D.K. (2015). *The Wisdom of Teams: Creating the High-Performance Organization*. Harvard Business Review Press.
Kock, N., Mayfield, M., Mayfield, J., Sexton, S. & De La Garza, L.M. (2019). Empathetic leadership: How leader emotional support and understanding fosters follower performance. *Journal of Leadership & Organizational Studies*, 26(2), 217–236.
Nadella, S. & Shaw, G. (2017). *Hit Refresh: The Quest to Rediscover Microsoft's Soul and Imagine a Better Future for Everyone*. New York: Harper Business.

Neale, P. (2025). Empathy is a non-negotiable leadership skill. Here's how to practice it. *Harvard Business Review*, 30 April. Available at: https://hbr.org/2025/04/empathy-is-a-non-negotiable-leadership-skill-heres-how-to-practice-itNewman A., Donohue R., & Eva, N. (2017). Psychological safety: A systematic review of the literature. *Human Resource Management Review*, 27(3), 521–535.

Roberson, Q.M. (2006). Disentangling the meanings of diversity and inclusion in organizations. *Group & Organization Management*, 31(2), 212–236.

Rozovsky, J. (2015). *The five keys to a successful Google team*. Google re:Work.

Wired (2017). Satya Nadella Rewrites Microsoft's Code. *Wired*, 26 September.

Chapter 8

Accenture (2022). *Inclusion and Diversity Report 2022*. Accenture.

Amabile, T.M. & Kramer, S.J. (2011). *The Progress Principle: Using Small Wins to Ignite Joy, Engagement, and Creativity at Work*. Boston, MA: Harvard Business Review Press.

Bersin, J. (2014). *High-Impact Learning Culture: The 40 Best Practices for Creating an Empowered Enterprise*. Oakland, CA: Bersin & Associates.

Bersin, J. (2019). *The company as a talent network: Unilever and Schneider Electric show the way*. Josh Bersin, 17 July.

Blanchard, K. & Johnson, S. (2015). *The New One Minute Manager*. New York: William Morrow.

Bock, L. (2015). *Work Rules!: Insights from Inside Google That Will Transform How You Live and Lead*. New York: Twelve.

Bourke, J. & Dillon, B. (2018). The diversity and inclusion revolution: Eight powerful truths. *Deloitte Review*, 22, 82–95.

Cappelli, P. & Tavis, A. (2016). The performance management revolution. *Harvard Business Review*, 94(10), 58–67.

Colquitt, J.A., Conlon, D.E., Wesson, M.J., Porter, C.O.L.H. & Ng, K.Y. (2001). Justice at the millennium: A meta-analytic review of 25 years of organizational justice research. *Journal of Applied Psychology*, 86(3), 425–445.

Conant, D.R. (2011). *TouchPoints: Creating Powerful Leadership Connections in the Smallest of Moments*. San Francisco: Jossey-Bass.

Covey, S.R. (1989). *The 7 Habits of Highly Effective People: Powerful Lessons in Personal Change*. New York: Free Press.

Deloitte (2017). *Diversity and Inclusion: The Reality Gap*. Deloitte University Press.

Department of Management Strategy, Policy and Compliance (DMSPC)/Office of Human Resources (OHR) (2023). *Compendium of Good Recognition and Rewards Practices in the UN Secretariat*.

Dhingra, N., Samo, A., Schaninger, B. & Schrimper, M. (2021). *Help your employees find purpose—or watch them leave*. McKinsey & Company, 5 April.

Gasta, M. R. (2016) *Driving employee engagement through greater purpose*. Doctoral dissertation, Pepperdine University. Available at: https://digitalcommons.pepperdine.edu/etd/664.

Gallup (2023). *State of the Global Workplace: 2023 Report*. Washington, DC: Gallup.

Harvard Business Review (2017). How Adobe structures feedback to drive performance. *Harvard Business Review*, 12 July.

IBM (2020). *Think Academy: Cultivating a learning and communication culture at IBM*. IBM.

LinkedIn (2023). *2023 Workplace Learning Report*. LinkedIn Learning.

Rosso, B.D., Dekas, K.H. & Wrzesniewski, A. (2010). On the meaning of work: A theoretical integration and review. *Research in Organizational Behavior*, 30, 91–127.

Salesforce (2019). *Annual Report and Accounts 2019*. London: Unilever.
Salesforce (2021). *Annual Equality Update 2021*. Salesforce.
Salesforce (2022). *Annual Equality Update: Accelerating progress*.
theEmployeeApp (2025). *Good employer and employee communication: The gold standard*. theEmployeeApp Blog, 7 June.
Towers Watson (2014). *Capitalizing on Effective Communication: How Courage, Innovation and Discipline Drive Business Results. 2013–2014 Change and Communication ROI Study Report*. Towers Watson.
Unilever (2019). *Annual Report and Accounts 2019*. London: Unilever.
Workhuman (2018). *Cisco: Connect People and Transform Culture*.

Chapter 9

Alabi, O.A., Ajayi, F.A., Udeh, C.A. & Efunniyi, C.P. (2024). Data-driven employee engagement: A pathway to superior customer service. *World Journal of Advanced Research and Reviews*, 23(03), 923–933. Available at: https://www.researchgate.net/publication/384141853.
Drucker, P.F. (2001). *The Essential Drucker: The Best of Sixty Years of Peter Drucker's Essential Writings on Management*. New York: HarperBusiness.
Gallup (2020). *State of the Global Workplace*. Gallup Press. Available at: https://www.gallup.com/workplace/257552/state-global-workplace-2020.aspx.
Harter, J.K., Schmidt, F.L. & Hayes, T.L. (2002). Business-unit-level relationship between employee satisfaction, employee engagement, and business outcomes: a meta-analysis. *Journal of Applied Psychology*, 87(2), 268–279.
IDC. (2023). Employee Experience and Customer Experience: The New Business Imperative. Available at: https://www.idc.com.
Lindblom, A., Kautto, M. & Mitronen, L. (2025). *Kaikkikanavainen kauppa*. Helsinki: Alma Insights.
Matsuda, A. (2025). Boosting CX through employee engagement: How 5 industry leaders are winning the workforce game. *NICE*. Available at: https://www.nice.com/blog/boosting-cx-through-employee-engagement-how-5-industry-leaders-are-winning-the-workforce-game.
Mittal, V., Han, K. & Westbrook, R.A. (2018). Customer Engagement and Employee Engagement: A Research Review and Agenda, in Palmatier, R.W. et al. (eds.) *Customer Engagement Marketing*. Cham: Springer, 173–200. Available at: https://link.springer.com/content/pdf/10.1007/978-3-319-61985-9_8.pdf.
Pavithra, S., Spoorthy, A.R. & Asha, K.C. (2018). Customer centricity for employee engagement: A new frontier in HRM. *International Journal of Research in Engineering, IT and Social Sciences*, 8(Special Issue), 71–80. Available at: https://indusedu.org/pdfs/IJREISS/IJREISS_1842_43724.pdf.
Repec (2020). Customer engagement and employee engagement: systematic review and research directions. *The Service Industries Journal*, 40(13–14), 932–959.
Rintamäki, T. (2016). *Managing Customer Value in Retailing – An Integrative Perspective*. Tampere: University of Tampere.
Robinson, D., Perryman, S. & Hayday, S. (2004). *The Drivers of Employee Engagement*. Brighton: Institute for Employment Studies.
Robertson-Smith, G. & Markwick, C. (2009). *Employee Engagement: A Review of Current Thinking*. Brighton: Institute for Employment Studies. Available at: https://www.employment-studies.co.uk/system/files/resources/files/469.pdf.
Saks, A.M. (2006). Antecedents and consequences of employee engagement. *Journal of Managerial Psychology*, 21(7), 600–619.

Yohn, D.L. (2023). Engaged Employees Create Better Customer Experiences. *Harvard Business Review*, 5 April. Available at: https://hbr.org/2023/04/engaged-employees-create-better-customer-experiences.

Chapter 10

15Five (2024) 'How to Recognize Employee Disengagement in the Workplace (And What to Do About It)', 15Five blog. Available at: https://www.15five.com/blog/how-to-recognize-employee-disengagement-in-the-workplace-and-what-to-do-about-it/.Alton

Alton,L. (2024). *Warning signs of employee disengagement*. Forbes, 6 March. Available at: https://www.forbes.com (Accessed: 21 August 2025).

Costa, A.C., Roe, R.A. & Taillieu, T. (2001). Trust within teams: The relation with trust, monitoring, and team performance. *The International Journal of Human Resource Management*, 12(2), 227–245.

Cross, R., Rebele, R. & Grant, A. (2016). Collaborative overload. *Harvard Business Review*, 94(1), 74–79.

CultureMonkey (2025). How does employee disengagement impact attrition? *CultureMonkey*, 2 May. Available at: https://www.culturemonkey.io/employee-engagement/disengaged-employees/.

De Smet, A., Mugayar-Baldocchi, M., Reich, A. & Schaninger, B. (2023). *Some employees are destroying value. Others are building it. Do you know the difference?* McKinsey & Company, McKinsey Quarterly, 11 September.

Edmondson, A.C. (1999). Psychological safety and learning behavior in work teams. *Administrative Science Quarterly*, 44(2), 350–383.

Frazier, M.L., Fainshmidt, S., Klinger, R.L., Pezeshkan, A. & Vracheva, V. (2017). Psychological safety: A meta-analytic review and extension. *Personnel Psychology*, 70(1), 113–165.

Gallup (2023). *State of the Global Workplace: 2023 Report*. Washington, DC: Gallup.

Gallup (2024). *State of the Global Workplace: 2024 Report*. Washington, DC: Gallup.

Goleman, D. (2000). *Working with Emotional Intelligence*. New York: Bantam.

Harter, J. (2022). *Disengagement Persists Among U.S. Employees*. Gallup Workplace Report.

PeopleHR (2024). *7 Signs of Disengaged Employees and How to Motivate Them*. PeopleHR Blog, 17 June. Available at: https://www.peoplehr.com/en-gb/resources/blog/signs-of-disengaged-employees/

Peter Barron Stark Companies (2024) *Rewarding Mediocrity Over Performers*, 23 July. Available at: https://peterstark.com/rewarding-mediocrity-over-performers/

Rastogi, A., Pati, S.P., Krishnan, T.N. & Krishnan, S. (2018). Causes, contingencies, and consequences of disengagement at work: An integrative literature review. *Human Resource Development Review*, 17(1), pp. 62–94.

SHRM (2024) *7 Strategies to Address Employee Disengagement*, SHRM. Available at: https://www.shrm.org/topics-tools/news/managing-smart/7-strategies-to-address-employee-disengagement

Teramind (2024). *Employee disengagement & productivity: The hidden toll*. Teramind Blog, 12 September. Available at: https://www.teramind.co/blog/how-does-employee-disengagement-influence-productivity/.

WebMD Health Services (2025). *7 signs of employee disengagement and how to solve it*. WebMD Health Services Blog, 26 February. Available at: https://www.webmdhealthservices.com/blog/signs-of-employee-disengagement/

Windon, S. (2023). *Employee Disengagement and the Impact of Leadership*. Penn State Extension.

Chapter 11

Amabile, T. & Kramer, S. (2011). *The Progress Principle: Using Small Wins to Ignite Joy, Engagement, and Creativity at Work*. Harvard Business Review Press.

Bass, B.M. & Avolio, B.J. (1990). *Transformational Leadership Development: Manual for the Multifactor Leadership Questionnaire*. Palo Alto, CA: Consulting Psychologists Press.

Been Remote (2024). *Remote Work Statistics: The Future of Work*. Available at: https://beenremote.com/remote-work-statistics.

Best Practice Institute (n.d.). Embracing Remote Work. Available at: https://blog.bestpracticeinstitute.org/embracing-remote-work.

Bloom, N., Liang, J., Roberts, J. & Ying, Z.J. (2015). Does working from home work? Evidence from a Chinese experiment. *Quarterly Journal of Economics*, 130(1), 165–218.

Day, A. (2025). *Remote Work Benefits for Employers*. Remote.com. Available.at: https://remote.com/blog/benefits/remote-work-benefits-for-employers.

Deloitte (2023). *2023 Global Human Capital Trends: New Fundamentals for a Boundaryless World*. Deloitte Insights.

Fatima, H., Javaid, Z.K., Arshad, Z., Ashraf, M. and Batool, H. (2024) 'A Systematic Review on the Impact of Remote Work on Employee Engagement', *Bulletin of Business and Economics*, 13(2), pp. 117–126. doi: 10.61506/01.00306.

FlexJobs (2024). *The Benefits of Remote Work for Employers and Employees*. Available at: https://www.flexjobs.com/blog/post/benefits-of-remote-work.

Forbes Advisor (2024). *Remote Work Statistics and Trends*. Available at: https://www.forbes.com/advisor/business/remote-work-statistics.

Fostervold, R., Ulleberg, P., Nilsen, M. & Halberg, T. (2024). The hidden costs of working from home: examining loneliness, role overload, and the role of social support during and beyond the COVID-19 lockdown. *Frontiers in Organizational Psychology*, April. DOI: 10.3389/forgp.2024.1380051.

Gallup (2025) *State of the Global Workplace*. Available at: https://www.gallup.com/workplace/349484/state-of-the-global-workplace.aspx (Accessed: 8 August 2025).

Gallup and WFH Research (2024). *Hybrid Work Insights*. Available at: https://wfhresearch.com.

Kahn, W.A. (1990). Psychological conditions of personal engagement and disengagement at work. *Academy of Management Journal*, 33(4), 692–724. iLab (2025): Available at: https://about.gitlab.com.

Madžak, A. (2025). *WORK2025: Työelämän murros digitalisaation ja tekoälyn aikakaudella*. LifeFactFuture-hanke, Turun yliopisto. Available at: https://sites.utu.fi/lifefactfuture/news/lff-work2025.

Microsoft (n.d.) *Employee Engagement Resources*. Available at: https://www.microsoft.com/en-us/microsoft-365/business-insights-ideas/resources/employee-engagement.

Neat (2024). *The State of Remote Work: 2024 Statistics*. Available at: https://neat.no/resources/top-remote-work-statistics.

Northouse, P.G. (2021). *Leadership: Theory and Practice. Leadership: Theory and Practice* (9th ed.). Thousand Oaks, CA: SAGE Publications.

Owl Labs (2024). *State of Remote Work Report*. Available at: https://www.owllabs.com/state-of-remote-work.

Prezi (2024). *Future of Work: Remote Work Trends*. Available at: https://prezi.com/blog/remote-work-trends.

Saks, A.M. (2006). Antecedents and consequences of employee engagement. *Journal of Managerial Psychology*, 21(7), 600–619.

Sweco Finland (2021). *Tulevaisuuden työ -raportti*. Available at: https://www.sweco.fi/wp-content/uploads/sites/7/2021/06/sweco_tulevaisuuden-tyo-raportti-2021.pdf.

Chapter 12

Bakker, A.B. & Demerouti, E. (2008). Towards a model of work engagement. *Career Development International*, 13(3), 209–223.

Bersin, J. (2019). Building a purpose-driven organization. *Josh Bersin Insights*.

Bersin, J. (2019). *AI Comes To HR: The Real Impact Of Artificial Intelligence On Human Resources*. Available at: https://joshbersin.com/2019/08/ai-comes-to-hr-the-real-impact-of-artificial-intelligence-on-human-resources/

Bessen, J. E. (2019). Automation and jobs: when technology boosts employment. *Economic Policy*, 34(100), pp. 585–615.

Chamorro-Premuzic, T. (2020). How to work with someone who's disengaged. *Harvard Business Review*, 98(2).

Chui, M., Manyika, J. & Miremadi, M. (2018). Notes from the AI frontier: Insights from hundreds of use cases. *McKinsey Global Institute Discussion Paper*. New York: McKinsey & Company.

Chui, M., Manyika, J. & Miremadi, M. (2018). What AI can and can't do (yet) for your business. *McKinsey Quarterly*.

Daugherty, P.R. & Wilson, H.J. (2018). *Human + Machine: Reimagining Work in the Age of AI*. Boston: Harvard Business Review Press.

Frey, C.B. & Osborne, M.A. (2017). The future of employment: How susceptible are jobs to computerisation?. *Technological Forecasting and Social Change*, 114, 254–280.

Gartner (2020). *Future of Work Trends Post-COVID-19*. Available at: https://www.gartner.com/en/articles/9-future-of-work-trends-post-covid-19

Gallup (2023). *State of the Global Workplace: 2023 Report*. Washington, DC: Gallup.

IBM (2020) *Think Academy: Cultivating a learning and communication culture at IBM*. Available at: https://www.ibm.com/blogs/think/think-academy/

Kahn, W.A. (1990). Psychological conditions of personal engagement and disengagement at work. *Academy of Management Journal*, 33(4), 692–724.

LinkedIn (2024). *2024 Workplace Learning Report*. Sunnyvale, CA: LinkedIn Learning.

Mateescu, A. & Nguyen, A. (2019). *Algorithmic Management in the Workplace*. Data & Society.

McKinsey & Company (2021). *The state of AI in 2021*. Available at: https://www.mckinsey.com/~/media/McKinsey/Business%20Functions/McKinsey%20Analytics/Our%20Insights/Global%20survey%20The%20state%20of%20AI%20in%202021/Global-survey-The-state-of-AI-in-2021.pdf

Chapter 13

Bryson, J.M., Crosby, B.C. & Bloomberg, L. (2014). *Public Value and Public Administration*. Washington, DC: Georgetown University Press.

Collins, J. (2001). *Good to Great: Why Some Companies Make the Leap . . . and Others Don't*. New York: Harper Business.

Drucker, P.F. (1990). *Managing the Non-Profit Organization: Principles and Practices*. New York: HarperCollins.

Gallup (2023). *State of the Global Workplace 2023 Report*. Washington, DC: Gallup.

Gallup (2025). *State of the Global Workplace 2025 Report*. Washington, DC: Gallup.

Felps, W., Mitchell, T.R. & Byington, E. (2006). How, when, and why bad apples spoil the barrel: Negative group members and dysfunctional groups. *Research in Organizational Behavior*, 27, 175–222.

Hofstede, G. (2001). *Culture's Consequences: Comparing Values, Behaviors, Institutions and Organizations Across Nations*. 2nd edn. Thousand Oaks, CA: Sage.

Inglehart, R. & Welzel, C. (2005). *Modernization, Cultural Change, and Democracy: The Human Development Sequence*. Cambridge: Cambridge University Press.
Kotter, J.P. (2012). *Leading Change*. Boston, MA: Harvard Business Review Press.
Lawrence, P.R. & Lorsch, J.W. (1967) *Organization and Environment: Managing Differentiation and Integration*. Boston, MA: Harvard Business School Press.
Lohr, S. (2017). Satya Nadella Rewrites Microsoft's Code. *The New York Times*, 24 June.
Raikaslehto, T., Mansukoski, S. & Mitronen, L. (2024). All About Management and Leadership – a Finnish perspective. Professional Publishing Finland.
Sarfraz, M., Bhutta, M. Khurrum & Ivascu, L. (2024). Leadership in cross-cultural contexts: Strategies for global success. *International Journal of Organizational Leadership*, 13 (First Special Issue 2024), 1–5.
Schein, E.H. (2010). *Organizational Culture and Leadership*. 4th edn. San Francisco: Jossey-Bass.
Sinek, S. (2019). *The Infinite Game*. New York: Portfolio/Penguin.

Chapter 14

Amabile, T.M. & Kramer, S.J. (2011). *The Progress Principle: Using Small Wins to Ignite Joy, Engagement, and Creativity at Work*. Boston, MA: Harvard Business Review Press.
Deloitte (2023). *2023 Global Human Capital Trends*. London: Deloitte.
Gallup (2023). *State of the Global Workplace 2023*. Washington, DC: Gallup.
IBM (2020). *Think Academy: Continuous Learning at IBM*. Armonk, NY: IBM Corporation.
Janssen, C. (1996). *The Four Rooms of Change: A Practical Everyday Psychology*. Stockholm: Claes Janssen Publishing.
Milkman, K. (2021). *How to Change: The Science of Getting from Where You Are to Where You Want to Be*. New York: Portfolio/Penguin.
PwC (2016). *Putting Purpose to Work: A Study of Purpose in the Workplace*. London: PwC.
Rozovsky, J. (2015). The five keys to a successful Google team, *re:Work* (Google). Mountain View, CA: Google.
Towers Watson (2014), *2014 Global Workforce Study*. New York: Towers Watson.

List of Figures

Figure I.1	Multidimensional representation of employee engagement —— 5	
Figure I.2	Annual cost of disengagement —— 7	
Figure 1.1	Improving organizational engagement across the five forces of engagement —— 12	
Figure 1.2	Global employee engagement (Gallup, 2023 vs. 2024) —— 15	
Figure 2.1	Multidimensional representation of employee engagement with the four levels of engagement —— 19	
Figure 3.1	Five forces of employee engagement —— 24	
Figure 4.1	The Model: Levels of and Five Forces of Engagement —— 31	
Figure 4.2	Comparison of Organizations —— 32	
Figure 4.3	Top and Bottom Quartile Engagement in the Same Organization —— 33	
Figure 4.4	Top and Bottom Quartile Engagement in the Same Organization —— 33	
Figure 4.5	Comparison of Groups in Different Engagement Level Groups—Department 1 —— 34	
Figure 4.6	Comparison of Groups in Different Engagement Level Groups—Department 2 —— 35	
Figure 4.7	Comparison of Engagement Profiles in Two Departments in the Same Retail Store —— 35	
Figure 4.8	Comparison of Employee Engagement in Two Similar Retail Stores in the Same Chain —— 36	
Figure 4.9	Comparison of Office and Factory Worker Engagements —— 36	
Figure 4.10	Comparison of Managers, Staff, and Factory Worker Engagement —— 37	
Figure 4.11	Example of an Individual Engagement Profile—Individual 1 —— 38	
Figure 4.12	Example of an Individual Engagement Profile—Individual 2 —— 38	
Figure 5.1	Multidimensional representation of employee engagement with individual PACT responsibility —— 44	
Figure 6.1	Multidimensional representation of employee engagement with leaders' IMPACT opportunities —— 63	
Figure 6.2	A typical example of engagement profiles for managers, office staff, and factory workers —— 64	
Figure 6.3	Managers vs. Individual Worker Engagement —— 64	
Figure 7.1	Multidimensional representation of employee engagement, focused on TEAMS responsibilities —— 88	
Figure 8.1	The five forces of engagement, with an emphasis on the company —— 98	
Figure 9.1	The five forces of engagement with emphasis on the customer —— 106	
Figure 10.1	A representation of Sam's engagement profile —— 119	
Figure 14.1	Four Rooms of change Model —— 152	

List of Tables

Table 5.1 Individual PACT actions to improve engagement —— **60**
Table 6.1 Leaders' actions supporting stronger employee engagement —— **86**
Table 7.1 Actions supporting stronger teams for engagement —— **97**

Index

accountability
- behaviors 50
- being trustworthy 52–53
- and collaboration 56
- encouraging 75–79
- engagement goals 103
- improving continuously 53
- and passion 53
- personal 148
- and responsibility 50
- taking ownership 51–52

Achievers Workforce Institute 68
actively disengaged employee
- causes of 121–122
- culture of engagement 117
- dealing with 122–124
- "disgruntled and disloyal" 117
- identifying 120–121
- leaders and managers, ten strategies for 122–124
- successes and failures 118–120
- workplace 150

adaptive learning platforms 133
Alabi, O.A. 108
Amabile, T.M. 102, 128, 154
Amazon and Workplace Intelligence 56
artificial intelligence (AI)
- adoption, individual opportunities in 137–138
- designing engagement 135–136
- empowering potential 132–133
- human side 139
- impact 134–135
- improving teamwork 138–139
- leadership capabilities 136–137
- risk of disengagement 133–134

Autism Hiring Program 103
autonomy factor 21, 25–27, 52, 58–59, 76–77, 83, 113, 121, 123, 132–135, 139–140, 143, 154

Bakker, A.B. 6, 27, 45, 55, 58, 133
Bandura, A. 59
Bersin, J. 99, 101, 135
Brazil corporate culture 144
building relationships 54–56

Campbell Soup Company 16, 22, 100
"Career Customization" framework 85

Cascio, W.F. 46
Chinese business culture 144
choice to engage
- accountability (*See* accountability)
- collaboration 53–56
- culture of engagement 43
- exceeding expectations 49–50
- finding joy 48–49
- meaningful work 46–48
- passion 46–50
- responsibility 43–46
- transformation 56–61

Clifton, J. 2
cognitive crafting 49
collaboration
- activities 53
- behaviors 54
- building relationships 55
- cross-functional 21, 135
- digital tools 129
- effective communication 55–56
- and individual engagement 55
- social environment 53
- spirit of engagement 61
- and teamwork 54
- valuing diversity 54

commitment to succeed acts 96–97
Communication ROI Study (Watson) 104
company impact on engagement
- best-known brands 99
- brand loyalty 98–99
- effective communication 103–105
- fairness and equity 101–102
- five forces 98
- growth and development, opportunities for 100–101
- inclusive and collaborative environment 103
- purpose-driven culture 99–100
- recognition and appreciation 102–103
- strong, trustworthy leadership 100

Conant, D. 11, 16, 22, 100
connect and engage 81
connecting personally with people 79
consensus-building processes 93
Cooper, C.L. 14
Costa, A.C. 52, 87, 89, 90, 93
Covey, S.R. 96, 100

COVID-19 pandemic 14–15, 122, 125
cultural differences 141, 144, 148
cultural intelligence 141
cultural norms 140, 145
customer
– committed staff 108
– companies and organizations 111–112
– competition 107
– engaged employees promote 110–111
– experience 109–110
– information technology, role of 108
– knowledge-based management 108
– leadership and management 112–113
– orientation 106, 107
– processes 113–114
– promise 109
– relationship and loyalty 109
– relationships and understanding 107
– value 108
customer-centric business 106
customer-centric operations 110
customer experience (CX) 27, 28, 47, 107–112
CVS Caremark 113

Delizonna, L. 68–70, 74, 82, 84, 87
Demerouti, E. 27, 45, 55, 58, 133
digital literacy 104, 107, 129, 136, 137
Dik, B.J. 14
disengaged employee. *See* actively disengaged employee
Duffy, R.D. 14
Dweck, C.S. 53

economic conditions 140
Edmondson, A.C. 70, 84, 87–90, 93
effective communication 55–56, 103–105
employee engagement 4
– academic literature 1
– beneficiary 6
– business leaders 1
– choice 5
– concrete actions 7–8
– engaged and disengaged 6, 7
– field of 3
– forces 11, 12, 106
– global percentage 14–15
– impact on customers 13–14
– innovation 12–13
– key findings 4–8

– knowledge economy 16–17
– leaders 7
– leadership principles 153–155
– multidimensionality 4, 5
– outcome improvement 11, 12
– people's level 6
– *vs.* positive outcomes 11
– productivity improvement 16
– scholarship 3
– well-being 14
– WIN-WIN-WIN proposition 5–6
– work environment 1
– *See also* remote work
Employee Engagement 2.0 (Kruse) 1
employee experience (EX) 107
empowering engagement 155–156
encourage collaboration 79–82
encouraging accountability
– autonomy 76
– environment 75
– feedback 77–79
– principles 76
– setting clear and measurable targets 76–77

Federal Aviation Administration (FAA) 84
financial incentives 66
Finnish business culture 144
Four Rooms of Change model 152–153
Frey, C.B. 133

Gallup Global Workplace Report 1
Gallup Workplace Research 20
Gartner, Inc. 133
German business culture 144
GitLab Inc. 130
global retail chain 67
Google's employee-centric approach 71
Google's Project Aristotle 69
"Great Resignation" 2
growth-oriented attitude 53

Halton Group Ltd. 13, 80
Harter, J.K. 4, 28, 117
Harvard Business Review 63
Harvard Business School case study 51
Hayes, T.L. 4, 28
Hirsch, A.S. 70
Hofstede, G. 140, 142–144, 148
human-centered approach 132, 135, 137, 139

IBM's Watson 133
incentives
– being fair 66–67
– effective 65
– financial 66
– organizational values and goals 65
– rewarding engagement 67–68
– setting boundaries 68–69
– strategic 68
– tangible rewards 65
– well-developed 65
individualism vs. collectivism 142, 143
indulgence vs. restraint culture 142, 143
In Search of Excellence: Lessons from America's Best-Run Companies (Peters & Waterman Jr.) 79
integrity 25, 52, 54, 89–90, 100
international multiculturalism
– business culture 144
– corporate culture 144
– cross-national differences 140
– cultural dimensions 142–143
– effective leadership and cooperation 141
– good cooperation 147–148
– incomplete/superficial assessments 145
– management 144–145
– multicultural environments 141
– multinational corporation 141
– multinational leaders 146–147
– organizational culture 145–146
– recognition program 140
– responsible employee 148
intrinsic investment 52

Japan business culture 144
Job Characteristics Model 21
Job Demands–Resources model 27

Kahn, W.A. 1, 14, 23, 27, 44, 55, 63, 67, 129, 133
Kohn, A. 65, 67, 71
Kotter, J.P. 145
Kramer, S.J. 102, 128, 154
Kruse, K.E. 1, 18

Latham, G.P. 49, 59, 77
leadership and trust 140
leadership principles 79, 89, 150, 153
leaders impact opportunities
– characteristics and behaviors 63, 64
– effective 63

– employee engagement 62, 63
– enlightening passion 72–75
– incentives and mutual respect 62
– managers and supervisors 62–63
– managers vs. individual worker engagement 62, 64
– quality 62
– team members 62
level of engagement
– actively disengaged 19–21
– continuum 18, 19
– engaged employees 20–22
– framework 18
– highly engaged employees 21
– nonengaged 20, 21
Locke, E.A. 49, 59, 77
London, M. 53, 58
long-term vs. short-term orientation 142, 143
Lowe's Companies, Inc. 113
Lysova, E.I. 46, 47

Macey, W.H. 59, 65, 68, 70, 71, 73, 75, 76
Markos, S. 23, 29
masculinity vs. femininity 142, 143
May, D.R. 27
Mazzetti, G. 26
Microsoft 13, 45
Microsoft Viva 130, 133
Milkman, K. 152, 155
Mittal, V. 107, 110
multidimensional engagement 4
– antecedents 23
– company 24–25, 28
– customers 27–28
– key factors/forces 23–24
– leaders and HR professionals 29
– leadership 25, 28
– own work assignment 26–27, 28
– teams 25–26, 28
mutual respect
– behaviors 69
– of culture 69
– encouraging life balance 70–71
– personalizing rewards 71–72
– psychological safety 69–70
Mvuyana, S. 5

Nadella, S. 13, 45, 90, 100, 145
natural language processing (NLP) systems 132

Netflix 76
Nooyi, I. 13

objective and key results (OKR) framework 77, 95
organizational justice theory 101
organization's support 24
Osborne, M.A. 133
ownership mentality 52, 66

passion, accountability, collaboration, and transformation or development (PACT) 43–44, 60, 62–64, 148–150
Pavithra, S. 107, 110
peer support 26
PepsiCo 13
Peters, T. 79
political environment 103
Post-it Notes 77
power distance cultures 143
principles of individual engagement 150
professional aspirations 70
profiles
– company culture 30
– customers 30
– departments *vs.* organizations *vs.* roles 34–37
– *vs.* individual engagement 37–39
– leadership 30
– levels and five forces 31
– organization 30, 31–32
– questionnaire 31
– top *vs.* bottom quartiles 32–33
Psychology Today 52
purpose-driven organizations 99–100, 154
recognition 67–68
– and appreciation 102–103
– competence and responsibilities 59
– and feedback 27
– program 144, 154
– public 67
– tools 136

relational crafting 49
remote work
– COVID-19 period 125
– customer impact 129
– development 125
– effects of 126
– full-time/full-week 125
– hybrid environment 125

– internal formal and informal communication 129
– maintaining engagement 130–131
– people and community 130
– resilience 129
– sense of progress 129
– support engagement things 126–128
– under- or overperformance, risk of 130
Robertson, I.T. 14
Rosso, B.D. 46, 47, 99

Saks, A.M. 21, 23, 24, 44, 129
Salanova, M. 6, 26
Schaufeli, W.B. 6
Schein, E.H. 141, 145
Schmidt, F.L. 4, 28
Schneider, B. 59, 65, 68, 70, 71, 73, 75, 76
self-driven development 58, 59
self-efficacy 45, 59
sense of community 126, 127, 144
service-profit chain 28
Smither, J.W. 53, 58
Sridevi, M.S. 23, 29
Steger, M.F. 14
support engagement things
– constant communication and communication 127
– giving feedback and supporting development 128
– leader and supervisor, role of 128
– leadership 126–127
– sense of community and culture 127
– visible support and proper resources 127–128
– work-life balance 128
supportive leadership approach 25
surveillance-driven environments 133
Sweco Finland company 130

task crafting 49
TD Bank 113
teams, engaging of
– appreciation 92–93
– "Deliver Results" 89
– empathy 90–91
– integrity 89–90
– mutual agreement 93–95
– people level role
– psychological safety 87
– synergy 95–97
– trust 88–89

- well-functioning 87
Training (magazine) 56
transformation
- behaviors 57
- challenges and opportunities 82
- contemporary workplace studies 56
- development 82, 85–86
- embracing mistakes 83–85
- encouraging innovation 83
- forward-looking component 56
- goals 59–61
- leaders 82–83
- learning and development opportunities 56–57
- new skills development 58–59
- owning your own future 58
- personal and professional growth 56
Travel + Leisure Co. 113
Trust, Empathy, Appreciation, Mutual agreements, and Synergy (TEAMS) 87, 88
trust-worthy behavior 52

2025 State of the Global Workplace 20

uncertainty avoidance 142, 143, 148
United States corporate culture 144
UN's Office of Human Resources 102

valuing diversity 54, 56, 92–93, 103
Vision, Values, Methods, Obstacles, Measures (V2MOM) process 95
voluntary disclosure programs (VDPs) 84

Waterman Jr. Robert 79
Whitener, E.M. 52
win-win attitude 96
work-life balance 128
Workplace Learning Report 101, 134
workplace structures 140

Yohn, D.L. 107, 108, 110

www.ingramcontent.com/pod-product-compliance
Lightning Source LLC
Chambersburg PA
CBHW082203220526
45470CB00010B/3034